BELLY LAUGHS FOR ALL!

**Adult Version
Volume 1**

ROBERTA CAVA

Copyright © 2013 by Roberta Cava

All rights reserved. No part of this work covered by the copyrights hereon may be reproduced or used in any form or by any means - graphic, electronic or mechanical, including photocopying, recording, taping or information storage and retrieval systems - without the prior written permission of the publisher.

Belly Laughs for All!
Adult Version
Volume 1
Roberta Cava

Published by Cava Consulting
105 / 3 Township Drive,
Burleigh Heads, 4220, Queensland, Australia
info@dealingwithdifficultpeople.info

       Discover other titles by Roberta Cava at
           www.dealingwithdifficultpeople.info

National Library of Australia
Cataloguing-in-publication data:

ISBN 978-0-9923402-8-5

BOOKS BY ROBERTA CAVA

Dealing with Difficult People
(21 publishers – in 16 languages)

Dealing with Difficult Situations – at Work and at Home
Dealing with Difficult Spouses and Children
Dealing with Difficult Relatives and In-Laws
Dealing with Domestic Violence and Child Abuse
Dealing with School Bullying
Dealing with Workplace Bullying
What am I going to do with the rest of my life?
Before tying the knot – Questions couples Must ask each other Before they marry!
How Women can advance in business
Survival Skills for Supervisors and Managers
Human Resources at its Best!
Easy Come – Hard to go – The Art of Hiring, Disciplining and Firing Employees
Time and Stress – Today's silent killers
Take Command of your Future – Make things Happen
Belly Laughs for All! – Volumes 1 to 4
Wisdom of the World! The happy, sad and wise things in life!
That Something Special

BELLY LAUGHS FOR ALL!

Volume 1

Table of Contents

Introduction	7
Chapter 1 – Couples	9
Chapter 2 – Males	53
Chapter 3 – Females	73
Chapter 4 – Singles	107
Chapter 5 – Lawyers	121
Chapter 6 – Doctors	135
Chapter 7 – Police	157
Chapter 8 – Airplane	165
Chapter 9 – Children	175
Chapter 10 – Seniors	209
Chapter 11 – Blondes	253
Conclusion	269

INTRODUCTION

This book is unlike any others I have written. Most of my books relate to how to deal with difficult people and situations. I had been feeling very depressed after writing my last three books - which focused around bullying - at home, at school and at work. This was a lovely change from that disturbing and depressing research.

I had collected jokes for years and enjoyed reading them whenever I felt down-in-the-dumps. This is what stimulated me to write a book on humour. It was soon evident that I had too many jokes for just one volume, hence I wrote Volumes 1, 2, 3 and 4. They discuss humour in different areas, so there's no repetition. I also realised that the books were meant for adult audiences and *are not suitable for children*.

I hope you enjoy this volume enough to want to obtain the other three volumes.

CHAPTER 1 COUPLES

Honeymoon

The morning after their honeymoon, the wife said to her husband, *'Y'know, you're really a lousy lover!'*

The husband replied, *'How would you know after only 30 seconds.'*

On the night of their wedding, a young couple finally retired to their hotel room. After making her preparations, the bride came out of the bathroom finding the bridegroom on his knees in front of the bed. *'What are you doing?'* she asked.

'I'm praying for guidance,' answered the young man.

'I'll take care of that,' she replied. *'You pray for endurance.'*

Just Married

Fred and Mary got married but can't afford a honeymoon, so they went back to Fred's Mom and Dad's for their first night together. In the morning, Johnny, Fred's little brother, gets up and has his breakfast. As he is going out the door to go to school, he asks his mom if Fred and Mary are up yet.

She replies, *'No.'*

Johnny asks, *'Do you know what I think?'*

His mom replies, *'I don't want to hear what you think! Just go to school.'*

Johnny comes home for lunch and asks his mom, *'Are Fred and Mary up yet?'*

She replies, *'No.'*

Johnny says, *'Do you know what I think?'*

His mom replies, *'Never mind what you think! Eat your lunch and go back to school.'*

After school, Johnny comes home and asks again, *'Are Fred and Mary up yet?'*

His mom says, *'No.'*

He asks, *'Do you know what I think?'*

His mom replies, *'OK, now tell me what you think?'*

He says: *'Last night Fred came to my room for the Vaseline and....I think I gave him my airplane glue.'*

The Neighbour

The middle-aged married couple finally moved into the condo of their dreams, but right next door to a very sexy fashion model. The husband had taken to borrowing this or that from their neighbour and it seemed to the wife that it always took him way too long to return.

One time the wife had had enough and actually pounded on the wall between the two apartments. There being no response, she telephoned, only to get the answering machine. Finally, she went to the model's door and kept ringing the bell.

When the model answered, the wife fumed, *'I would like to know why it is my husband takes so damn long to get something over here.'*

'Well sweetie,' the model purred, *'All these interruptions sure aren't helping none.'*

A week after their marriage, the Arkansas newlyweds, Bubba and Arlene, paid a visit to their doctor.

'You ain't gonna believe this, Doc,' said the husband. *'My thingy's turnin' blue.'*

'That's pretty unusual,' said the doctor. *'Let me examine you.'*

The doctor took a look. Sure enough, the redneck's 'thingy' was really blue.

The doctor turns to the wife, *'Are you using the diaphragm that I prescribed for you?'*

'Yep, shore am,' she replied brightly.

'And what kind of jelly are you using with it?'

'Grape.'

A typical macho man married a typical good-looking lady and after the wedding, he laid down the following rules: *'I'll be home when I want, if I want and at what time I want - and I don't expect any hassles from you. I expect a great dinner to be on the table unless I tell you otherwise. I'll go hunting, fishing, boozing and card-playing when I want with my old buddies and don't you give me a hard time about it. Those are my rules. Any comments?'*

His new bride said, *'No, that's fine with me. Just understand that there'll be sex here at seven o'clock every night - whether you're here or not.'*

Then there was the couple that got married and was happy about the whole thing. He was happy about the hole, she was happy about the thing.

It has been determined that the most used sexual position for married couples is a doggie position. The husband sits up and begs. The wife rolls over and plays dead.

The Wedding night

On their wedding night, the young bride approached her new husband and asked for $20.00 for their first lovemaking encounter. In his highly aroused state her husband readily agreed. This scenario was repeated each time they made love for the next 30 years, with him thinking that it was a cute way for her to afford new clothes and other incidentals that she needed.

Arriving home around noon one day, she was surprised to find her husband at home in a very drunken state. During the next few minutes, he explained that his employer was going through a process of corporate downsizing and his position had been eliminated. It was unlikely that at the age of 55 he'd be able to find another position that paid anywhere near what he'd been earning and therefore, they were financially ruined.

Calmly, his wife handed him a bank book which showed thirty years of deposits and interest totalling nearly $1 million. Then she showed him certificates of deposits issued by the bank that were worth over $2 million and informed him that they were one of the largest depositors in the bank. She explained that for the 30 years she had charged him for sex, these holdings had multiplied and these were the results of her savings and investments.

Faced with evidence of cash and investments worth over $3 million, her husband was so astounded he could barely speak, but finally he found his voice and blurted out, *'If I'd had any idea what you were doing, I would have given you all my business!'*

That's when she shot him. You know, sometimes men just don't know when to keep their mouths shut.

The Rodeo

A man took his wife to the rodeo and one of their first stops was the breeding bull exhibit. They went up to the first pen and there was a sign attached that said, *'This bull mated fifty times last year.'*

The wife playfully nudged her husband in the ribs and said, *'See. He mated fifty times last year ...once-a-week.'*

They walked to the second pen which had a sign attached that said, *'This bull mated one hundred and twenty times last year.'*

The wife gave her husband a healthy jab and said, *'That's more than twice a week! You could learn a lot from him.'*

They walked to the third pen and it had a sign attached that said, in capital letters, *'This bull mated three hundred and sixty five times last year.'*

The wife, so excited that her elbow nearly broke her husband's ribs, said, *'That's once-a-DAY. You could REALLY learn something from this one.'*

The husband looked at her and said, *'Go over and ask him if it was with the same cow.'*

Note: The husband's condition has been upgraded from critical to stable and the doctors say after months of rehab and a couple more operations he will be okay.

The Love Dress

A woman stopped by, unannounced, at her son's house. She knocked on the door then immediately walked in. She was shocked to see her daughter-in-law lying on the couch, totally naked. Soft music was playing and the aroma of perfume filled the room.

'What are you doing?' she asked.

'I'm waiting for Justin to come home from work.' The daughter-in-law answered.

'But you're naked!' the mother-in-law exclaimed.

'This is my love dress,' the daughter-in-law explained.

'Love dress? But you're naked!'

'Justin loves me to wear this dress,' she explained. *'Every time he sees me in this dress, he instantly becomes romantic and ravages me for hours.'*

The mother-in-law left. When she got home she undressed, showered, put on her best perfume, dimmed the lights, put on a romantic CD and lay on the couch waiting for her husband to arrive. Finally, her husband came home. He walked in and saw her lying there so provocatively.

'What are you doing?' he asked.

'This is my love dress,' she whispered, sensually.

'Needs ironing,' he said, *'What's for dinner?'*

Living Will

Last night, my wife and I were sitting in the living room and I said to her, *'I never want to live in a vegetative state, dependent on some machine and fluids from a bottle. If that ever happens, just pull the plug.'*

She got up, unplugged the TV and threw out my beer.

If I should die ...?

Ralph and Mary were sitting around the breakfast table one lazy morning. Ralph suddenly said, *'Mary, if I were to die suddenly, I want you to immediately sell all my stuff.'*

'Now why would you want me to do something like that?' Mary asked.

'I figure that you would eventually remarry and I don't want some other asshole using my stuff...'

'What makes you think I'd marry another asshole?'

Hillbilly Mirror

After living in the remote wilderness of Kentucky all his life, an old hillbilly decided it was time to visit the big city. In one of the stores he picks up a mirror and looks in it. Not ever having seen one before, he remarked at the image staring back at him, *'How about that! Here's a picture of my daddy.'*

He bought the 'picture', but on the way home he remembered his wife didn't like his father. So he hung it in the barn and every morning before leaving for the fields, he would go there and look at it. His wife began to get suspicious of these many trips to the barn.

One day after her husband left, she searched the barn and found the mirror. As she looked into the glass, she fumed, *'So that's the ugly bitch he's runnin' around with.'*

Lingerie

A husband walked into Victoria's Secret to purchase some sheer lingerie for his wife. He is shown several possibilities that range from $250 to $500 in price, the sheerer, the higher the price. He opts for the sheerest item, pays the $500 and takes the lingerie home.

He presents it to his wife and asks her to go upstairs, put it on and model it for him. Upstairs, the wife thinks, *'I have an idea. It's so sheer that it might as well be nothing. I won't put it on, but I'll do the modelling naked, return it tomorrow and keep the $500 refund for myself.'*

So she appears naked on the balcony and strikes a pose. Her husband says, *'Good Lord! You'd think that for $500, they'd at least iron it!'*

He never heard the shot.

Critical Evaluation

Harvey and Gladys are getting ready for bed. Gladys is standing in front of her full-length mirror, taking a long, hard look at herself.

'You know, Harvey,' she comments, *'I stare into this mirror and I see an ancient creature. My face is all wrinkled, my boobs sag so much that they dangle to my waist, my arms and legs are as flabby as popped balloons and my butt looks like a sad, deflated version of the Hindenburg!'*

She turns to face her husband and says, *'Dear, please tell me just one positive thing about my body so I can feel better about myself.'*

Harvey studies Gladys critically for a moment and then says in a soft, thoughtful voice, *'Well ... there's nothing wrong with your eyesight.'*

Henry never heard the shot.

Marriage

A woman marries a man expecting he will change, but he doesn't. A man marries a woman expecting that she won't change - but she does.

Sign on the door of a marriage licence bureau. *'By all means, marry. If you get a good wife, you'll be happy. If you get a bad one, you'll become a philosopher.'* Socrates.

'I was married by a judge. I should have asked for a jury.' George Burns

'Never go to bed mad. Stay up and fight!' Phyllis Diller.

'I think men who have a pierced ear are better prepared for marriage. They've experienced pain and bought jewellery.' Rita Rudner

'I haven't spoken to my mother-in-law for two years. I don't like to interrupt her.' Roseanne

'Behind every successful man stands a surprised mother-in-law.'

'You know your marriage is in trouble when your current husband introduces you to people as his 'first wife.''

'Never marry a man who refers to the rehearsal dinner as 'The Last Supper.''

'Why does a woman work for years to change a man's habits and then complain that he's not the man she married?' Barbara Streisand.

'Only two things are necessary to keep one's wife happy. One is to let her think she is having her own way and the other is to let her have it.'

'An archaeologist is the best husband a woman can have – the older she gets, the more interested he is in her.' Agatha Christie.

'When you're in love, it's the most glorious two-and-a-half days of your life.'

'Love: a temporary insanity curable by marriage.'

'Do you know what it means to come home at night to a woman who'll give you a little love, a little affection and a little tenderness? It means you're in the wrong house!' Henry Youngman.

'One of the best ways to get most husbands to do something is to suggest that perhaps they're too old to do it.' Anne Bancroft.

'Your marriage is in trouble if your wife says, 'You're only interested in one thing!' and you can't remember what it is!' Milton Berle.

'A man in the house is worth two in the street.' Mae West

'I told my mother-in-law that my house was her house and she said, 'Get the hell off my property.'' Joan Rivers

'During sex my wife wants to talk to me. The other night she called me from a hotel.' Rodney Dangerfield.

'The first part of our marriage was very happy. But then, on the way back from the ceremony ...' Henry Youngman.

'Whenever you want to marry someone who has been married before, go have lunch with his ex-wife.'

'You know what I did before I got married? Anything I wanted to!'

'When a man brings his wife flowers for no reason - there's a reason.'

'Some people ask the secret of our long marriage. We take time to go to a restaurant two times a week - a little candlelight, dinner, soft music and dancing. She goes Tuesdays and I go Fridays.' Henry Youngman.

'I hate housework! You make the beds, you do the dishes ...and six months later you have to start all over again!' Joan Rivers.

'Give a man a fish and he eats for a day. Teach him how to fish and you get rid of him for the whole weekend.'

'The honeymoon is over when he phones that he'll be late for supper and she's already left a note that it's in the refrigerator.'

'My husband makes love to me almost every day of the week – almost on Monday, almost on Tuesday and almost on Wednesday.'

'I was the best man at the wedding. If I'm the best man, why is she marrying him?' Jerry Seinfeld.

'To keep your marriage brimming with love in the marriage cup: whenever you're wrong, admit it ...whenever you're right – shut up!'

A cute quote from '53 things women don't understand about men book: 'Why is it that men can throw a softball with pinpoint accuracy, but they can't aim and hit the toilet?'

A man spoke frantically into the phone, 'My wife is pregnant and her contractions are only two minutes apart!'

'Is this her first child?' the doctor asked.

'No, you idiot!' the man shouted. 'This is her husband.'

Oops

Wife: *'What would you do if I died? Would you get married again?'*
Husband: *'Definitely not!'*
Wife: *'Why not - don't you like being married?'*
Husband: *'Of course I do.'*
Wife: *'Then why wouldn't you remarry?'*
Husband: *'Okay, I'd get married again.'*
Wife: *'You would?'* (With a hurtful look on her face).
Husband: (Makes audible groan).
Wife: *'Would you live in our house?'*
Husband: *'Sure, it's a great house.'*
Wife: *'Would you sleep with her in our bed?'*
Husband: *'Where else would we sleep?'*
Wife: *'Would you let her drive my car?'*
Husband: *'Probably, it's almost new.'*
Wife: *'Would you replace my pictures with hers?'*
Husband: *'That would seem like the proper thing to do.'*
Wife: *'Would she use my golf clubs?'*
Husband: *'No, she's left-handed.'*
Wife: (Silence)
Husband: *'Sssshit!!'*

A guy dials his home and a strange woman answers. The guy says, *'Who is this?'*

'This is the maid,' answers the woman.

'We don't have a maid,' says the man.

'I was hired this morning by the lady of the house.' She replied.

The man says, *'Well, this is her husband. Is she there?'*

The woman replies, *'She's upstairs in the bedroom with someone who I figured was her husband.'*

The guy is fuming. He says to the maid, *'Listen, would you like to make $50,000?'*

The maid says, *'What will I have to do?'*

'I want you to get my gun from the desk and shoot the bitch and the jerk she's with.'

The maid puts the phone down. The man hears footsteps and then two gunshots. The maid comes back to the phone, *'What should I do with the bodies?'*

The man replies, *'Throw them into the swimming pool.'*

Puzzled, the maid answers, *'But we don't have a pool.'*

A long pause later the man says, *'Is this 832-5831?'*

Saying the right thing at the right time

Jack wakes up with a huge hangover after a night at a business function. He forces himself to open his eyes and the first thing he sees is a couple of aspirins next to a glass of water on the side table. And, next to them, a single red rose!

Jack sits up and sees his clothing in front of him, all clean and pressed. Jack looks around the room and sees that it is in perfect order, spotlessly clean. He takes the aspirins, cringes when he sees a huge black eye staring back at him in the bathroom mirror and notices a note on the table: *'Honey, breakfast is on the stove, I left early to go shopping - Love you!!'*

His son is also at the table, eating. Jack asks, *'Son, what happened last night?'*

'Well, you came home after 3 am, drunk and out of your mind. You broke the coffee table, puked in the hallway and got that black eye when you walked into the door.'

'So, why is everything in such perfect order, so clean, I have a rose and breakfast is on the table waiting for me?'

His son replies, *'Oh, THAT! Mum dragged you to the bedroom and when she tried to take your pants off, you screamed, 'Leave me alone, b*tch, I'm married!!!''*

> Broken table - $580
> Hot breakfast - $22
> Red Rose bud - $15
> Two aspirins - $1
> Saying the right thing, at the right time ... Priceless

Watching TV

My wife and I were watching 'Who Wants To Be A Millionaire' while we were in bed. I turned to her and said, *'Do you want to have sex?'*

'No.' she answered.

I then said, *'Is that your final answer?'*

'Yes.' She replied.

Then I said, *'I'd like to phone a friend.'*

That's the last thing I remember.

Your cheating heart....

She came home early and found her husband in their bedroom making love to a very attractive young woman. The wife was VERY upset!

'You are a disrespectful pig!' she cried. 'How dare you do this to me - a faithful wife, the mother of your children?' I'm leaving you. I want a divorce straight away!'

And he replied: 'Hang on just a minute luv, so at least I can tell you what happened'

'Fine, go ahead,' she sobbed, 'but they'll be the last words you'll say to me!'

And he began: 'Well, I was getting into the car to drive home and this young lady here asked me for a lift. She looked so down and out and defenceless that I took pity on her and let her into the car. I noticed that she was very thin, not well dressed and very dirty.

'She told me that she hadn't eaten for three days! So, in my compassion, I brought her home and warmed up the enchiladas I made for you last night, the ones you wouldn't eat because you're afraid you'll put on weight.

'The poor thing devoured them in moments. Since she needed a good clean-up I suggested a shower and while she was doing that I noticed her clothes were dirty and full of holes so I threw them away. Then, as she needed clothes, I gave her the designer jeans that you have had for a few years, but don't wear because you say they are too tight. I also gave her the underwear that was your anniversary present, which you don't wear because I don't have good taste. I found the sexy blouse my sister gave you for Christmas that you don't wear just to annoy her and I also donated those boots you bought at the expensive boutique and don't wear because someone at work has a pair like them.'

He took a quick breath and continued: 'She was so grateful for my understanding and help and as I walked her to the door she turned to me with tears in her eyes and said, 'Please ... do you have anything else that your wife doesn't use?''

Friendship amongst women

A woman didn't come home one night. The next morning she told her husband that she had slept over at a friend's house. The man called his wife's ten best friends. None of them knew anything about it.

Friendship amongst men

A man didn't come home one night. The next morning he told his wife that he had slept over at a friend's house. The woman called her husband's ten best friends. Eight confirmed that he had slept over and two said he was still there.

The Hypnotist

A woman comes home from the hypnotist and tells her husband: *'Remember those headaches I've been having all these years? Well, they're gone.'*

'No more headaches?' the husband asks, *'What happened?'*

His wife replies: *'Margie referred me to a hypnotist He told me to stand in front of a mirror, stare at myself and repeat 'I do not have a headache. I do not have a headache. I do not have a headache.' It worked! The headaches are all gone.'*

The husband replies: *'Well, that's wonderful.'*

His wife then says: *'You know you haven't been exactly a ball of fire in the bedroom these last few years. Why don't you go see the hypnotist and see if he can do anything for that?'*

The husband agrees to try it. Following his appointment, the husband comes home, rips off his clothes, picks up his wife and carries her into the bedroom. He puts her on the bed and says: *'Don't move. I'll be right back.'*

He goes into the bathroom and comes back a few minutes later and jumps into bed and makes passionate love to his wife like never before.

His wife says: *'Boy that was wonderful!'*

The husband says: *'Don't move! I will be right back.'* He goes back into the bathroom, comes back and round two was even better than the first time. The wife sits up and her head is spinning.

Her husband again says: *'Don't move, I'll be right back.'* With that, he goes back in the bathroom. This time, his wife quietly follows him and there, in the bathroom, she sees him standing at the mirror saying: *'She's not my wife. She's not my wife. She's not my wife!'*

The Old Outhouse

For those of you who remember the 'Old Outhouse,' it will make you smile, the rest of you just use your imagination.

Ma was in the kitchen fiddling around when she hollered out, *'Pa! You need to go out and fix the outhouse!'*

Pa replies, *'There ain't nuthin wrong with the outhouse.'*

Ma yells back, *'Yes there is. Now git out there and fix it.'*

So, Pa mosies out to the outhouse, looks around and yells back, *'Ma! There ain't nuthin wrong with the outhouse!'*

Ma replies, *'Stick yur head in the hole!'*

Pa yells back, *'I ain't stickin my head in that hole!'*

Ma says, *'Ya have to stick yur head in the hole to see what to fix.'*

So with that, Pa sticks his head in the hole, looks around and yells back, *'Ma! There ain't nuthin wrong with this outhouse!'*

Ma hollers back, *'Now take your head out of the hole!'*

Pa proceeds to pull his head out of the hole and then starts yelling, *'Ma! Help! My beard is stuck in the cracks in the toilet seat!'*

To which Ma replies, *'Hurt's, don't it?'*

The Affairs

The 1st Affair

A married man was having an affair with his secretary. One day they went to her place and made love all afternoon. Exhausted, they fell asleep and woke up at 8 pm. The man hurriedly dressed and told his lover to take his shoes outside and rub them in the grass and dirt. He put on his shoes and drove home.

'Where have you been?' his wife demanded.

'I can't lie to you,' he replied, *'I'm having an affair with my secretary. We had sex all afternoon.'*

She looked down at his shoes and said: *'You lying bastard! You've been playing golf!'*

The 2nd Affair

A middle-aged couple had two beautiful daughters but always talked about having a son. They decided to try one last time for the son they always wanted. The wife got pregnant and delivered a healthy baby boy. The joyful father rushed to the nursery to see his new son. He was horrified at the ugliest child he had ever seen.

He told his wife: *'There's no way I can be the father of this baby. Look at the two beautiful daughters I fathered! Have you been fooling around behind my back?'*

The wife smiled sweetly and replied: *'Not this time!'*

The 3rd Affair

A mortician was working late one night. He examined the body of Mr. Schwartz, about to be cremated and made a startling discovery. Schwartz had the largest private part he had ever seen!

'I'm sorry Mr. Schwartz,' the mortician commented, *'I can't allow you to be cremated with such an impressive private part. It must be saved for posterity.'*

So, he removed it, stuffed it into his briefcase and took it home. *'I have something to show you that you won't believe,'* he said to his wife, opening his briefcase.

'My God!' the wife exclaimed, *'Schwartz is dead!'*

The 4th Affair
A man walked into a cafe, went to the bar and ordered a beer. *'Certainly, sir, that'll be one cent.'*

'One Cent?' the man exclaimed. He glanced at the menu and asked: *'How much for a nice juicy steak and a bottle of wine?'*

'A nickel,' the barman replied.

'A nickel?' exclaimed the man. *'Where's the guy who owns this place?'*

The bartender replied: *'Upstairs, with my wife.'*

The man asked: *'What's he doing upstairs with your wife?'*

The bartender replied: *'The same thing I'm doing to his business down here.'*

The 5th Affair
Jake was dying. His wife sat at the bedside. He looked up and said weakly: *'I have something I must confess.'*

'There's no need to,' his wife replied.

'No,' he insisted, *'I want to die in peace. I slept with your sister, your best friend, her best friend and your mother!'*

'I know,' she replied, *'now just rest and let the poison work.'*

The 6th Affair
A wealthy man was giving an affair with an Italian woman for several years. One night, during one of their rendezvous, she confided in him that she was pregnant. Not wanting to ruin his reputation or his marriage, he paid her a large sum of money if she would go to Italy to secretly have the child. If she stayed in Italy to raise the child, he would also provide child support until the child turned eighteen.

She agreed, but asked how he would know when the baby was born. To keep it discreet, he told her to simply mail him a post card and write 'Spaghetti' on the back. He would then arrange for child support payments to begin.

One day, about nine months later, he came home to his confused wife. *'Honey,'* she said, *'you received a very strange post card.'*

'Oh, just give it to me and I'll explain it.' He said. The wife obeyed and watched as her husband read the card, turned white and fainted.

On the card was written: *'Spaghetti, Spaghetti, Spaghetti. Two with meatballs, one without.'*

The 7th Affair

A woman was having a passionate affair with an inspector from a pest-control company. One afternoon they were carrying on in the bedroom together when her husband arrived home unexpectedly.

'Quick,' said the woman to her lover, *'into the closet!'* and she pushed him into the closet, stark naked.

The husband, however, became suspicious and after a search of the bedroom discovered the man in the closet. *'Who are you?'* he asked him.

'I'm an inspector from Bugs-B-Gone,' said the exterminator.

'What are you doing in there?' the husband asked.

'I'm investigating a complaint about an infestation of moths,' the man replied.

'And where are your clothes?' asked the husband. The man looked down at himself and said ... *'Those little bastards.'*

Pregnancy News

A young husband comes home one night and his wife throws her arms around his neck, *'Darling, I have great news: I'm a month overdue. I think we're going to have a baby! The doctor gave me a test today, but until we find out for sure, we can't tell anybody.'*

The next day, a guy from the electric company rings the doorbell, because the young couple hasn't paid their last bill. *'Are you Mrs. Smith? You're a month overdue, you know!'*

'How do YOU know?' stammers the woman.

'Well, ma'am, it's in our files!' says the man from the electric company.

'What are you saying? It's in your files?????'

'Absolutely.'

'Well, let me talk to my husband about this tonight.'

That night, she tells her husband about the visit and he, mad as a bull, rushes to the electric company offices the first thing the next morning.

'What's going on here? You have it on file that my wife is a month overdue? What business is that of yours?' the husband shouts.

'Just calm down,' says the clerk, *'it's nothing serious. All you have to do is pay us.'*

'PAY you? And if I refuse?'

'Well, in that case, sir, we'd have no option but to cut you off.'

'And what would my wife do then?' the husband asks.

'I don't know. I guess she'd have to use a candle.'

Golf Stories

A guy out on the golf course takes a high-speed ball right in the crotch. Writhing in agony, he falls to the ground. When he finally gets himself to the doctor, he says, *'How bad is it doc? I'm getting married next week and my fiancée is still a virgin in every way.'*

The doc said, *'I'll have to put your penis in a splint to let it heal and keep it straight. It should be okay by next week.'* So he took four tongue depressors and formed a neat little 4-sided bandage and tied it all together - an impressive work of art.

The guy mentions none of this to his fiancée. They get married and on the honeymoon night in their hotel room, she rips open her blouse to reveal a gorgeous set of breasts. This was the first time he had seen them (believe it or not). She says, *'You'll be the first. No one has ever touched these breasts before.'*

He whips down his pants and says, *'Well look at this. It's still in its original crate!'*

Two women were playing golf one sunny Saturday afternoon. The first of the twosome teed off and watched in horror as her ball headed directly toward a foursome of men standing on the tee box on the next fairway. Sure enough, the ball hit one of the men. He immediately clasped his hands over his crotch and fell to the ground in agony.

The woman rushed over to the man and began to apologise. *'Please allow me to help,'* she begged. *'I'm a professional physiotherapist and I can quickly relieve your pain.'*

'No I'll be okay, just give me a minute,' he said, as he rolled on the ground in the foetal position, still clasping his hands over his crotch. The woman persisted and insisted she could help, so the man finally agreed.

She gently took his hands away from his crotch and laid them at his side. Then she loosened his pants and began to gently massage his privates.

'Does that feel better?' she asked.

'It feels great,' he said, *'but my thumb still hurts like a bitch.'*

One day, a man came home and was greeted by his wife dressed in a very sexy nightie. *'Tie me up,'* she purred, *'And you can do anything you want.'*

So he tied her up and went golfing.

A man staggered into a hospital with a concussion, multiple bruises, two black eyes and a five iron wrapped tightly around his throat. Naturally the Doctor asked him, *'What happened to you?'*

'Well, I was having a quiet round of golf with my wife when, at a difficult hole, we both sliced our golf balls into a field of cattle. We went to look for them and, while I was looking around, I noticed one of the cows had something white in its rear end. I walked over, lifted its tail and sure enough there was a golf ball with my wife's monogram on it - stuck right in the middle of the cow's fanny! Still holding the cow's tail up, I yelled to my wife, 'Hey, this looks like yours!''

'I don't remember much after that!

BBQ Rules

We are about to enter the summer and BBQ season. Therefore it's important to refresh your memory on the etiquette of this sublime outdoor cooking activity, as it's the only type of cooking a 'real' man will do, probably because there is an element of danger involved.

When a man volunteers to do the BBQ the following chain of events are put into motion: Routine:

1. The woman buys the food.
2. The woman makes the salad, prepares the vegetables and makes dessert.
3. The woman prepares the meat for cooking, places it on a tray along with the necessary cooking utensils and sauces and takes it to the man who is lounging beside the grill - beer in hand.
   Here comes the important part:
4. The man places the meat on the grill.
5. The woman goes inside to organise the plates and cutlery.
6. The woman comes out to tell the man that the meat is burning. He thanks her and asks if she will bring another beer while he deals with the situation. Important again:
7. The man takes the meat off the grill and hands it to the woman.
8. The woman prepares the plates, salad, bread, utensils, napkins, sauces and brings them to the table.
9. After eating, the woman clears the table and does the dishes.
   And most important of all:
10. Everyone praises the man and thanks HIM for his cooking efforts.
11. The man asks the woman how she enjoyed 'her night off.' And, upon seeing her annoyed reaction, concludes that there's just no pleasing some women.

The Fight

Walking into the bar, Mike said to Charlie the bartender, *'Pour me a stiff one - just had another fight with the little woman.'*

'Oh yeah?' said Charlie *'And how did this one end?'*

'When it was over,' Mike replied, 'she came to me on her hands and knees.'

'Really,' said Charles, 'now that's a switch! What did she say?'

She said, 'Come out from under the bed you chicken!'

Relationship

Marriage is a relationship in which one person is always right and the other is a husband.

Bouquet of flowers

When I go to a local discount store to get oil and filters for my car, I buy my wife a bouquet of flowers on display near the checkout counter. During one trip, some women in line behind me were oohing and aahing about a husband getting flowers for his wife. 'How often do you do that?' one asked.

Before I could answer, the cashier, more than familiar with my routine, said, 'Every three months or 3,000 miles, whichever comes first.'

Vacation

Billy Bob and Luther were talking one afternoon when Billy Bob tells Luther, 'Ya know, I reckon I'm 'bout ready for a vacation. Only this year I am gonna do it a little different. The last few years, I took your advice about where to go. Three years ago, you said to go to Hawaii. I went to Hawaii and Earlene got pregnant. Then two years ago, you told me to go to the Bahamas and Earlene got pregnant again. Last year you suggested Tahiti and darned if Earlene didn't get pregnant again.'

Luther asks Billy Bob, 'So, what you gonna do this year that's different?'

Billy Bob says, 'This year I'm taking Earlene with me.'

The Inheritance

When Dan found out he was going to inherit a fortune when his sickly father died, he decided he needed a woman to enjoy it with. So one evening he went to a singles bar where he spotted the most beautiful woman he had ever seen. Her natural beauty took his breath away 'I may look like just an ordinary man,' he said as he walked up to her, 'but in just a week or two, my father will die and I'll inherit 20 million dollars.' Impressed, the woman went home with him that evening and, three days later, she became his stepmother.

Women are so much smarter than men.

Won the Lottery

A woman came home, screeching her car into the driveway and ran into the house. She slammed the door and shouted at the top of her lungs, *'George, pack your bags. I won the lottery!'*

The husband said, *'Oh my God! What should I pack, beach stuff or mountain stuff?'*

'Doesn't matter,' she said. *'Just get out.'*

More Butter

A wife was making a breakfast of fried eggs for her husband. Suddenly, her husband burst into the kitchen. *'Careful,'* he said, *'Careful! Put in some more butter! Oh my God! You're cooking too many at once. Too many! Turn them! Turn them now! We need more butter. Oh my God! Where are we going to get more butter? They're going to stick! Careful. Careful! I said be Careful! You never listen to me when you're cooking! Never! Turn them! Hurry up! Are you Crazy? Have you lost your mind? Don't forget to salt them. You know you always forget to salt them. Use the salt. Use the salt! The salt!'*

The wife stared at him. *'What in the world is wrong with you? 'You think I don't know how to fry a couple of eggs?'*

The husband calmly replied, *'I just wanted to show you what it feels like when I'm driving.'*

The Sandals

A married couple walked into a Jamaican Sandals Shop. The Jamaican said to them, *'I have some special sandals I think you would be interested in. Dey make you wild at sex.'*

Well, the wife was really interested in buying the sandals after what the man claimed, but her husband felt he really didn't need them, being the sex god he was.

The husband asked the man, *'How could sandals make you into a sex freak?'*

The Jamaican replied, *'Just try dem on, Mon.'*

So, the husband, after some badgering from his wife, finally gave in and tried them on.

As soon as he slipped them onto his feet, he got this wild look in his eyes, something his wife hadn't seen in many years! In the blink of an eye, the husband grabbed the Jamaican, bent him violently over a table, yanked down his pants, ripped down his own pants and grabbed a firm hold of the Jamaican's hips.

The Jamaican then began screaming, *'You got dem on da wrong feet Mon!'*

Butt measurement

A man and his wife were working in their garden one day and the man looks over at his wife and says: *'Your butt is getting really big, I mean really big. I'll bet your butt is bigger than the barbecue.'*

With that, he proceeded to get a measuring tape and measured the grill and then went over to where his wife was working and measured his wife's bottom.

'Yes, I was right. Your butt is two inches wider than the barbecue!!!'

The woman chose to ignore her husband. Later that night in bed, the husband is feeling a little frisky. He makes some advances towards his wife who completely brushes him off.

'What's wrong?' he asks.

She answers: *'Do you really think I'm going to fire up this big-ass grill for one little weenie?'*

The Cowboy Boots

An elderly couple, Margaret and Bert, live in Alberta. Bert always wanted a pair of authentic cowboy boots, so, seeing some on sale one day, he buys them and wears them home, walking proudly.

He walks into the house and says to his wife, *'Notice anything different about me?'*

Margaret looks him over, *'Nope.'*

Frustrated, Bert storms off into the bathroom, undresses and walks back into the room completely naked except for the boots. Again he asks, a little louder this time, *'Notice anything different NOW?'*

Margaret looks up and says, *'Bert, what's different? It's hanging down today, it was hanging down yesterday and it'll be hanging down again tomorrow.'*

Furious, Bert yells, *'And do you know why it's hanging down, Margaret?'*

'Nope,' she replies.

'It's hanging down, because it's looking at my new boots!!!!'

Margaret replies ... *'Shoulda bought a hat, Bert. Shoulda bought a hat.'*

The Hormone Hostage

The Hormone Hostage knows that there are days in the month when all a man has to do is open his mouth and he takes his life in his own hands! This is a handy guide that should be as common as a driver's license in the wallet of every husband, boyfriend, co-worker or significant other:

Dangerous: What's for dinner?
Safer: Can I help you with dinner?
Safest: Where would you like to go for dinner?
Ultra Safe: Here, have some wine.

Dangerous: Are you wearing that?
Safer: Wow, you sure look good in brown!
Safest: WOW! Look at you!
Ultra Safe: Here, have some wine.

Dangerous: What are you getting so worked up about?
Safer: Could you be over-reacting?
Safest: Here's my pay cheque.
Ultra Safe: Here, have some wine.

Dangerous: Should you be eating that?
Safer: You know, there are a lot of apples left.
Safest: Can I get you a piece of chocolate with that?
Ultra Safe: Here, have some wine.

Dangerous: What did you DO all day?
Safer: I hope you didn't over-do it today.
Safest: I always loved you in that robe.
Ultra Safe: Here, have some wine.

Why we split up!

She told me we couldn't afford beer anymore and I'd have to quit. Then I caught her spending $65.00 on make-up. And I asked how come I had to give up stuff and not her.

She said she needed the make-up to look pretty for me.

I told her that was what the beer was for. I don't think she's coming back.

13 Things PMS Stands for:

1. Pass My Shotgun
2. Psychotic Mood Shift
3. Perpetual Munching Spree
4. Puffy Mid-Section
5. People Make me Sick
6. Provide Me with Sweets

7. Pardon My Sobbing
8. Pimples May Surface
9. Pass My Sweat pants
10. Pissy Mood Syndrome
11. Plainly; Men Suck
12. Pack My Stuff (and my favourite one)
13. Potential Murder Suspect

Husband and Wife

A husband and wife are in bed together. She feels his hand rubbing against her shoulder.

'Oh honey, that feels good,' she said.

His hand moves to her breast. *'Gee, honey, that feels wonderful,'* she said.

His hand moves to her leg. *'Oh, honey, don't stop,'* she begged. But he stops... *'Why did you stop???'* she cried.

'I found the remote ...' he replied.

Hotel Bill Too High?

The next time you think your hotel bill is too high, you might want to consider this ...

A husband and wife are travelling by car from Key West to Boston. After almost twenty-four hours on the road, they're too tired to continue and they decide to stop for a rest. They stop at a nice hotel and take a room, but they only plan to sleep for four hours and then get back on the road.

When they check out four hours later, the desk clerk hands them a bill for $350.00. The man explodes and demands to know why the charge is so high. He tells the clerk although it's a nice hotel the rooms certainly aren't worth $350.00.

When the clerk tells him $ 350.00 is the standard rate, the man insists on speaking to the Manager.

The Manager appears, listens to the man and then explains that the hotel has an Olympic-sized pool and a huge conference centre that were available for the husband and wife to use.

'But we didn't use them,' the man complains.

'Well, they are here and you could have,' explains the Manager. He goes on to explain they could have taken in one of the shows for which the hotel is famous. *'The best entertainers from New York, Hollywood and Las Vegas perform here,'* the Manager says.

'But we didn't go to any of those shows,' complains the man again.

'Well, we have them and you could have,' the Manager replies. No matter what amenity the Manager mentions, the man replies, *'But we didn't use it!'*

The Manager is unmoved and eventually the man gives up and agrees to pay. He writes a check and gives it to the Manager. The Manager is surprised when he looks at the check. *'But sir,'* he said, *'this check is only made out for $50.00.'*

'That's correct,' says the man. *'I charged you $300.00 for sleeping with my wife.'*

'But I didn't!' exclaims the Manager.

'Well, too bad.' the man replies. *'She was here and you could have!'*

The Anniversary Gift

Ed was in trouble. He forgot his wedding anniversary. His wife was really angry. She told him *'Tomorrow morning, I expect to find a gift in the driveway that goes from 0 to 200 in less than 6 seconds AND IT HAD BETTER BE THERE!!'*

The next morning Ed got up early and left for work. When his wife woke up, she looked out the window and sure enough there was a box gift wrapped in the middle of the driveway. Confused, the wife put on her robe and ran out to the driveway and brought the box back in the house.

She opened it and found a brand new bathroom scale.

Ed has been missing since Friday.

Birthday present

A wife decides to take her husband to a strip club for his birthday. They arrive at the club and the doorman said, *'Hey, Dave! How ya doin'?'*

His wife is puzzled and asks if he's been to this club before.

'Oh, no,' says Dave. *'He's on my bowling team.'*

When they are seated, a waitress asks Dave if he'd like his usual and brings over a Budweiser. His wife is becoming increasingly uncomfortable and said, *'How did she know that you drink Budweiser?'*

'She's in the Ladies' Bowling League, honey. We share lanes with them.'

A stripper then comes over to their table, throws her arms around Dave and says *'Hi Davey. Want your usual table dance, big boy?'*

Dave's wife, now furious, grabs her purse and storms out of the club. Dave follows and spots her getting into a cab. Before she can slam the door, he jumps in beside her. He tries desperately to explain how the stripper must have mistaken him for someone else, but his wife is having none of it. She is screaming at him at the top of her lungs, calling him every name in the book.

The cabby turns his head and says, *'Looks like you picked up a real bitch tonight, Dave.'*

Ear Rings

A man is at work one day when he notices that his co-worker is wearing an earring. This man knows his co-worker to be a normally conservative fellow and is curious about his sudden change in 'fashion sense.'

The man walked up to him and said, *'I didn't know you were into earrings.'*

'Don't make such a big deal out of this, it's only an earring,' he replies sheepishly.

His friend falls silent for a few minutes, but then his curiosity prods him to say, *'So, how long have you been wearing one?'*

'Ever since my wife found it in my truck ...'

[I always wondered how this trend got started].

Gentleman Take Note

When I was married twenty-five years, I took a look at my wife one day and said, *'Honey, twenty-five years ago, we had a cheap apartment, a cheap car, slept on a sofa bed and watched a 10-inch black and white TV, but I got to sleep every night with a hot twenty-five-year-old blonde. Now, we have a nice house, nice car, big bed and plasma screen TV, but I'm sleeping with a 50-year-old woman. It seems to me that you are not holding up your side of things.'*

My wife is a very reasonable woman. She told me to go out and find a hot twenty-five-year-old blonde and she would make sure that I would once again be living in a cheap apartment, driving a cheap car, sleeping on a sofa bed.

Aren't older women great? They really know how to solve your mid-life crises!

Stumpy Grinder

Every year, Stumpy Grinder and his wife Martha went to their local fair and every year Stumpy said, *'Ya know Mahtha, I'd like ta get a ride in that theah aihplane.'* And every year Martha would say, *'I know Stumpy, but that ahplane ride costs ten dollahs ... and ten dollahs is ten dollahs.'*

So Stumpy says, *'By Jeebers Mahtha, I'm 71 yeahs old, if I don't go this time, I may nevah go.'* Martha replies, *'Stumpy, that there aihplane ride is ten dollahs .and ten dollahs is ten dollahs.'*

The pilot overhears them and says, *'Folks, I'll make you a deal. I'll take you both up for a ride, if you can stay quiet for the entire ride and not say one word, I won't charge you, but just one word and it's ten dollars.'*

They agree and up they go. The pilot does all kinds of twists and turns, rolls and dives, but not a word is heard, he does it one more time, still nothing ... so he lands.

He turns to Stumpy as they come to a stop and says, *'By golly, I did everything I could think of to get you to holler out, but you didn't.'*

And Stumpy replies, *'Well, I was gonna say something when Mahtha fell out ...but ten dallahs is ten dollahs!'*

Sex in the Dark

There was this couple that had been married for 20 years. Every time they made love the husband always insisted on shutting off the light. Well, after twenty years the wife felt this was ridiculous. She figures she would break him out of this crazy habit. So, one night while they were in the middle of a wild, screaming, romantic session, she turned on the lights. She looked down and saw her husband was holding a battery-operated leisure device ... a vibrator! Soft, wonderful and larger than a real one, she went completely ballistic. *'You impotent bastard,'* she screamed at him. *'How could you be lying to me all of these years? You'd better explain yourself.'*

The husband looks her straight in the eyes and said calmly: *'I'll explain the toy if you explain the kids.'*

Onions & Christmas Trees

A family was at the dinner table. The son asked his father, *'Dad, how many kinds of boobies are there?'*

The father, surprised, answers, *'Well, son, there's three kinds of breasts. In her twenties, a woman's breasts are like melons, round and firm. In her thirties to forties, they're like pears, still nice but hanging a bit. After fifty, they're like onions.'*

'Onions?'

'Yes, you see them and they make you cry.'

This infuriated his wife and daughter so the daughter said, *'Mom, how many kinds of 'willies' are there?'*

The mother, surprised, smiles and answers, *'Well dear, a man goes through three phases. In his twenties, his willy is like an oak*

tree, mighty and hard. In his thirties and forties, it is a birch, flexible but reliable. After his fifties, it is like a Christmas tree.'
'A Christmas tree?'
'Yes, dead from the root up and the balls are for decoration.'

The Mistress

A married couple was enjoying a dinner out when a statuesque blonde walked over to their table, exchanged warm greetings with the husband and walked off.
'Who was that?' the wife demanded.
'If you must know,' the husband replied, 'that was my mistress.'
'Your mistress! That's it! I want a divorce!' the wife fumed.
The husband looked her straight in the eye and said, 'Are you sure you want to give up our big house in the suburbs, your Mercedes, your furs, your jewellery and our vacation home in Mexico?'
For a long time they continued dining in silence. Finally, the woman nudged her husband and said, 'Isn't that Howard over there? Who's he with?'
'That's his mistress,' her husband replied.
'Hrmmph ...' she said, taking a bite of dessert, 'Ours is much cuter.'

Bad Behaviour

Dear Mrs. Price,
Over the past six months, your husband, Mr. Lee Price has been causing quite a commotion in our store. We cannot tolerate this type of behaviour and have considered banning the entire family from shopping in our stores.

We have documented all incidents on our video surveillance equipment. Three of our clerks are attending counselling from the trouble your husband has caused. All complaints against Mr. Price have been compiled and listed below.

Mr. Wally, President and CEO Wal-Mart Complaint Department
MEMO: Re: Mr. Lee Price - Complaints - 15 things Mr. Lee Price has done while his spouse/partner was shopping:
1. June 15: Took 24 boxes of condoms and randomly put them in people's carts when they weren't looking.
2. July 2: Set all the alarm clocks in housewares to go off at 5-minute intervals.
3. July 7: Made a trail of tomato juice on the floor leading to the rest rooms.

4. July 19: Walked up to an employee and told her in an official tone, 'Code 3' in house wares - and watched what happened.
5. August 4: Went to the Service Desk and asked to put a bag of M&Ms on lay-away.
6. September 14: Moved a 'Caution - Wet Floor' sign to a carpeted area.
7. September 15: Set up a tent in the camping department and told other shoppers he'd invite them in if they'll bring pillows from the bedding department.
8. September 23: When a clerk asks if they can help him, he begins to cry and asks *'Why can't you people just leave me alone?'*
9. October 4: Looked right into the security camera, used it as a mirror and picked his nose.
10. November 10: While handling guns in the hunting department, asked the clerk if he knew where the anti-depressants were.
11. December 3: Darted around the store suspiciously loudly humming the 'Mission Impossible' theme.
12. December 6: In the auto department, practiced his 'Madonna look' using different sized funnels.
13. December 18: Hid in a clothing rack and when people browsed through yelled, *'Pick me. Pick me!'*
14. December 21: When an announcement came over the loud speaker, he assumed the foetal position and screamed, *'No! No! It's those voices again!'*
15. December 23: Went into a fitting room, shut the door and waited a while, then yelled very loudly, *'There's no toilet paper in here!'*

Cheating

A man wanted to determine if both his wife and mistress were faithful to him, so he decided to send them on the same cruise and then later question each one on the other's behaviour.

When his wife returned, he asked her about the people on the trip in general, then casually asked her about the specific behaviour of the passenger he knew to be his mistress. *'She slept with nearly every man on the ship,'* his wife reported.

The disheartened man then rendezvoused with his cheating mistress to ask her the same questions about his wife. *'She was a real lady,'* his mistress said.

'How so?' the encouraged man asked.

'She came on board with her husband and never left his side.'

Efficiency

A businessman taking a seminar on efficiency completed a case study of his wife's routine for fixing breakfast and presented the results to the class. *'After a few days of observation, I quickly determined the practices that were robbing her of precious time and energy,'* the man reported. *'Taking note of how many trips she made from the kitchen to the dining room carrying just one item, I suggested that in future she carry several items at one time'*

'Did it work?' the teacher asked.

'It sure did,' replied the businessman. *'Instead of it taking her twenty minutes to fix my breakfast, it now takes me seven.'*

Talking too much

A husband had always been disdainful of people who, in his estimation, talked too much. Recently, he proudly told his wife that he'd heard that men use 2,200 words a day, while women use 4,400. The wife thought about that a moment, then concluded, *'That's because women have to repeat everything they say to their husbands,'* to which he looked up and asked, *'Come again?'*

'I rest my case!'

First man: *'I'm going to get a divorce. My wife hasn't spoken to me in six months.*

Second man: *'Better think it over, wives like that are hard to get.'*

Amorous Hubby

Her husband was in a rather amorous mood and figured he would try for the shock effect to bring this to his wife's attention. So when the computer asked him to enter his password, he made it plainly obvious to his wife that he was keying in:

P
E
N
I
S

His wife fell out of her chair because she was laughing so hard. The computer had replied ... *'Password invalid ... .Not long enough.'*

The Ribbon

A woman learned from her vet that if she put a ribbon around her snoring dog's penis, that he'd roll over and stop snoring. The next night her dog was snoring, so she tied a red ribbon around his penis. His snoring stopped immediately.

Later that night her husband was snoring, so she did the same to him only this time with a blue ribbon. He stopped snoring. The next morning when he woke up, he looked at his dog then at himself and said to his dog, *'I don't know what happened last night, but we came in first and second.'*

Who wears the pants?

A young couple, just married, were in their honeymoon suite on their wedding night. As they were undressing for bed, the husband who was a big burley man tossed his pants to his bride and said, *'Here, put these on.'*

She put them on and the waist was twice the size of her body. *'I can't wear your pants,'* she said.

'That's right,' said the husband, *'and don't you ever forget it. I'm the man and I wear the pants in this family.'*

With that, she flipped him her panties and said, *'Try these on.'* He tried them on and found he could only get them on as far as his kneecaps.

'Heck,' he said, *'I can't get into your panties!'*

She replied, *'That's right and that's the way it's going to be until you change your attitude!'*

The Statue

A woman was in bed with her lover when she heard her husband opening the front door. *'Hurry!'* she said, *'Stand in the corner.'* She quickly rubbed baby oil all over him then dusted him with talcum powder.

'Don't move till I tell you to,' she whispered. *'Just pretend you're a statue.'*

'What's this, honey?' the husband inquired as he entered the room.

'Oh, it's just a statue,' she replied nonchalantly. *'The Smiths bought one for their bedroom. I liked it so much; I got one for us too.'* No more was said about the statue, not even later that night when they went to sleep.

Around two in the morning the husband got out of bed, went to the kitchen and returned a while later with a sandwich and a glass of milk.

'Here,' he said to the 'statue,' *'eat something. I stood like an idiot at the Smith's for three days and nobody offered me as much as a glass of water.'*

Why men don't write advice columns

Dear Walter

I hope you can help me here. The other day I set off for work leaving my husband in the house watching the TV as usual. I hadn't gone more than a mile down the road when my engine conked out and the car shuddered to a halt. I walked back home to get my husband's help. When I got home I couldn't believe my eyes. He was in the bedroom with a neighbour lady making passionate love to her. I am 32, my husband is 34 and we have been married for twelve years. When I confronted him, he broke down and admitted that he'd been having an affair for the past six months.

I told him to stop or I would leave him. He was let go from his job six months ago and he says he has been feeling increasingly depressed and worthless. I love him very much, but ever since I gave him the ultimatum he has become increasingly distant. I don't feel I can get through to him anymore.

Can you please help?

Sincerely
Mrs Sheila Usk

Dear Sheila:

A car stalling after being driven a short distance can be caused by a variety of faults with the engine. Start by checking that there is no debris in the fuel line. If it is clear, check the jubilee clips holding the vacuum pipes onto the inlet manifold. If none of these approaches solves the problem, it could be that the fuel pump itself is faulty, causing low delivery pressure to the carburettor float chamber.

I hope this helps.
Walter

Wifely Duties

Three men were sitting together bragging about how they had given their new wives duties.

Terry had married a woman from America and bragged that he had told his wife she needed to do all the dishes and housework. He said that it took a couple days but on the third day he came home to a clean house and the dishes were all washed and put away.

Jimmie had married a woman from Canada. He bragged that he had given his wife orders that she was to do all the cleaning, dishes and the cooking. He told them that the first day he didn't see any results, but the next day it was better. By the third day, his house was clean, the dishes were done and he had a huge dinner on the table.

The third man had married an Australian girl. He boasted that he told her that her duties were to keep the house cleaned, dishes washed, laundry and ironing twice a week, lawns mowed, windows cleaned and hot meals on the table for every meal. He said the first day he didn't see anything, the second day he didn't see anything, but by the third day most of the swelling had gone down and he could see a little out of his left eye enough to fix himself a bite to eat, load the dishwasher and call a handyman.

God bless Australian women.

Code Word

A husband and wife decided they needed to use a code word to indicate that they wanted to have sex, without letting their children in on the idea, so they decided on the word 'typewriter.' One day, the husband told his five-year-old daughter, *'Dear, go tell your mommy that Daddy needs to type a letter.'*

The child went into the next room and told her mom what Daddy had said and her mother responded, *'Honey, tell your Daddy that he can't type a letter right now because there's a red ribbon in the typewriter.'*

The child went back to tell her dad what her mom had said. A few days later, the mother told her daughter, *'Honey, go tell Daddy that he can type that letter now.'* The child went into the next room and gave her dad the message. A few minutes later, she returned to her mother and announced, *'Daddy said never mind with the typewriter, he already wrote the letter by hand.'*

Costume Party

A couple was going to a costume party. The husband was unsure of what costume to wear. His wife was telling him to hurry or they'd be late for the party. She walked down the stairs from the bedroom, completely naked except for a big old floppy pair of boots on her feet.

'Where's your costume?' the husband asked.

'This is it,' replied his wife.

'What the heck kind of costume is that?' asked the husband.

'I'm going as Puss and Boots,' explains the wife. *'Now hurry and get your costume on.'*

The husband went upstairs and was back in about two minutes. He also was completely naked except he had a rose vase slid over his penis.

'What the heck kind of costume is that?' asked the wife.
'I'm a fire alarm?' he replied.
'A fire alarm?' she repeated laughing.
'Yes,' he replied. *'In case of fire break the glass, pull twice and I'll come.'*

Unique Store

A store that sells new husbands has just opened in New York City, where a woman may go to choose a husband. Among the instructions at the entrance is a description of how the store operates.

'You may visit this store ONLY ONCE! There are six floors and the attributes of the men increase as the shopper ascends the flights. There is however a catch: you may choose any man from a particular floor or you may choose to go up a floor, but you cannot go back down except to exit the building!'

So, a woman goes to the Husband Store to find a husband ... On the first floor the sign on the door reads: Floor 1 - These men have jobs.

The second floor sign reads: Floor 2 - These men have jobs and love kids. The third floor sign reads: Floor 3 - These men have jobs, love kids and are extremely good looking.

'Wow,' she thinks, but feels compelled to keep going. She goes to the fourth floor and sign reads: Floor 4 - These men have jobs, love kids, are drop-dead gorgeous and help with the housework. *'Oh, mercy me!'* she exclaims, *'I can hardly stand it!'*

Still, she goes to the fifth floor and sign reads: Floor 5 - These men have jobs, love kids, are drop-dead gorgeous, help with the house-work and have a strong romantic streak.

She is so tempted to stay, but she goes to the sixth floor and the sign reads: Floor 6 - *'You are visitor 31,456,012 to this floor. There are no men on this floor. This floor exists solely as proof that women are impossible to please. Thank you for shopping at the Husband Store.'*

A New Wives store opened across the street. The first floor has wives that love sex. The second floor has wives that love sex and have money. The third through sixth floors have never been visited ...

The Best Comeback line ever?

Marine Corp's General Reinwald was interviewed on the radio the other day and you have to read his reply to the lady who interviewed him concerning guns and children. Regardless of how you feel about gun laws you gotta love this!!!! This is one of the best comeback lines of all time. It is a portion of National Public Radio (NPR) interview between a female broadcaster and US Marine Corps General Reinwald who was about to sponsor a Boy Scout Troop visiting his military installation.

Female interviewer: *'So, General Reinwald, what things are you going to teach these young boys when they visit your base?'*
General Reinwald: *'We're going to teach them climbing, canoeing, archery and shooting.'*
Female interviewer*: 'Shooting! That's a bit irresponsible, isn't it?'*
General Reinwald: *'I don't see why, they'll be properly supervised on the rifle range.'*
Female Interviewer: *'Don't you admit that this is a terribly dangerous activity to be teaching children?'*
General Reinwald: *'I don't see how. We will be teaching them proper rifle discipline before they even touch a firearm.'*
Female Interviewer: *'But you're equipping them to become violent killers!'*
General Reinwald: *'Well, Ma'am, you're equipped to be a prostitute, but you're not one, are you?'*
The radio went silent and the interview ended. You gotta love the Marines.

Morning Blindness

Men and women are different in the morning. Men wake up aroused in the morning. They can't help it. They just wake up and they want you. And the women are thinking, *'How can he want me the way I look in the morning?'*

It's because they can't see you! They have no blood anywhere near their optic nerve.

Special Men's Classes

Winter classes for men at the learning centre for adults. Registration must be completed by Tuesday February 28th. Note: due to the complexity and difficulty level of their contents, class sizes will be limited to a maximum of 8 participants.
Class 1: How to fill up the ice cube trays: Step by step, with slide presentation. Meets 4 weeks, Monday and Wednesday for 2 hours beginning at 7:00 pm.
Class 2: The toilet paper roll: Does it change itself? Round table discussion. Meets 2 weeks, Saturday 12:00 for 2 hours.
Class 3: Is it possible to urinate using the technique of lifting the seat and avoiding the floor, walls and nearby bathtub? Group Practice. Meets 4 weeks, Saturday 10:00 am. for 2 hours.

Class 4: Fundamental differences between the laundry hamper and the floor: Pictures and explanatory graphics. Meets Saturdays at 2:00 pm for 3 weeks.
Class 5: After dinner dishes: Can they levitate and fly into the kitchen sink? Examples on Video. Meets 4 weeks, Tuesday and Thursday for 2 hours beginning at 7:00 pm.
Class 6: Loss of identity: Losing the remote to your significant other. Help line support and support groups. Meets 4 Weeks, Friday and Sunday 7:00 pm.
Class 7: Learning how to find things: Starting with looking in the right places and not turning the house upside down while screaming. Open Forum. Monday at 8:00 pm - 2 hours.
Class 8: Health watch: Bringing her flowers is not harmful to your health. Graphics and audio tapes. Three nights; Monday, Wednesday, Friday at 7:00 pm for 2 hours.
Class 9: Real men ask for directions when lost: Real life testimonials. Tuesdays at 6:00 pm Location to be determined.
Class 10: Is it genetically impossible to sit quietly while she parallel parks? Driving simulations. 4 weeks, Saturdays - noon, 2 hours.
Class 11: Learning to live: Basic differences between mother and wife. Online classes and role-playing. Tuesdays at 7:00 pm, location to be determined.
Class 12: How to be the ideal shopping companion. Relaxation exercises, meditation and breathing techniques. Meets 4 weeks, Tuesday and Thursday for 2 hours beginning at 7:00 pm.
Class 13: How to fight cerebral atrophy: Remembering birthdays, anniversaries and other important dates and calling when you're going to be late. Cerebral shock therapy sessions and full lobotomies offered. Three nights; Monday, Wednesday, Friday at 7:00 pm for 2 hours.
Class 14: The stove/oven: What it is and how it is used. Live demonstration. Tuesdays at 6:00 pm, location to be determined.
Upon completion of any of the above courses, diplomas will be issued to the survivors.

Drive-through banking

A sign in a bank lobby states:
Please note that this bank is installing new drive-through teller machines enabling customers to withdraw cash without leaving their vehicles. Customers using this new facility are requested to use the procedures outlined below when accessing their accounts.
After months of careful research, Male and Female procedures have been developed. Please follow the appropriate steps for your gender:

Male Procedure:
- Drive up to the cash machine.
- Put down your car window.
- Insert card into machine and enter PIN.
- Enter amount of cash required and withdraw.
- Retrieve card, cash and receipt.
- Put window up.
- Drive off.

Female Procedure:
- Drive up to cash machine.
- Reverse and back up the required amount to align car window with the machine.
- Set parking brake, put the window down.
- Find handbag, remove all contents onto passenger seat to locate card.
- Tell person on cell phone you will call them back and hang up.
- Attempt to insert card into machine.
- Open car door to allow easier access to machine due to its excessive distance from the car.
- Insert card.
- Re-insert card the right way.
- Dig through handbag to find diary with your PIN written on the inside back page.
- Enter PIN.
- Press cancel and re-enter correct PIN.
- Enter amount of cash required.
- Check makeup in rear view mirror.
- Retrieve cash and receipt.
- Empty handbag again to locate wallet and place cash inside.
- Write debit amount in check register and place receipt in back of chequebook.
- Re-check makeup.
- Drive forward two feet.
- Reverse back to cash machine.
- Retrieve card.
- Re-empty handbag, locate cardholder and place card into slot provided.
- Give dirty look to irate male driver waiting behind you.
- Restart stalled engine and pull off.
- Redial person on cell phone.
- Drive for 2 or 3 kilometres

- Release the parking brake.

Lord, they're finally together

She married and had 13 children. Her husband died. She married again and had 7 more children. Again, her husband died. But, she remarried and this time had 5 more children. Alas, she finally died.
Standing before her coffin, the preacher prayed for her. He thanked the Lord for this very loving woman and said, *'Lord, they're finally together.'*

One mourner leaned over and quietly asked her friend, *'Do you think he means her first, second or third husband?'*

The friend replied, *'I think he means her legs.'*

The Girdle

One morning while making breakfast, a man walked up to his wife and pinched her on her butt and said, *'You know, if you firmed this up, we could get rid of your girdle.'*

While this was on the edge of intolerable, she thought herself better and replied with silence.

The next morning the man woke his wife with a pinch on the breast and said, *'You know if you firmed these up, we could get rid of your bra.'*

This was beyond a silent response, so she rolled over and grabbed him by his penis. With a death grip in place she said, *'You know if you firmed this up, we could get rid of the postman, the gardener, the pool man and your brother.'*

The Mother-in law

A man answers the phone and has the following conversation:

'Yes, mother, I've had a hard day. Gladys has been most difficult. I know I ought to be firmer, but it's hard. Well, you know how she is. Yes, I remember you warned me. I remember you told me that she was a vile creature who would make my life miserable and you begged me not to marry her. You were perfectly right. You want to speak with her? All right ...'

He looks up from the telephone and calls to his wife in the next room: *'Gladys, your mother wants to talk to you!'*

The Dog

A couple were going out for the evening. They were ready, dressed, had put out the dog and were ready to leave. The taxi arrived and as the couple left the house, the dog shot back into the house. They didn't want the dog shut in the house, so the wife went out to the taxi while the husband went upstairs to chase the dog out. The wife, not wanting it known that the house would be empty explains to the taxi driver, *'He's just going upstairs to say good-bye to my mother.'*

A few minutes later, the husband gets into the taxi. *'Sorry I took so long'* he says. *'The stupid bitch was hiding under the bed and I had to poke her with a coat hanger to get her to come out! Then I had to wrap her in a blanket to keep her from scratching and biting me as I hauled her ass downstairs and tossed her into the back yard! She'd better not shit in the vegetable garden again!'*

The silence in the taxi was deafening.

Caught Ya!

This is a true story that happened at a huge wedding with about 300 guests. At the wedding reception, the groom got up on the stage at the microphone to talk to the crowd. He said that he wanted to thank everyone for coming and from long distances, to support them on their wedding day. He said, he wanted to especially thank the bride's family for such a beautiful wedding and reception, knowing it cost a considerable amount of money.

Then he said, *'To thank everyone for coming, I have a gift for you. Taped to the bottom of everyone's chair is a manila envelope.'*
Everyone reached for his or her envelope. Inside was an 8 x 10 picture of his bride having sex with the best man. (He had become suspicious of them and hired a private detective to follow them.) After he stood there and watched people's reactions for a couple of minutes, he turned to the best man and said, *'(Expletive) you!'* He turned to the bride and said, *'(Expletive) you too!'* And then he said, *'I'm out of here.'*

He got the marriage annulled the next day. While most of us would have broken it off immediately after we found out about the affair, this guy went through with it anyway. His revenge: making the bride's parents pay for a 300 guest wedding and reception, letting everyone know exactly what happened and trashing the bride and best man's reputations in front of family and friends.

Pancakes

Brenda and Steve took their six-year-old son to the doctor. With some hesitation, they explained that although their little angel appeared to be in good health, they were concerned about his rather small penis.

After examining the child, the doctor confidently declared, *'Just feed him pancakes. That should solve the problem.'*

The next morning when the boy arrived at breakfast, there was a large stack of warm pancakes in the middle of the table.

'Gee, Mom,' he exclaimed. 'For me?'

'Just take two,' Brenda replied. 'The rest are for your father.'

Newborn son

One night a wife watched her husband as he held their baby over their newborn baby's crib. Silently she watched him. As he stood looking down at the sleeping infant, she saw on his face a mixture of emotions: disbelief, doubt, delight, amazement, enchantment and scepticism.

Touched by this unusual display and the deep emotions it aroused, with eyes glistening, she slipped her arms around her husband. 'A penny for your thoughts,' she whispered in his ear.

'It's amazing!' he replied. 'I just can't see how anybody can make a crib like that for only $46.50!

The Scots

A Scotsman asks the dentist the cost for a tooth extraction. '$85 for an extraction sir,' was the dentist's reply.

'$85? Huv ye no' got anythin' cheaper?'

'That's the normal charge,' said the dentist.

'Whit aboot if ye didnae use any anesthetic?'

'That's unusual, sir, but I could do it and knock $15 off.'

'Whit aboot if ye used wan o yer dentist trainees and still withoot the anaesthetic?'

'I can't guarantee their professionalism and it'll be painful. But the price could drop to $40.'

'How aboot if ye make it a trainin' session, 'ave yer student do the extraction wae' the other students watchin' and learnin?'

'It'll be good for the students,' mulled the dentist. 'OK, I'll charge you $5. But it will be traumatic.'

'Och, now yer talkin' laddie! It's a deal,' said the Scotsman. 'Can ye confirm an appointment for the wife next Tuesday then?'

Mr. McTavish was very sick. His wife sat at his bedside after the doctor had said no more could be done. The man said, 'I don't think I'm going to make it through the night.'

The wife replied, 'I've got to finish my chores, but if you feel yourself slipping away before I return, please be sure to call me.'

A Scot meets a friend at a train station and explains he's off to Glasgow on his honeymoon. His friend asks, 'And just where is your wife?'

'She's been to Glasgow before.' the groom replied.

The Scot told his wife, *'Be sure now to take off your new eye glasses if you're not looking at anything.'*

Looking after your wife

When our lawn mower wouldn't run, my wife kept hinting to me that I should get it fixed. But, somehow I always had something else to take care of first, the truck, the car and fishing: always something more important to me.

Finally she thought of a clever way to make her point. When I arrived home one day, I found her seated in the tall grass, busily snipping away with a tiny pair of sewing scissors. I watched silently for a short time and then went into the house. I was gone only a few minutes.

When I came out again I handed her a toothbrush. *'When you finish cutting the grass,'* I said, *'you might as well sweep the sidewalk.'*

The Anniversary

'What do you want for our 40th anniversary?' John asked his wife, Mary. *'Would you like a new mink coat?'* he asked.
  'Not really,' replied Mary.
  'Well, how about a new Mercedes sports car?' said John.
  'No,' she responded.
  'What about a vacation home in the country?' he suggested.
  She again rejected his offer with a *'No thanks.'*
  'Well what would you like for your anniversary?' John asked.
  'John, I'd like a divorce,' answered Mary.
  'Sorry, I wasn't planning on spending that much,' said John.

Wants a Divorce

A married couple is driving down the interstate going 90 kph. The husband is behind the wheel. His wife looks over at him. *'Honey, I know we've been married for fifteen years, but I want a divorce.'*

The husband says nothing, but slowly increases speed to 100 kph. *'I don't want you to try to talk me out of it, because I've been having an affair with your best friend and he's a better lover than you.'*

Again the husband stays quiet and just speeds up as his anger increases. *'I want the house also.'*

Again the husband speeds up and now is going 135 kph. *'I want the kids too.'* The husband just keeps driving faster and faster until he's up to 150 kph. *'And I want the car, the cheque account and all the credit cards.'*

The husband slowly starts to veer towards a bridge overpass piling as the speedometer reaches 160 kph. *'You're taking this incredibly calmly,'* the wife says. *'Isn't there anything that you want?'*

'No, I have everything I need.'
'What's that?'
'The air bag.'

Family Spat

A husband is at home watching a football game when his wife interrupts, *'Honey, could you fix the light in the hallway? It's been flickering for weeks now.'*

He looks at her and says sarcastically, *'Fix the light? Now? Does it look like I have a G.E. logo printed on my forehead? I don't think so.'*

'Well then, could you fix the fridge door? It won't close right.'

To which he replied, *'Fix the fridge door? Does it look like I have Westinghouse written on my forehead? I don't think so.'*

'Fine,' she says, *'Then you could at least fix the steps to the front door. They're about to break.'*

'I'm not a damned carpenter and I don't want to fix the steps,' he says. *'Does it look like I have Ace Hardware written on my forehead? I don't think so. I've had enough of you. I'm going to the bar!'*

So he goes to the bar and drinks for a couple of hours. He starts to feel guilty about how he treated his wife and decides to go home and help out. As he walks into the house, he notices the steps are already fixed; the hall light is working and when he goes to get a beer, he notices the fridge door is fixed. *'Honey, how'd all this get fixed?'*

She replied, *'Well, when you left, I sat outside and cried. Just then a nice young man asked me what was wrong and I told him. He offered to do all the repairs and all I had to do was either go to bed with him or bake a cake.'*

He said, *'So, what kind of cake did you bake him?'*

She replied, *'Hellooooo ... Do you see Betty Crocker written on my forehead?'*

The Young and the Old

Two guys, one old and one young, are pushing their carts around a furniture warehouse when they collide. The old guy says to the young guy, *'Sorry about that. I'm looking for my wife and I guess I wasn't paying attention to where I was going.'*

The young guy says, *'That's okay. It's a coincidence. I'm looking for my wife, too. I can't find her and I'm getting a little desperate.'*

The old guy says, *'Well, maybe we can help each other. What does your wife look like?*

The young guy says, *'Well, she is 27 yrs old, tall, with red hair, blue eyes, long legs, big boobs and she's wearing tight white shorts. What does your wife look like?'*

The old guy says, *'Doesn't matter - let's look for yours.'*

The Good, the Bad and the Ugly

Good: Your hubby and you agree, no more kids.
Bad: You can't find your birth control pills.
Ugly: Your daughter has taken them.

Good: Your son studies a lot in his room.
Bad: You find several porn movies hidden there.
Ugly: You're in them.

Good: Your husband understands fashion.
Bad: He's a cross-dresser.
Ugly: He looks better than you.

Good: Your son's finally maturing.
Bad: He's involved with the woman next door.
Ugly: So are you.

Good: You give the birds and bees talk to your daughter.
Bad: She keeps interrupting.
Ugly: With corrections.

Good: Your wife's not talking to you.
Bad: She wants a divorce.
Ugly: She's a lawyer.

Good: The postman's early.
Bad: He's wearing fatigues and carrying an AK47.
Ugly: You gave him nothing for Christmas.

Good: Your daughter got a new job.
Bad: She's a hooker
Ugly: Your co-workers are her best clients.
Way Ugly: She makes more money than you do.

Good: Your son is dating someone new.
Bad: It's another man.
Ugly: He's your best friend.

Good: Your wife is pregnant.
Bad: It's triplets.
Ugly: You had a vasectomy five years ago.

Random Thoughts

1. Now that food has replaced sex in my life, I can't even get into my own pants.
2. Marriage changes passion. Suddenly you're in bed with a relative.
3. I saw a woman wearing a shirt with *'Guess'* on it. So I said *'Implants?'* She hit me.
4. I don't do drugs. I get the same effect just standing up fast.
5. I live in my own little world. But it's okay. They know me* here.
6. I got a jumper for Christmas. I really wanted a screamer or a moaner.
7. If flying is so safe, why do they call the airport the terminal?
8. I don't approve of political jokes. I've seen too many of them get elected.
9. There are two sides to every divorce: Yours and fatheads.
10. I love being married. It's so great to find that one special person you want to annoy for the rest of your life.
11. I am a nobody and nobody is perfect; therefore, I am perfect!
12. Every day I beat my own previous record for number of consecutive days I've stayed alive.
13. How come we choose from just two people to run for president and 50 for Miss America?
14. Isn't having a smoking section in a restaurant like having a peeing section in a swimming pool?
15. Why is it that most nudists are people you don't want to see naked?
16. Snowmen fall from Heaven unassembled.
17. Every time I walk into a singles bar, I can hear mom's wise words: *'Don't pick that up - you don't know where it's been.'*

Emotional needs

A husband and wife were getting all snugly in bed. The passion is heating up, but then the wife says, *'I don't feel like it. I just want you to hold me.'*

The husband says, *'What!'*

The wife explains that he must not be in tune with her emotional needs as a woman. The husband realises that nothing is going to happen that night so he might as well deal with it.

The next day the husband takes her shopping at a big department store. He walks around and has her try on three very expensive outfits. She can't decide, so he tells her to take all three of them.

Then they pick up matching shoes at about $100 each. Then they go to the jewellery department where she gets a set of diamond earrings.

The wife is jumping up and down so excited she cannot even believe what is going on. She says, *'I'm ready to go. Let's go to the cash register.'*

The husband stops and says, *'No, honey I don't feel like buying all this stuff now.'*

The wife's face goes blank.

He says, *'Honey - I just want you to hold this stuff for a while.'*

The look on her face is indescribable and she is about to explode and the husband says, *'You must not be in tune with my financial needs as a man.'*

Definitions by Gender

Thingy (thing-ee) n.
Female: Any part under a car's hood.
Male: The strap fastener on a woman's bra.

Vulnerable (vul-ne-ra-bel) adj.
Female: Fully opening up one's self emotionally to another.
Male: Playing football without a helmet.

Communication (ko-myoo-ni-kay-shon) n.
Female: The open sharing of thoughts and feelings with one's partner.
Male: Scratching out a note before suddenly taking off for a weekend with the boys.

Butt (but) n.
Female: A body part that every item of clothing manufactured makes 'look bigger.'
Male: What you slap when someone's scored a touchdown, home run or goal. Also good for mooning.

Commitment (ko-mit-ment) n.
Female: A desire to get married and raise a family.

Male: Not trying to pick up other women while out with one's girlfriend.

Entertainment (en-ter-tayn-ment) n.
Female: A good movie, concert, play or book.
Male: Anything that can be done while drinking.

Flatulence (flachu-u-lens) n.
Female: An embarrassing by-product of digestion.
Male: An endless source of entertainment and self-expression.

Making Love (may-king luv) n.
Female: The greatest expression of intimacy a couple can achieve.
Male: Call it whatever you want, just as long as we end up in bed.

Remote Control (ri-moht kon-trohl) n.
Female: A device for changing from one TV channel to another
Male: A device for scanning through all 75 channels every three minutes.

Red Skelton's recipe for the perfect marriage

1. Twice a week we go to a nice restaurant, have a little beverage, good food and companionship. She goes on Tuesdays; I go on Fridays.
2. We also sleep in separate beds. Hers is in California and mine is in Texas.
3. I take my wife everywhere ... but she keeps finding her way back.
4. I asked my wife where she wanted to go for our anniversary. *'Somewhere I haven't been in a long time!'* she said. So I suggested the kitchen.
5. We always hold hands. If I let go, she shops.
6. She has an electric blender, electric toaster and electric bread maker. She *said 'There are too many gadgets and no place to sit down!'* So I bought her an electric chair.
7. My wife told me the car wasn't running well because there was water in the carburettor. I asked where the car was. She told me, *'In the lake.'*
8. She got a mud pack and looked great for two days. Then the mud fell off.
9. She ran after the garbage truck, yelling, *'Am I too late for the garbage?'* The driver said, *'No, jump in!'*
10. Remember: Marriage is the number one cause of divorce.

11. I married Miss Right. I just didn't know her first name was Always.
12. I haven't spoken to my wife in 18 months. I don't like to interrupt her.
13. The last fight was my fault though. My wife asked, *'What's on the TV?'* I said, *'Dust!'*

Can't you just hear him say all of these? I love it. These were the good old days when humour didn't have to start with a four-letter word. It was just clean and simple fun. And he always ended his programs with the words *'God Bless.'*

CHAPTER 2 - MALE JOKES

Bachelors:

A bachelor who lived at home with his mother and pet cat went on a trip to Europe. Before he left, he told his best friend to inform him of any emergencies. A few days after his departure, his cat climbed up on the roof, fell off and was killed. His friend immediately wired him with the message: *'Your cat died!'*

In a few hours he was back home, having cut short his trip in grief and anger at his friend whom he told, *'Why didn't you break the news to me gradually? You know how close I was to my cat! You could have sent a message 'Your cat climbed up on the roof today,' and the next day you could have written, 'Your cat fell off the roof' and let me down slowly that he died.'*

After a quick memorial service, the bachelor left again to continue his trip. A few days later he returned to his hotel and there was a message waiting for him from his friend. He read, *'Your mother climbed up on the roof today.'*

The Nudist Colony

Bob joins a very exclusive nudist colony. On his first day he takes off his clothes and starts wandering around. A gorgeous blonde walks by him and the man immediately gets and erection. The woman notices his erection, comes over to him grinning sweetly and says: *'Sir, did you call for me?'*

Bob replies, *'No, what do you mean?'*

She replies, *'You must be new here; let me explain. It's a rule here that if I give you an erection, it implies that you called for me.'*

Smiling, she then leads him to the side of the pool, lies down on a towel, eagerly pulls him to her and happily lets him have his way with her.

He sees a sauna, sits down and farts. Within a few moments a huge, horribly corpulent hairy man with a firm erection lumbers out of the steam towards him. The huge man says, *'Sir did you call for me?'*

Bob replies, *'No what do you mean?'*

'You must be new here. It's the rule that when you fart, it implies you called for me.'

The huge man easily spins Bob around, bends him over the bench and lets him have it.

Bob rushes back to the colony office. The smiling naked receptionist greets him. *'May I help you sir?'*

Bob says, *'Here is your card and key back and you can keep the $500 joining fee.'*

'But sir, you've only been here a couple of hours; you only saw a small fraction of our facilities.'

Bob interrupts, *'Listen lady, I am 68 years old, I get a hard-on about once a month, but I fart 15 times a day. No thanks!'*

Lonesome guy

A fellow checked into a hotel on a business trip recently and was a bit lonely so he thought he'd get one of those girls you see advertised in the phone books under 'Escorts and Massages.' He opened the phone book to an ad for a girl calling herself Erogonique, a lovely girl, bending over in the photo. She had all the right curves in all the right places, beautiful long wavy hair and long graceful legs all the way up. You know the kind. So he is in his room and figures, what the hell, he gave her a call.

'Hello?' the woman says. God she sounded sexy!

'Hi, I hear you give a great massage and I'd like you to come to my room and give me one. No, wait, I should be straight with you. I'm in town all alone and what I really want is sex. I want it hard, I want it hot and I want it now. I'm talking kinky the whole night long. You name it; we'll do it. Bring implements, toys, everything you've got in your bag of tricks. We'll go hot and heavy all night; tie me up, cover me in chocolate syrup and whip cream, anything you want baby. Now, how does that sound?'

She says, *'That sounds fantastic, but for an outside line you need to press 9.'*

The Hunters

Two guys go hunting. Jerry has never gone hunting while Joe has hunted all his life. When they get to the woods, Joe tells Jerry to sit by a tree and not make a sound while Joe checks out a deer stand. After he gets about a quarter of a mile away, Joe hears a blood-curdling scream. He rushes back to Jerry and yells, *'I thought I told you to be quiet!'*

Jerry says, *'Hey, I tried - I really did. When those snakes crawled over me, I didn't make a sound. When that bear was breathing down my neck, I didn't make a peep. But when those two chipmunks crawled up my pants leg and said, 'Should we take them with us or eat them here?' I couldn't keep quiet any more!'*

Why men are never depressed:

Men are just happier people – Why?

- Your last name stays put.
- The garage is all yours.
- Wedding plans take care of themselves.
- Chocolate is just another snack.
- You can be President.
- You can never be pregnant.
- You can wear a white T-shirt to a water park.
- You can wear NO shirt to a water park.
- Car mechanics tell you the truth.
- The world is your urinal. You never have to drive to another gas station restroom because this one is just too icky.
- You don't have to stop and think of which way to turn a nut on a bolt.
- Same work, more pay.
- Wrinkles add character.
- Wedding dress $5,000. Tux rental - $100.
- People never stare at your chest when you're talking to them.
- New shoes don't cut, blister or mangle your feet.
- One mood all the time.
- Phone conversations are over in 30 seconds flat.
- You know stuff about tanks.
- A five-day vacation requires only one suitcase.
- You can open all your own jars.
- You get extra credit for the slightest act of thoughtfulness.
- If someone forgets to invite you, s/he can still be your friend.
- Your underwear is $8.95 for a three-pack.
- Three pairs of shoes are more than enough.
- You almost never have strap problems in public.
- The occasional well-rendered belch is practically expected.
- Your belly usually hides your big hips.
- You are unable to see wrinkles in your clothes.
- Everything on your face stays its original colour.
- The same hairstyle lasts for years, maybe decades.
- You only have to shave your face and neck.
- You can play with toys all your life.
- One wallet and one pair of shoes -- one colour for all seasons.
- You can wear shorts no matter how your legs look.
- You can 'do' your nails with a pocket knife.
- You have freedom of choice concerning growing a moustache.
- You can do Christmas shopping for 25 relatives on December 24 in 25 minutes.

No wonder men are happier!

Making a hit with the ladies

Patrick, who was holidaying from Ireland on Bondi beach couldn't seem to make it with any of the girls. So he asked the local lifeguard for some advice.

'Mate, it's obvious,' says the lifeguard, *'You're wearing them old baggy swimming trunks that make you look like an old geezer. They're years out of style. Your best bet is to grab yourself a pair of Speedos - about two sizes too small - and drop a fist-sized potato down inside them. I'm telling you man ... You'll have all the babes you want!'*

The following weekend, Patrick hits the beach with his spanking new tight Speedos and his fist-sized potato. Everybody on the beach was disgusted as he walked by, covering their faces, turning away and laughing, looking sick!

So Patrick went back to the lifeguard again and asked him, *'What's wrong now?'*

'JAHEESUS!' said the lifeguard, *'Mate. The potato goes in front!'*

Male Bashing

1. Why do men become smarter during sex? Because they're plugged into a genius.
2. Why don't women blink during foreplay? They don't have time.
3. Why does it take 1 million sperm to fertilise 1 egg? They won't stop for directions.
4. Why did God put men on earth? Because a vibrator can't mow the lawn.
5. Why don't women have men's brains? Because they don't have penises to put them in.
6. What do electric trains and breasts have in common? They're intended for children, but it's the men who usually end up playing with them.
7. Why do men snore when they lay on their backs? Because their balls fall over their assholes and they have vapour lock.
8. Why do men masturbate? It's sex with someone they love.
9. Why is air a lot like sex? Because it's no big deal unless you're not getting any.
10. What's the difference between a boyfriend and a husband? 45 minutes.
11. What's the difference between a girlfriend and a wife? 45 kgs.

12. What's the fastest way to a man's heart? Through his chest with a sharp knife.
13. Why do men want to marry virgins? They can't stand criticism.
14. Why is it so hard for women to find men that are sensitive, caring and good-looking? Because those men already have boyfriends.
15. What's the difference between a new husband and a new dog? After a year, the dog is still excited to see you.
16. What makes men chase women they have no intention of marrying? The same urge that makes dogs chase cars they have no intention of driving.
17. Why did God make men before women? You need a rough draft before you have a final copy.
18. Why is a man's urine yellow and his sperm white? So he can tell if he's coming or going.
19. Why do men find it difficult to make eye contact? Breasts don't have eyes.
20. How many men does it take to put the toilet seat down? Nobody knows. It hasn't happened yet.
21. Why are men given larger brains than dogs? So they won't hump women's legs at cocktail parties.
22. Why don't men do laundry? Because the washer and dryer don't have a remote control.
23. What's a man's idea of protected sex? A padded headboard.
24. What do you call a woman that works like a man? A lazy bitch.
25. What do men and pantyhose have in common? They cling, run or don't fit right in the crotch.
26. How do we know men invented maps? Who else would make an inch into a mile?
27. Why is psychoanalysis a lot quicker for men than for women? When it's time to go back to his childhood, he's already there.
28. How are men like parking space? The good ones are always taken and all that's left are handicapped.
29. Why do women fake orgasms? Because men fake foreplay.
30. How many men does it take to screw in a light bulb? Only one – men are good at screwing things up!
31. What's the difference between government bonds and men? Government bonds mature.
32. What is the same about a condom and Kodak film? They both catch that special moment.
33. Why was Adam so jealous of his firstborn? He didn't know what an umbilical cord was.
34. How many men does it take to change a roll of toilet paper? No one knows. It's never happened.

35. Why did Moses wander in the desert for 40 years? Because even back then, men wouldn't stop and ask for directions.
36. Santa Claus, the Tooth Fairy, a non-lazy man (who helps out around the house) and a lazy man are about to jump off a bridge into water. Who makes the biggest splash? The lazy man - the other three don't exist.
37. What were Adam's first words to Eve? *'Stand back. I don't know how big it'll get.'*
38. What's a 'Yankee?' It's like a 'Quickee,' but you're by yourself.
39. Why did the condom fly around the room? Because it was pissed off.
40. What did the elephant say to the naked man? How do you breathe through something that little?
41. A man would say: *'Woman: Without her man, is nothing.'* A woman would say: *'Woman: Without her, man is nothing.'*
42. What's a man's idea of helping with the housework? Lifting his legs so you can vacuum.
43. How does a man keep his youth? By giving her money, furs and diamonds.
44. What is the most common cause of hearing loss among men? A woman saying she wants to talk to him.
45. Where do you have to go to find a man who is truly into commitment? A mental hospital.
46. How are men like bank machines? Once they withdraw they lose interest.
47. How can you tell when a man is well hung? When you can just barely slip your finger between his neck and the noose.
48. Why do men prefer the woman to be on top? Because men always screw up.
49. How do you keep your husband from reading your e-mail? Rename the mail folder to 'instruction manuals.'
50. How does a man show that he's planning for the future? He buys two cases of beer.
51. Why are blonde jokes so short? So men can remember them.
52. How are men and parking spots alike? Good ones are always taken. Free ones are mostly handicapped or extremely small.
53. A woman of 35 thinks of having children. What does a man of 35 think of? Dating children.
54. How can you tell soap operas are fictional? In real life, men aren't affectionate out of bed.
55. Why do black widow spiders kill their males after mating? To stop the snoring before it starts.

56. Why don't men have mid-life crisis? They're stuck in adolescence.
57. How is being in a singles bar different from going to the circus? At the circus, the clowns don't talk.
58. What do you do with a bachelor who thinks he's God's gift? Exchange him.
59. Arguments: A woman has the last word in any argument. Anything a man says after that is the beginning of a new argument.
60. Why are husbands like lawn mowers? 'They are hard to get started, emit foul odours and don't work half the time.'
61. What's the difference between a man and E.T.? E.T. phoned home.

Five tips for a woman ...

1. It's important that a man helps you around the house and has a job.
2. It's important that a man makes you laugh.
3. It's important to find a man you can count on and doesn't lie to you.
4. It's important that a man loves you and spoils you.
5. It's important that these four men don't know each other!

If men really ruled the world

1. Nodding and looking at your watch would be deemed an acceptable response to, *'I love you.'*
2. Hallmark would make, *'Sorry, what was your name again?'* cards.
3. When your girlfriend really needed to talk to you during the game, she'd appear in a little box in the corner of the screen during a time-out.
4. Breaking up would be a lot easier. A smack to the ass and a *'Nice hussle, you'll get 'em next time,'* would pretty much do it every time.
5. The funniest guy in the office would get to be CEO.
6. The only show opposite Monday Night Football would be Monday Night Football from a different camera angle.
7. Phones would automatically cut off after one minute of conversation.
8. When a cop gave you a ticket, smart-ass responses would actually reduce your fine.

Double entendres

Mike Hallett discussing missed snooker shots on Sky Sports: *'Stephen Hendry jumps on Steve Davis's misses every chance he gets.'*

Jack Burnicle was talking about Colin Edwards' tyre choice on World Superbike racing: *'Colin had a hard on in practice earlier and I bet he wished he had a hard on now.'*

Winning Post's Stewart Machin commentating on jockey Tony McCoy's formidable lead: *'Tony has a quick look between his legs and likes what he sees.'*

Ross King discussing relays with champion runner Phil Redmond: *'Well Phil, tell us about your amazing third leg.'*

Clair Frisby talking about a jumbo hot dog on Look North said: *'There's nothing like a big hot sausage inside you on a cold night like this.'*

James Allen interviewing Ralf Schumacher at the Grand Prix, asked, *'What does it feel like being rammed up the backside by Barrichello?'*

Steve Ryder covering the US Masters: *'Ballesteros felt much better today after a 69.'*

A female news anchor who, the day after it was supposed to have snowed and didn't, turned to the weatherman and asked, *'So Bob, where's that eight inches you promised me last night?'* Not only did he have to leave the set, but half the crew did too, because they were laughing so hard.

US PGA Commentator - *'One of the reasons Arnie (Arnold Palmer) is playing so well is that, before each tee shot, his wife takes out his balls and kisses them. - Oh my God!!!! What have I just said?!!!!'*

Metro Radio: *'Julian Dicks is everywhere. It's like they've got eleven Dicks on the field.'*

Harry Carpenter at the Oxford-Cambridge boat race 1977 - *'Ah, isn't that nice. The wife of the Cambridge President is kissing the Cox of the Oxford crew.'*

Ted Walsh - Horse Racing Commentator - *'This is really a lovely horse. I once rode her mother.'*

Pat Glenn, weightlifting commentator - *'And this is Gregoriava from Bulgaria. I saw her snatch this morning and it was amazing!'*

The Wedding Ring

Recently a man had to go to the hospital to have his wedding ring cut off from his penis after his mistress found the ring in his pants

pocket and got so mad at him she stuck it on him while he was asleep. I don't know what's worse:
1. Having your mistress find out you're married.
2. Explaining to your wife how your wedding ring got on your penis.
3. Or finding out your penis fits through your wedding ring.

Because I'm a Man

When I catch a cold, I need someone to bring me soup and take care of me while I lie in bed and moan. You're a woman. You never get as sick as I do, so for you this isn't a problem.

I can be relied upon to purchase basic groceries at the store, like milk or bread. I cannot be expected to find exotic items like 'cumin' or 'tofu.' For all I know, these are the same thing. And never, under any circumstances, expect me to pick up anything for which 'feminine hygiene product' is a euphemism. (F.Y.I. guys: cumin is a spice and not a bodily function).

When one of our appliances stops working, I will insist on taking it apart, despite evidence that this will just cost me twice as much, once the repair person gets here and has to put it back together.

I must hold the television remote control in my hand while I watch TV. If the thing has been misplaced, I may miss an entire show looking for it though one time I was able to survive by holding a calculator (applies to engineers mainly).

There is no need to ask me what I'm thinking about. The answer is always mainly sex, cars or sports. I have to make up something else when you ask, so don't ask.

I do not want to visit your mother or have your mother come visit us or talk to her when she calls or think about her any more than I have to. Whatever you got her for Mother's Day is okay; I don't need to see it. And don't forget to pick up something for my mother too.

You don't have to ask me if I liked the movie. Chances are, if you're crying at the end of it, I didn't ... and if you are feeling amorous afterwards ... then I will certainly at least remember the name and recommend it to others.

I think what you're wearing is fine. I thought what you were wearing five minutes ago was fine, too. Either pair of shoes is fine. With the belt or without it, looks fine. Your hair is fine. You look fine. Can we just go now?

Because this is, after all, the year 2013, I will share equally in the housework. You just do the laundry, the cooking, the cleaning, the vacuuming and the dishes and I'll do the rest, like looking for my socks or like wandering around in the garden with a beer wondering what to do.

When I lock my keys in the car, I will fiddle with a wire clothes hanger and ignore your suggestions that we call a road service, until long after hypothermia has set in. Oh and when the car isn't running very well, I will pop the hood and stare at the engine as if I know what I'm looking at. If another guy shows up, one of us will say to the other, *'I used to be able to fix these things, but now with all these computers and everything, I wouldn't know where to start.'* We will then drink beer.

I don't think we're all that lost and no, I don't think we should stop and ask someone. Why would you listen to a complete stranger - how the heck could he know where we're going?

I'm capable of announcing, *'One more beer and I really have to go'* and mean it every single time I say it, even when it gets to the point that the one bar closes and my buddies and I have to go hunt down another. I will find it increasingly hilarious to have my friends call you to tell you I'll be home soon and no, I don't understand why you threw all my clothes into the front yard. What's the connection?

Yes, I have to turn up the radio when Bruce Springsteen or The Doors comes on and then, yes, I have to tell you every single time about how Bruce and his picture on the cover of Time and Newsweek the same day or how Jim Morrison is buried in Paris and everyone visits his grave. Please do not behave as if you do not find this fascinating.

The Cruise

A man goes to a travel agent and books a two-week cruise for himself and his girlfriend. A couple of days before the cruise, the travel agent phones and says the cruise has been cancelled, but he can get them on a three-day cruise instead. The man agrees and then goes to the pharmacy to buy three Dramamine tablets and three condoms.

The next day, the agent calls back and says that he can now book a five-day cruise. The man takes it and returns to the same pharmacy and buys two more Dramamine tablets and two more condoms.

The following day, the travel agent calls again and says he can now book an eight-day cruise. The man accepts it and goes back to the pharmacy and asks for three more Dramamine and three more condoms.

Finally, the pharmacist asks, *'Look, if it makes you sick, why do you keep doing it?'*

Shipwrecked

A young man was shipwrecked on a remote island. Although he had plenty of food and water, there was nothing for him to do except play with himself. After many years, even that became so monotonous that he couldn't even get and erection. Completely without happiness, he started to lose his sanity. One morning, as he was lying on the beach, he thought he saw a cruise ship in the distance. He quickly started a fire and threw wet seaweed on top until smoke billowed high in the air. The ship started to come his way!

He got all excited and thought, *'Finally! I'm going to be saved! The first thing I want to do is to take a long, hot shower. Then they're going to give me some clothes and I'm going to have a nice dinner. I'll find a nice lady to dance with, then I'll take her to her cabin and we can kiss and I can fondle her body. She'll start to take off her clothes and she'll be wearing red silk panties!'*

At this, he starts to get an erection. He slips his hand into his shorts and yells, *'Ho! Ha! Ha! I lied about the ship!'*

A very successful and ambitious yuppie finally decided to take a vacation. He booked himself on a Caribbean cruise and proceeded to have the time of his life. Until the boat sank.

The man found himself swept up on the shore of an island with no other people, no supplies ... nothing! Only bananas and coconuts. After about four months, he is lying on the beach when the most gorgeous woman he has ever seen rows up to him. In disbelief, he asks her, *'Where did you come from? How did you get here?*

'I rowed from the other side of the island,' she says. *'I landed here when my cruise ship sank.*

'Amazing,' he says. *'You were really lucky to have a row boat wash up with you.'*

'Oh this?' replied the woman. *'I made the rowboat out of raw material that I found on the island. The oars were whittled from gum tree branches. I wove the bottom from palm branches and the sides and stern came from a Eucalyptus tree.'*

'But-but, that's impossible,' stutters the man. *'You had no tools or hardware. How did you manage?'*

'Oh that was no problem,' replied the woman. *'On the south side of the island there is a very unusual strata of alluvial rock exposed. I found if I fired it to a certain temperature in my kiln, it melted in to forgeable ductile iron. I used that for tools and used the tools to make the hardware.'*

The guy is stunned. *'Let's row over to my place,'* she says.

After a few minutes of rowing, she docks the boat at a small wharf. As the man looks onto shore, he nearly falls out of the boat. Before him is a stone walk leading to an exquisite bungalow painted blue and white. While the man ties up the rowboat with an expertly woven hemp rope, the man can only stare ahead dumbstruck. As they walk into the house she says casually, *'It's not much, but I call it home. Sit down please. Would you like to have a drink?'*

'No, no thank you,' he says still dazed. *'I can't take any more coconut juice.'*

'Oh it's not coconut juice,' the woman replied. *'I have a still. How about a Pinna Colada?'*

Trying to hide his continued amazement, the man accepts and they sit down on her couch to talk. After they have exchanged their stories, the woman announces, *'I'm going to slip into something more comfortable. Would you like to take a shower and shave? There is a razor upstairs in the bathroom cabinet.'*

No longer questioning anything, the man goes into the bathroom. There, in the cabinet, is a razor made from a bone handle. Two shells honed to a hollow ground edge are fastened onto its end inside of a swivel mechanism.

'This woman is amazing,' he muses. *'What's next?'* When he returns, she greets him wearing nothing but vines - strategically positioned and smelling faintly of gardenias. She beckons him to sit down next to her.

'Tell me,' she begins, suggestively slithering closer to him, *'We've been out here for a really long time. You've been lonely. There's something I'm sure you really feel like doing right now, something you've been longing for all these months?'*

She stares into his eyes. He can't believe what he's hearing: *'You mean ...?'* he swallows excitedly, *'I can check my e-mail from here?'*

A man is stranded on a desert island and one day a lady gets washed up onto shore. They talk and get to know each other. Later on that day, the woman asks him, *'I don't suppose you smoked before you were stranded here did you'*

The man replies, *'Why yes I did.'*

So she produces a cigarette from her bag and they smoke it together. A little while later she says, *'I don't suppose you drank before you were stranded did you?'*

'Why yes I did.'

The woman produces a flask from her bag and they have a drink. More time passes and the woman says, *'So you've been on this island for ten years without a woman?'*

'Yes I have.'

'I don't suppose you'd like to play around?'

The man shouts, *'Good God lady, you have a set of clubs in that bag too?'*

Fighting back

After all those male-bashing jokes floating around, someone finally fought back:

How many men does it take to open a beer? None. It should be opened by the time she brings it.

Why is a Laundromat a really bad place to pick up a woman? Because a woman who can't even afford a washing machine will never be able to support you.

Why do women have smaller feet than men? So they can stand closer to the kitchen sink.

How do you know when a woman's about to say something smart? When she starts her sentence sith, 'A man once told me ...'

Why do men pass gas more than women? Because women don't shut up long enough to build up pressure.

If your dog is barking at the back door and your wife is yelling at the front door, whom do you let in first? The dog of course. At least he'll shut up after you let him in.

All wives are alike, but they have different faces so you can tell them apart.

What's worse than a Male Chauvinist Pig? A woman that won't do what she's told.

What do you call a woman with two brain cells? Pregnant.

I haven't spoken to my wife for 18 months - I don't like to interrupt her.

What do you call a woman who has lost 95% of her intelligence? Divorced.

Bigamy is having one wife too many. Some say monogamy is the same.

Scientists have discovered one certain food that diminishes a woman's sex drive by 90% ... wedding cake.

Girls Night Out

Why females should avoid a girls night out after they are married!

The other night I was invited out for a night with 'the girls.' I told my husband that I would be home by midnight, *'I promise!'* Well, the hours passed and the margaritas went down way too easy.

Around 3 am, a bit loaded, I headed for home. Just as I got in the door, the cuckoo clock in the hall started up and cuckooed 3 times. Quickly, realising my husband would probably wake up, I cuckooed another 9 times. I was really proud of myself for coming up with such a quick-witted solution, in order to escape a possible conflict with him. (Even when totally smashed ... 3 cuckoos plus 9 cuckoos totals 12 cuckoos equals MIDNIGHT!)

The next morning my husband asked me what time I got in and I told him *'Midnight.'* He didn't seem pissed off at all. Whew! Got away with that one! Then he said, *'We need a new cuckoo clock.'*

When I asked him why, he said, *'Well, last night our clock cuckooed three times, then said, 'Oh. Shit,' cuckooed 4 more times, cleared it's throat, cuckooed another 3 times, giggled, cuckooed twice more and then tripped over the coffee table and farted.'*

*1950's **Rules for Wives*** (Obviously written by a man!)

1. Have dinner ready: Plan ahead, even the night before, to have a delicious meal - on time. This is the way of letting him know that you have been thinking about him and are concerned about his needs. Most men are hungry when they come home and the prospect of a good meal is part of the warm welcome needed at the end of a day.
2. Prepare yourself: Take fifteen minutes to rest so you will be refreshed when he arrives. Touch up your make-up, put a ribbon in your hair and be fresh looking. He has just been with a lot of work-weary people. Be a little gay and interesting. His boring day may need a lift.
3. Clear away clutter: Make one last rip through the main part of the home just before our husband arrives, gathering up school books, toys, paper, etc. Then run a dust cloth over the tables. Your husband will feel he has reached a haven of rest and order and it will give you a lift too.
4. Prepare the children: Take a few minutes to wash the children's hands and faces if they are small, comb their hair and if necessary, change their clothes. They are little treasures and he would like them to greet him as he arrives home.
5. Greet him with a warm smile: Be glad to see him. Minimise the noise. At the time of his arrival, eliminate all noise of washer, dryer or vacuum. Encourage the children to sit quietly.

Some don'ts (more of his nonsense)

1. Don't greet him with problems or complaints.
2. Don't complain if he's late for dinner. Count this as minor compared with what he might have gone through that day.
3. Make him comfortable. Have him lean back in a comfortable chair or suggest he lay down in the bedroom. Have a cool or

warm drink ready for him. Arrange his pillow and offer to take off his shoes. Speak in a low, soft, soothing and pleasant voice. Allow him to relax and unwind.
4. Listen to him. You may have a dozen things to tell him, but the moment of his arrival home is not the time. Let him talk first.
5. Make the evening his. Never complain if he does not take you out to dinner or to other places of entertainment; instead try to understand his world of strain and pressure and his need to be home and relax.
6. The Goal: Try to make your home a place of peace and order where your husband can relax.

The Updated Version for the New Millennium woman

1. Have dinner ready: Make reservations ahead of time. If your day becomes too hectic, just leave him a voice mail message regarding where you'd like to eat and at what time. This lets him know that your day has been crappy and gives him an opportunity to change your mood.
2. Prepare yourself: A quick shop at the Lancome counter on your way will do wonders for your outlook and will keep you from becoming irritated every time he opens his mouth. (Don't forget to use his credit card!)
3. Clear away the clutter: Call the housekeeper and tell her that any miscellaneous items left on the floor by the children can be placed in the Goodwill box in the garage.
4. Prepare the children: Send the children to their rooms to watch television or play Nintendo. After all, both of them are from his previous marriages.
5. Minimise the noise: If you happen to be home when he arrives, be in the bathroom with the door locked.

Some Don'ts

1. Don't greet him with problems and complaints. Let him speak first and then your complaints will get more attention and remain fresh in his mind throughout dinner.
2. Don't complain if he's late for dinner, simply remind him that the left-overs are in the fridge and you left the dishes for him to do.
3. Make him comfortable. Tell him where he can find a blanket if he's cold. This will really show you care.
4. Listen to him: But don't ever let him get the last word.
5. Make the evening his: Never complain if he does not take you out to dinner or other places of entertainment - go with a friend

or go shopping (using his credit card). Familiarise him with the phrase, 'girls' night out'
6. The Goal: Try to keep things amicable without reminding him that he only thinks the world revolves around him. Obviously he's wrong - it revolves around you.

The Moocher

'I'm ashamed of the way we live,' a young wife says to her lazy husband who refuses to find a job. *'My father pays our rent. My mother buys all our food. My sister buys our clothes. My aunt bought us a car. I'm just so ashamed.'*

The husband rolls over on the couch. *'And you damned well should be,'* he agrees. *'Those two worthless brothers of yours ain't never give us a cent!'*

Soldiers

Three soldiers had just been released from the Army. To celebrate, they decided to take a helicopter ride around the town. The first soldier was eating a banana. *'Hmmm. I wonder. If we throw this peel out of the helicopter, will we see it land?'* The other two soldiers shrugged and said to go ahead and throw it out. They watched with anticipation, but they didn't see it land.

The second soldier had a rock. He threw it out of the helicopter and said, *'This is bigger than the peel. We oughta be able to see this land.'* The soldiers all watched again, but nothing happened. The third soldier pulled out a grenade, pulled the pin and threw it. *'Now we'll see this land.'* The soldiers watched again. Nothing happened.

After the ride, the soldiers were walking home. They saw a little girl crying on the sidewalk. *'What's wrong?'* the soldiers asked. *'Well,'* said the little girl, *'I was just walking along and slipped on a banana peel that came out from no where.'* The soldiers explained what had happened in the helicopter and carried the girl home.

As they were walking along once more, they saw a little boy crying on the side of the road. *'What's the matter son?'*

'Well,' said the little boy, *'I was just walking along when a rock hit me on the head.'* The soldiers again told their story and helped the little boy home.

'I wonder what happened with the grenade,' said one soldier. *'Me, too,'* said another, so the soldiers went down the road where they saw an old woman laughing hysterically. *'Ma'am, what's so funny?'*

The old woman between giggles said, *'Well, I farted and my house blew up.'*

Beer Facts

You have to hope that this study is flawed, but the evidence seems irrefutable. Yesterday, scientists for Health Canada suggested that, considering the results of a recent analysis that revealed the presence of female hormones in beer, men should take a look at their beer consumption. The theory is that drinking beer makes men turn into women.

To test the theory, 100 men were fed six pints of beer each within a one-hour period. It was then observed that 100% of the men gained weight, talked excessively without making sense, became overly emotional, couldn't drive, failed to think rationally, argued over nothing, had to sit down while urinating, couldn't perform sexually and refused to apologise when wrong.

No further testing is planned.

Natural Selection

A herd of buffalo can move only as fast as the slowest buffalo and when the herd is hunted, it is the slowest and weakest ones at the back that are killed first.

This natural selection is good for the herd as a whole, because the general speed and health of the whole group keeps improving by the regular attrition of the weakest members. In much the same way, the human brain can only operate as fast as the slowest brain cells.

Excessive intake of alcohol, as we all know, kills brain cells, but naturally it attacks the slowest and weakest brain cells first. In this way, regular consumption of beer eliminates the weaker brain cells, making the brain a faster and more efficient machine.

And that is why you always start feeling smarter after a few beers.

GST Update

The Prime minister announced today that the GST would definitely apply to the Penis because it provides a service. This was due to the fact that:

- 40% of the time it is hanging around unemployed.
- 30% of the time it is hard up.
- 20% of the time it is pissed off.
- 10% of the time it is in a hole.

On top of that, it has two dependents and they're both nuts. Effective from July 1st, 2014, a penis will be taxed according to size:

- 10-12 inches - Luxury tax.
- 8-10 inches - Pole tax.

- 5-6 inches - Privilege tax.
- 4-5 inches - Nuisance tax.
- Males with penises exceeding 12 inches must file under capital gains. Please do not ask for an extension.

The taxpayers association is still waiting clarification on a number of questions raised on this new tax including:
- Are there penalties for late withdrawals?
- Do multiple partners count as a corporation?
- Are condoms deductible as work clothes?

The Trade

'I just got a car for my wife. Good trade, huh?'

Texan Baby

A Texan is drinking in a New York bar when he got a call on his cell phone. He hung up, grinning from ear to ear and ordered a round of drinks for everybody in the bar. He announces that his wife has just produced a typical Texas baby boy weighing 25 pounds. Nobody can believe that any new baby can weigh in at 25 pounds, but the Texan just shrugs, *'That's about average down South folks. Like I said, my boy's a typical Texan baby boy.'*

Congratulations showered him from all around and many exclamations of *'Wow!'* were heard. One woman actually fainted due to sympathy pains.

Two weeks later the Texan returns to the bar. The bartender says, *'Say, you're the father of that Texan baby that weighed 25 pounds at birth, aren't you? Everybody's been making bets about how big he'd be in two weeks. We were gonna call you. So how much does he weigh now?'*

The proud father answers, *'Twenty-three pounds.'* The bartender is puzzled and concerned. *'What happened? He already weighed 25 pounds the day he was born.'*

The Texan father takes a slow swig from his Budweiser, wipes his lips on his shirt sleeve, leans into the bartender and proudly says, *'Had him circumcised'*

Spanish Restaurant

An American touring in Spain stopped at a local restaurant following a day of sightseeing. While sipping his sangria, he noticed a sizzling, scrumptious looking platter being served at the next table. He asked the waiter, *'What is that you just served?'*

The waiter replied, *'Ah senor, you have excellent taste! Those are the bull's testicles from the bullfight this morning. A delicacy!'*

The American, though momentarily daunted, said, *'What the Hell, I'm on vacation! Bring me an order!'*

The waiter replied, *'I am sorry senor. There is only one serving per day because there is only one bullfight each morning. If you come early tomorrow and place your order, we will be sure to save you this delicacy!'*

The next morning, the American returned, placed his order and then that evening he was served the one and only special delicacy of the day. After a few bites and inspecting the contents of his platter, he called to the waiter and said, *'These are delicious, but they are much, much smaller than the ones I saw you serve yesterday!'*

The waiter shrugged his shoulders and replied, *'Si senor. Sometimes the bull he wins.'*

CHAPTER 3 - FEMALES

It's good to be a woman:

- We got off the Titanic first.
- We can scare male bosses with mysterious gynaecological disorder excuses.
- Taxis stop for us.
- We don't look like a frog in a blender when dancing.
- No fashion faux pas we make could ever rival the Speedo.
- We don't have to pass gas to amuse ourselves.
- If we forget to shave, no one has to know.
- We can congratulate our teammate without ever touching her rear end.
- We never have to reach down every so often to make sure our privates are still there.
- We have the ability to dress ourselves.
- We can talk to the opposite sex without having to picture them naked.
- If we marry someone twenty years younger, we are aware that we will look like an idiot.
- We will never regret piercing our ears.
- There are times when chocolate really can solve all your problems.
- We can make comments about how silly men are when in their presence - because they aren't really listening anyway.
- We can be groupies. Male groupies are stalkers.
- We can cry and get off speeding fines.
- Free drinks, free dinners.
- New lipstick gives us a whole new lease on life.
- If we're dumb, some people will find it cute.
- I've found at my age going bra-less pulls all the wrinkles out of my face.
- Behind every successful woman - is herself.
- Why is virginity like a balloon? All it needs is one little prick and it's gone.

Just a thought for all you women out there: MENtal illness; MENstrual cramps; MENtal breakdown; MENopause. Ever notice how all of women's problems start with men? And when we have real problems, it's a HISterectomy?

- First God created man. Then he had a better idea.
- Ginger Rogers did everything Fred Astaire did, but she did it backwards and in high heels!
- A woman is like a tea bag. You don't know how strong she is until you put her in hot water.
- So many men, so few who can afford me.
- Coffee, chocolate and men - some things are just better rich.
- Don't treat me any differently than you would the queen.
- How can I miss you if you won't go away?
- Of course I don't look busy. I did it right the first time.
- If you want breakfast in bed, sleep in the kitchen.

Female Facts

- There are three billion women who don't look like super models and only eight who do - and they're all beautiful in their own way.
- Marilyn Monroe wore a size 14.
- If Barbie were a real woman, she'd have to walk on all fours due to her proportions.
- The average American woman weighs 144 pounds (65.3 kg) and wears between a size 12 and 14.
- One out of every four college-aged women has an eating disorder.
- The models in magazines are airbrushed; they are not perfect!
- A psychological study found that three minutes spent looking at models in a fashion magazine caused 70% of women to feel depressed, guilty and shameful.
- Models who twenty years ago weighed 8% less than the average woman, today weigh 23% less.

A Short Course In Marketing, Advertising And Public Relations

The buzz Word in today's business world is MARKETING. However, people often ask for a simple explanation of 'Marketing.' Well, here it is:

1. You're a woman and you see a handsome guy at a party. You go up to him and say, *'I'm fantastic in bed.'* That's Direct Marketing.
2. You're at a party with a bunch of friends and see a handsome guy. One of your friends goes up to him and, pointing at you, says, *'She's fantastic in bed.'* That's Advertising.

3. You see a handsome guy at a party. You go up to him and get his telephone number. The next day you call and say, *'Hi, I'm fantastic in bed.'* That's Telemarketing.
4. You see a guy at a party; you straighten your dress. You walk up to him and pour him a drink. You say, *'May I?'* and reach up to straighten his tie, brushing your breast lightly against his arm and then say, *'By the way, I'm fantastic in bed.'* That's Public Relations.
5. You're at a party and see a handsome guy. He walks up to you and says, *'I hear you're fantastic in bed.'* That's Brand Recognition.
6. You're at a party and see a handsome guy. He fancies you, but you talk him into going home with your friend. That's a Sales Rep.
7. Your friend can't satisfy him so he calls you. That's Tech Support.
8. You're on your way to a party when you realise that there could be handsome men in all these houses you're passing, so you climb onto the roof of one situated towards the centre and shout at the top of your lungs, *'I'm fantastic in bed!'* That's Junk Mail.
9. You are at a party; this well-built man walks up to you and grabs your ass. that's Bill Clinton.
10. You liked it, but twenty years later your attorney decides you were offended; that's America.

Every woman should have

- One old love she can imagine going back to and one who reminds her how far she has come.
- Enough money within her control to move out and rent a place of her own, even if she never wants to and needs to.
- Something perfect to wear if the employer or date of her dreams wants to see her in an hour.
- A youth she's content to leave behind.
- A past juicy enough that she's looking forward to retelling it in her old age.
- The realisation that she is actually going to have an old age and some money set aside to fund it.
- A set of screwdrivers, a cordless drill and a black lace bra.
- One friend who always makes her laugh and one who lets her cry.
- A good piece of furniture not previously owned by anyone else in her family.

- Eight matching plates, wine glasses with stems and a recipe for a meal that will make her guests feel honoured.
- A resume that is not even a slightest bit padded.
- A feeling of control over her destiny.

Every woman should know

- How to fall in love without losing herself.
- How to quit a job, break up with a lover and confront a friend without ruining the friendship.
- When to try harder - and when to walk away.
- How to have a good time at a party she'd never choose to attend.
- How to ask for what she wants in a way that makes it most likely she'll get it.
- That she can't change the length of her calves, the width of her hips or the nature of her parents.
- That her childhood may not have been perfect - but it's over.
- What she would and wouldn't do for love or more.
- How to live alone, even if she doesn't like it.
- Whom she can trust, whom she can't and why she shouldn't take it personally.
- Where to go, be it her best friend's kitchen table or a charming inn in the woods, when her soul needs soothing.
- What she can and can't accomplish in a day, a month and a year.

The Lonely Brain Cell

Once upon a time there was a female brain cell that, by mistake, happened to end up in a man's head. She looked around nervously because it was all empty and quiet.

'Hello?' she cried, but no answer. *'Is there anyone here?'* she cried a little louder, but still no answer.

Now the female brain cell started to feel alone and scared because there were no brain cells around and she yelled at the top of her voice, *'HELLO, IS THERE ANYONE HERE?'*

Then she heard a faint voice from far, far away....

'We're down here.'

Women's Strengths

- Women have strengths that amaze men:
- Women wait by the phone for a 'safe at home call' from a friend after a snowy drive home.

- Women have special qualities about them. They volunteer for good causes. They are pink ladies in hospitals, they bring food to shut-ins. They are child-care workers, executives, attorneys, stay-at-home moms, biker babes and your neighbours.
- They fight for what they believe in and they stand up for injustice. They are in the front row at PTA meetings. They vote for the person that will do the best job for family issues.
- They walk and talk the extra mile to get their children in the right schools and for getting their family the right health care.
- They write to the editor, their congressmen and to the 'powers that be' for things that make for a better life.
- They don't take 'No' for an answer when they believe there is a better solution.
- They stick a love note in their husband's lunch box.
- They do without new shoes so their children can have them.
- They go to the doctor with a frightened friend.
- They love unconditionally.
- Women are honest, loyal and forgiving. They are smart, knowing that knowledge is power. But they still know how to use their softer side to make a point.
- Women want to be the best for their family, their friends and themselves.
- They cry when their children excel and cheer when their friends win awards.
- A woman's touch can cure any ailment.
- They can make a romantic evening unforgettable.
- They e-mail you to show how much they care about you.
- They give moral support to their family and friends. And all they want back is a hug, a smile and for you to do the same to the people in your life.

TV Ads

Languishing in bed last week with a bad cold, I spent four days in the company of Oprah and Maury Povitch and General Hospital. I was astonished to discover that most daytime TV commercials have one clear message: women leak, dribble and smell. They're overweight and they're constipated. Women have dandruff, split ends, bad breath and bad breasts; both the under- and over-endowed require special bras.

Apparently women must buff, douche, diet, gargle and primp constantly if they want to overcome their basic vileness. Then I thought, '*Maybe men get the same messages when they watch their programs. Maybe advertising during sporting events is geared* towards products that men need to make them socially acceptable. So I turned on a golf tournament and spent an hour and 12 minutes watching the commercials.'

Evidently men are fine just the way they are. They have a small problem with weight gain and greying hair, but mainly they are handsome, playful and successful. They get to go fishing with their buddies, using leaves for toilet paper. They could probably come home from their trip and hop right into the sack for a romantic encounter and think they were just fine. No rushing off to shower or spray here.

Around this time I needed to get some caught syrup. The first thing I noticed when I got to the pharmacy was a huge sign, 'Feminine Hygiene,' hanging above an aisle filled with thousands of products designed for women's 'special' needs. There were a variety of pads in a multitude of shapes for heavy periods, light periods and bladder control, as well as for women who wanted to feel fresh all day.

There were yeast-infection medications, vaginal deodorants, vaginal lubricants, douches, personal towelettes, pregnancy tests and germicides to do away with feminine odour. There were laxatives, haemorrhoid creams and gas-relief tablets.

The packages for feminine products usually featured a woman in a gauzy dress running through a meadow full of spring flowers (daisies were very popular) as her sparkling clean hair billowed behind her.

I looked all over, but there was no aisle for 'Masculine Hygiene.' Now I've been around enough men to know that some of them could use piddle pads and penis towelettes and deodorants, products for crabs and crotch rot and athlete's foot and gas, so couldn't understand why the drugstore didn't at least label the aisle 'Feminine/Masculine Hygiene.' The closest I came to anything specifically target to men was a large display of condoms next to a shelf of K-Y jelly.

As the female pharmacist explained to me - most shoppers for hygiene products were women whether the product was for male or female usage. I guess that explains it.

Home Depot

Charlie was fixing a door and found that he needed a new hinge, so he sent his wife Mary to Home Depot.

At Home Depot, Mary saw a beautiful teapot on a top shelf while she was waiting for Walt, the manager, to finish waiting on a customer. When Walt was finished, Mary asked *'How much for the teapot?'*

Walt replied, *'That's silver and it costs $300.'*

'My goodness! That sure is a lot of money!' Mary exclaimed. Then she proceeded to describe the hinge that Charlie had sent her to buy and Walt went to the back room to find it.

From the back room Walt yelled, *'Mary, you wanna screw for that hinge?'*

Mary replied, *'No, but I will for the teapot.'*

This is why you can't send a woman to Home Depot.

Women are evil by nature

A sexy woman went up to the bar in a quiet rural pub; she gestured alluringly to the bartender who approached her immediately. She seductively signalled that he should bring his face closer to hers. As he did, she gently caressed his full beard. *'Are you the manager?'* she asked, softly stroking his face with both hands.

'Actually, no,' he replied.

'Can you get him for me? I need to speak to him,' she said, running her hands beyond his beard and into his hair.

'I'm afraid I can't,' breathed the bartender. *'Is there anything I can do?'*

'Yes. I need for you to give him a message,' she continued, running her forefinger across the bartender's lips and slyly popping a couple of her fingers into his mouth and allowing him to suck them gently.

'What should I tell him?' the bartender managed to say.

'Tell him,' she whispered, *'there's no toilet paper, hand soap or paper towels in the ladies room.'*

The ugly woman

An ugly woman walks into a shop with her two kids. The shopkeeper asks: *'Are they twins?'*

The woman says: *'No, he's 9 years old and she's 7. Why? Do you think they look alike?'*

'No,' he replies *'I just can't believe the fellow did it with you twice.'*

It will never fit

The woman entered the room and with a knowing smile teasing her full lips, she sank into the comfort of the plush chair in the corner. The handsome stranger turned, having sensed her approach. Locking his steely grey eyes on hers, he moved slowly toward her, his experienced gaze measuring her, hypnotising her with his soft murmurs of assurance. He sank to his knees before her and without a word, smoothly released her from her constraining attire.

With a sigh of surrender, she allowed his foreign hands to unleash her bare flesh. He expertly guided his hands through this tender, often hidden territory, his movements deliberate, confident in his ability to satisfy her every need. Her senses swam. She was overcome with an aching desire that had gone unfulfilled for so long. And, just as it seemed that ecstasy was within her grasp, he paused and for one heart-stopping moment, she thought, *'It's too big! - it will never fit!'*

Then, with a sudden rush, it slid into place as if it had been made only for her. As pleasure and contentment washed over her, she met his steady gaze, tears of gratitude shining in her eyes. And he knew it wouldn't be long before she returned. Oh, yes, this woman would want more. She would want to do it again and again and again.

Don't ya just love shopping for shoes?

One Flaw In Women

By the time the Lord made woman, He was into his sixth day of working overtime. An angel appeared and said, *'Why are you spending so much time on this one?'*

And the Lord answered, *'Have you seen my spec sheet on her? She has to be completely washable, but not plastic, have over 200 movable parts, all replaceable and able to run on diet coke and leftovers, have a lap that can hold four children at one time, have a kiss that can cure anything from a scraped knee to a broken heart - and she will do everything with only two hands.'*

The angel was astounded at the requirements. *'Only two hands!? No way! And that's just on the standard model? That's too much work for one day. Wait until tomorrow to finish.'*

'But I won't,' the Lord protested. *'I am so close to finishing this creation that is so close to my own heart. She already heals herself when she is sick AND can work 18 hour days.'*

The angel moved closer and touched the woman. *'But you have made her so soft, Lord.'*

'She is soft,' the Lord agreed, *'but I have also made her tough. You have no idea what she can endure or accomplish.'*

'Will she be able to think?' asked the angel.

The Lord replied, *'Not only will she be able to think, she will be able to reason and negotiate.'*

The angel then noticed something and reaching out, touched the woman's cheek. *'Oops, it looks like you have a leak in this model. I told you that you were trying to put too much into this one.'*

'That's not a leak,' the Lord corrected, *'that's a tear!'*

'What's the tear for?' the angel asked.

The Lord said, *'The tear is her way of expressing her joy, her sorrow, her pain, her disappointment, her love, her loneliness, her grief and her pride.'*

The angel was impressed. *'You are a genius, Lord. You thought of everything! Woman is truly amazing.'*

And she is! Women have strengths that amaze men. They bear hardships and they carry burdens, but they hold happiness, love and joy. They smile when they want to scream. They sing when they want to cry. They cry when they are happy and laugh when they are nervous. They fight for what they believe in. They stand up to injustice. They don't take 'no' for an answer when they believe there is a better solution.

They go without so their family can have. They go to the doctor with a frightened friend. They love unconditionally. They cry when their children excel and cheer when their friends get awards. They are happy when they hear about a birth or a wedding. Their hearts break when a friend dies. They grieve at the loss of a family member, yet they are strong when they think there is no strength left.

They know that a hug and a kiss can heal a broken heart. Women come in all shapes, sizes and colours. They'll drive, fly, walk, run or e-mail you to show how much they care about you. The heart of a woman is what makes the world keep turning. They bring joy, hope and love. They have compassion and ideals. They give moral support to their family and friends. Women have vital things to say and everything to give.

However, if there is one flaw in women, it is that they forget their worth.

Preparing for the Annual Mammogram

Many women are afraid of their first mammogram and even if they have had them before, there is fear. But there is no need to worry. By taking a few minutes each day for a week preceding the exam and doing the following practice exercises, you will be totally prepared for the test and best of all - you can do these simple practice exercises right in or around your home!

Exercise 1: Open your refrigerator door and insert one breast between the door and the main box. Have one of your strongest friends slam the door shut as hard as possible and lean on the door for good measure. Hold that position for five seconds. Repeat in case the first time wasn't effective. Repeat for second breast.

Exercise 2: Visit your garage at 3:00 am when the temperature of the cement floor is just perfect. Take off all your clothes and lie comfortably on the floor sideways with one breast wedged under the rear tire of the car. Ask a friend to slowly back the car up until your breast is sufficiently flattened and chilled. Switch sides and repeat for the other breast.

Exercise 3: Freeze two metal bookends over night. Strip to the waist. Invite a stranger into the room. Have the stranger press the book ends against either side of one of your breasts and smash the bookends together as hard as s/he can. Set an appointment with the stranger to meet next year to do it again. Now - you're properly prepared for the real thing. Read on ...

Ode to a Mammogram

For years and years they told me, be careful of your breasts,
    Don't ever squeeze or bruise them and give them monthly tests.
    So I heeded all their warnings and protected them by law.
    Guarded them very carefully and always wore my bra.
    After 30 years of astute care, my doctor found a lump.
    He ordered up a mammogram, to look inside that lump.
    'Stand up very close,' he said, as he got my boob in line,
    'And tell me when it hurts,' he said, 'Ah yes! There, that's just fine.'
    He stepped upon a pedal; I could not believe my eyes!
    A plastic plate pressed down and down - my boob was in a vice!
    My skin was stretched and stretched, from way up under my chin,
    My poor boob was being squashed, to Swedish pancake thin.
    Excruciating pain I felt, within its vice-like grip,
    A prisoner in this vicious thing - my poor defenceless tit!
    'Take a deep breath,' he said to me - who does he think he's kidding?
    My chest is mashed in his machine and woozy I am getting.
    'There, that was good,' I heard him say as the room was slowly swaying.
    'Now let's have a go at the other one. 'Lord have mercy,' I was praying.
    It squeezed me from up and down; it squeezed me from both sides,
    I'll bet he's never had this done - not to his tender hide!
    If I had no problem when I came in, I surely have one now.
    If there had been a cyst in there, it would have popped, ker-pow!
    This machine was designed by a man; of this I have no doubt.

I'd like to stick his balls in there and see how they come out!

Power outage during a mammogram

I actually kept my mammogram appointment. I was met with, *'Hi! I'm Belinda!'* This perky clipboard carrier smiled from ear to ear, tilted her head to one side and crooned, *'All I need you to do is step into this room right hereee, strip to the waist, then slip on this gown. Everything clearrrr?'*

'I'm thinking, 'Belinda, try decaf. This ain't rocket science.' Belinda skipped away to prepare the chamber of horrors.

Call me crazy, but I suspect a man invented this machine. It takes a perfectly healthy cup size of 36-B to a size 38-LONG in less than 60 seconds. Also, girls aren't made of sugar and spice and everything nice. It's Spandex. We can be stretched, pulled and twisted over a cold 4-inch piece of square glass and still pop back into shape.

With the right side finished, Belinda flipped me (literally) to the left and said, *'Hmmmm. Can you stand on your tippy toes and lean in a tad so we can get everything?'* Fine, I answered. I was freezing, bruised and out of air, so why not use the remaining circulation in my legs and neck and finish me off? My body was in a holding pattern that defied gravity (with my other boob wedged between those two 4' pieces of square glass) when we heard, then felt a zap! Complete darkness and the power went off! *'What?'* I yelled.

'Oh, maintenance is working. Bet they hit a snag.' Belinda headed for the door.

'Excuse me! You're not leaving me in this vise alone, are you?' I shouted Belinda kept going and said, *'Oh, you fussy puppy. The door's wide open so you'll have the emergency hall lights. I'll be rightttt backkkk.'*

Before I could shout *'NOOOO!'* she disappeared. And that's exactly how Bubba and Earl, maintenance men extraordinaire, found me, half-naked and part of me dangling from the Jaws of Life and the other part smashed between the glass!

After exchanging polite *'Hi, how's it going'* type greetings, Bubba (or possibly Earl) asked, to my utter disbelief, if I knew the power was off. Trying to disguise my hysteria, I replied with as much calmness as *possible 'Uh, yes, yes I did thanks'*

'You bet, take care' Bubba replied and waved good-bye as though I'd been standing in the line at the grocery store.

Two hours later, Belinda breezes in wearing a sheepish grin and making no attempt to suppress her amusement, she said. *'Oh I am soooo sorry! The power came back on and I totally forgot about you! And silly me, I went to lunch. Are we upset?'*

'And that, Your Honour, is exactly how her head ended up between the clamps.'

If my body were a car

If my body were a car, this is the time I would be thinking about trading it in for a newer model:

I've got bumps and dents and scratches in my finish and my paint job is getting a little dull, but that's not the worst of it.

My headlights are out of focus and it's especially hard to see things up close.

My traction is not as graceful as it once was. I slip and slide and skid and bump into things even in the best of weather.

My whitewalls are stained with varicose veins.

It takes me hours to reach my maximum speed.

My fuel rate burns inefficiently. But here's the worst of it: Almost every time I sneeze, cough or sputter - either my radiator leaks or my exhaust backfires!

Santa Claus

There was a perfect man who met a perfect woman. After a perfect courtship, they had a perfect wedding. Their life together was, of course, perfect.

One snowy, stormy Christmas Eve this perfect couple was driving along a winding road when they noticed someone at the roadside in distress. Being a perfect couple, they stopped to help. There stood Santa Claus with a huge bundle of toys. Not wanting to disappoint any children on the eve of Christmas, the perfect couple loaded Santa and his toys into their vehicle. Soon they were driving along delivering the toys. Unfortunately, the driving conditions deteriorated and the perfect couple and Santa Claus had an accident.

Only one of them survived the accident. Who was the survivor?

The perfect woman. Everyone knows there is no Santa Claus and no such thing as a perfect man.

(Male response to this)
So if there is no perfect man and no Santa Claus, the perfect woman must have been driving. This explains why there was a car accident! (So there!)

Christmas Blues

When four of Santa's elves got sick and the trainee elves did not produce the toys as fast as the regular ones, Santa was beginning to feel the pressure of being behind schedule. Then Mrs Claus told

Santa that her Mom was coming to visit. This stressed Santa even more.

When he went to harness the reindeer, he found that three of them were about to give birth and two had jumped the fence and were out, heaven knows where.
More stress.

Then when he began to load the sleigh one of the boards cracked and the toy bag fell to the ground and scattered the toys. So, frustrated, Santa went into the house for a cup of apple cider and a shot of rum. When he went to the cupboard he discovered that the elves had hidden the liquor and there was nothing to drink. In his frustration he accidentally dropped the cider pot and it broke into hundreds of little pieces all over the kitchen floor.

He went to get the broom and found that mice had eaten the straw end of the broom. Just then the doorbell rang and irritable Santa trudged to the door.

He opened the door and there was a little angel with a great big Christmas tree. The angel said very cheerfully, *'Merry Christmas, Santa. Isn't it a lovely day? I have a beautiful tree for you. Where would you like me to stick it?'*

And so began the tradition of the little angel on top of the Christmas tree!

So that's what happened!

You've heard about people who have been abducted and had their kidneys removed by black-market organ thieves. My thighs were stolen from me during the night a few years ago. I went to sleep and woke up with someone else's thighs. It was just that quick. The replacements had the texture of cooked oatmeal. Whose thighs were these and what happened to mine? I spent the entire summer looking for my thighs. Finally, hurt and angry, I resigned myself to living out my life in jeans. And then the thieves struck again.

My butt was next. I knew it was the same gang, because they took pains to match my new rear-end to the thighs they had stuck me with earlier. But my new butt was attached at least three inches lower than my original! I realised I'd have to give up my jeans in favour of long skirts.

Two years ago I realised my arms had been switched. One morning I was fixing my hair and was horrified to see the flesh of my upper arm swing to and fro with the motion of the hairbrush. This was really getting scary - my body was being replaced one section at a time. What could they do to me next?

When my poor neck suddenly disappeared and was replaced with a turkey neck, I decided to tell my story. Women of the world,

Wake up and smell the coffee! Those 'plastic' surgeons are using REAL replacement body parts - stolen from you and me! The next time someone you know has something 'lifted,' look again - was it lifted from you?

THIS IS NOT A HOAX. This is happening to women everywhere every night. WARN YOUR FRIENDS!

P.S. Last year I thought someone had stolen my boobs. I was lying in bed and they were gone! But when I jumped out of bed, I was relieved to see that they had just been hiding in my armpits as I slept. Now I keep them hidden in my waistband.

A Woman's Random Thoughts

Skinny people piss me off. Especially when they say things like, *'You know, sometimes I forget to eat.'* Now, I've forgotten my address, my mother's maiden name and my keys. But I've never forgotten to eat. You have to be a special kind of stupid to forget to eat.

They say you shouldn't say anything about the dead unless it's good. *'He's dead. Good.'*

A friend of mine confused her Valium with her birth control pills. She had 14 kids, but she didn't give a crap.

I wonder who coined the phrase 'Drop dead gorgeous?' It was probably a nerd who would go into convulsions if a gorgeous female even looked at him.

The trouble with some women is that they get all excited about nothing (and marry him.)

I read this article that said the typical symptoms of stress are eating too much, smoking too much, impulse buying and driving too fast. Are they kidding? That is my idea of a perfect day.

I know what Victoria's Secret is. The secret is that nobody older than 30 can fit into their stuff.

You have two choices in life: You can stay single and be miserable or get married and wish you were dead.

A lady inserted an ad in the classifieds: *'Husband Wanted.'* Next day she received a hundred letters. They all said the same thing: *'You can have mine.'*

When a woman steals your husband, there is no better revenge than to let her keep him.

A man is incomplete until he is married. Then he is completely finished.

A little boy asked his father, *'Daddy, how much does it cost to get married?'* Father replied, *'I don't know son, I'm still paying.'*

A young son asked, *'Is it true Dad that in some parts of Africa a man doesn't know his wife until he marries her?'* Dad replied, *'That happens in every country, son.'*

At a cocktail party, one woman said to another, *'Aren't you wearing your wedding ring on the wrong finger?'*

'Yes, I am. I married the wrong man.'

Then there was a woman who said, *'I never knew what real happiness was until I got married and by then, it was too late.'*

Marriage is the triumph of imagination over intelligence.

What is the one thing you should not ask your partner while having sex? Do you accept VISA?

If you want your spouse to listen and pay strict attention to every word you say - talk in your sleep.

Just think if it weren't for marriage, men would go through life thinking they had no faults at all.

First guy says, *'My wife's an angel!'* Second guy remarks, *'You're lucky, mine's still alive.'*

Husband and wife are waiting at the bus stop with their nine children. A blind man joins them after a few minutes. When the bus arrives, they find it over-loaded and only the wife and the nine kids are able to fit onto the bus. So the husband and the blind man decide to walk.

After a while, the husband gets irritated by the ticking of the stick of the blind man as he taps it on the sidewalk and says to him, *'Why don't you put a piece of rubber at the end of your stick? That ticking sound is driving me crazy.'* The blind man replies, *'If you would've put a rubber at the end of your stick, we'd be riding the bus.'*

The world's shortest fairy tale

Once upon a time, a girl asked a guy, *'Will you marry me?'* The guy said, *'No,'* and the girl lived happily ever after and went shopping, dancing, drank martinis, always had a clean house, never had to cook, stayed skinny and farted whenever she wanted.

The end ...

Separate but equal

My company enrolled me in a sales training class, where the instructor subscribed to a philosophy of constant abuse - but in his own gentlemanly fashion. That is, he addressed the men in the class as 'swines' and the women as 'swinettes.' A male student was a 'schmuck' and a female was a 'schmuckette.'

I found this Equal Opportunity harassment fascinating and after several sessions, was inspired to extend the concept further - right in front of the class.

'By your own rules of grammatical logic,' I pointed out, *'If a man is an 'ass,' then a woman is obviously an 'asset!''*

A Woman's Prayer

'Dear Lord, I pray for: Wisdom, to understand a man, to Love and to forgive him and for Patience, for his moods. Because Lord, if I pray for Strength - I'll just beat him to death '

Now I lay me down to sleep,
I pray for a man, who's not a creep.
One who's handsome, smart and strong.
He's not afraid to admit when he's wrong.
One who thinks before he speaks.
When he promises to call, he doesn't wait six weeks.
I pray that he is gainfully employed,
Won't lose his cool when he's annoyed.
Pulls out my chair and opens my door,
Massages my back and begs to do more.
Oh! Send me a man who will make love to my mind,
Knows what to say when I ask, 'How fat is my behind?'
One who'll make love till my body's a'twitchin,
He brings ME a sandwich too, when he goes to the kitchen!
I pray that this man will love me to no end,
And would never compare me with my best friend.
Thank You in advance and now I'll just wait,
For I know You will send him before it's too late.
Amen.

Advice for Women ... decades too late!!

- If you want someone who will bring you the paper without first tearing it apart to remove the sports section - Buy a dog.
- If you want someone willing to make a fool of himself simply over the joy of seeing you - Buy a dog.
- If you want someone who will eat whatever you put in front of him and never says it's not quite as good as his mother makes - Buy a dog.
- If you want someone always willing to go out, at any hour, for as long and wherever you want - you know the answer.

- If you want someone who will never touch the remote, doesn't care about watching football and can sit next to you as you watch romantic movies - ditto.
- If you want someone who is content to get up on your bed just to warm your feet and whom you can push off if he snores - Buy a dog.
- If you want someone who never criticises what you do, doesn't care if you are pretty or ugly, fat or thin, young or old, who acts as if every word you say is especially worthy of listening to and loves you unconditionally and perpetually- you know what I'm going to say ...
- But, on the other hand, if you want someone who will never come when you call, ignores you totally when you come home, leaves hair all over the place, walks all over you, runs around all night and only comes home to eat and sleep and acts as if your entire existence is solely to ensure his happiness - then buy a cat!

The car accident

A woman and a man are involved in a car accident; a bad one. Both of their cars are totally demolished, but amazingly neither of them is hurt. After they crawl out of their cars, the woman says, *'Wow just look at our cars! There nothing left, but fortunately we were not hurt. This must be a sign from God that we should meet and be friends.'*

The man replies, *'I agree with you completely. This must be a sign from God!'* The woman continued, *'And look at this. Here's another miracle. My car is completely demolished, but this bottle of wine didn't break. Surely God wants us to drink this wine and celebrate our good fortune.'*

Then she hands the bottle to the man. He nods his head in agreement, opens it and drinks half the bottle and hands it back to the woman. The woman takes the bottle and puts the cap back on and hands it back to the man. The man asks, *'Aren't you having any?'*

The woman replies, *'No, I think I'll just wait for the police.'*

Women over 40 (By Andy Rooney)

A woman over 40 will never wake you in the middle of the night to ask *'What are you thinking?'* She doesn't care what you think.
If a woman over 40 doesn't want to watch the game, she doesn't sit around whining about it. She does something SHE wants to do. And it's usually something more interesting.

A woman over 40 knows herself well enough to be assured in who she is, what she is, what she wants and from whom. Few women past the age of 40 give a damn what you might think about her or what she's doing. Women over 40 are dignified.

They seldom have a screaming match with you at the opera or in the middle of an expensive restaurant. Of course, if you deserve it, they won't hesitate to shoot you, if they think they can get away with it.

Older women are generous with praise, often undeserved. They know what it's like to be unappreciated.

A woman over 40 has the self-assurance to introduce you to her women friends. A younger woman with a man will often ignore even her best friend because she doesn't trust the guy with other women. Women over 40 couldn't care less if you're attracted to her friends because she knows her friends won't betray her.

Women get psychic as they age. You never have to confess your sins to a woman over 40. They always know.

A woman over 40 looks good wearing bright red lipstick. This is not true of younger women or drag queens. Once you get past a wrinkle or two, a woman over 40 is far sexier than her younger counterpart.

Older women are forthright and honest. They'll tell you right off if you're a jerk or if you're acting like one! You don't ever have to wonder where you stand with her.

Yes we praise women over 40 for a multitude of reasons. Unfortunately, it's not reciprocated. For every stunning, smart well-coiffed hot woman of 40+ there is a bald, paunchy relic in yellow pants making a fool of himself with some 22-year-old waitress. Ladies, I apologise.

Female Jokes

It has long been contended that there are male jokes and there are female jokes. And there are unisex jokes. Here is a joke I consider a true female joke. I offer it to you in the hopes that women will love it and men will pass it along to a woman who will love it.

A woman was sitting at a bar enjoying an after work cocktail with her girlfriends when an exceptionally tall, handsome, extremely sexy middle-aged man entered. He was so striking that the woman could not take her eyes off him. The young-at-heart man noticed her overly attentive stare and walked directly towards her (as all men will).

Before she could offer her apologies for so rudely staring, he leaned over and whispered to her, *'I'll do anything, absolutely* *anything, that you want me to do, no matter how kinky, for $20.00 - on one condition.'*

Flabbergasted, the woman asked what the condition was. The man replied, *'You have to tell me what you want me to do in just three words.'*

The woman considered his proposition for a moment and then slowly removed a $20 bill from her purse, which she pressed into the man's hand along with her address. She looked deeply into his eyes and slowly and meaningfully said ...

'Clean my house.'

Steroids

A female Olympic swimmer was discussing steroid use with one of her team members. She claimed that she was going to cease using steroids because she was growing hair where she had not previously had any. When asked where this hair was growing, she responded, *'On my balls.'*

For Bright Women

I'm not offended by all the dumb blonde jokes because I know I'm not dumb ... and I also know that I'm not blonde. Dolly Parton

You see a lot of smart guys with dumb women, but you hardly ever see a smart woman with a dumb guy. Erica Jong.

My husband and I are either going to buy a dog or have a child. We can't decide whether to ruin our carpet or ruin our lives. Rita Rudner.

I want to have children, but my friends scare me. One of my friends told me she was in labour for 36 hours. I don't even want to do anything that feels good for 36 hours! Rita Rudner.

I've been on so many blind dates; I should get a free dog. Wendy Liebman.

Never lend your car to anyone to whom you have given birth. Erma Bombeck.

If high heels were so wonderful, men would still be wearing them. Sue Grafton.

I think - therefore I'm single. Lizz Winstead.

When women are depressed, the either eat or go shopping. Men invade another country. Maryon Pearson.

Behind every successful man is a surprised woman. Maryon Pearson.

I base most of my fashion taste on what doesn't itch. Gilda Radner.

In politics, if you want anything said, ask a man; if you want anything done, ask a woman. Margaret Thatcher.

I have yet to hear of a man ask for advice on how to combine marriage and a career. Gloria Steinhem.

Some of us are becoming the men we wanted to marry. Gloria Steinhem.

I never married because there was no need. I have three pets at home that answer the same purpose as a husband. I have a dog that growls every morning, a parrot that swears all afternoon and a cat that comes home late at night. Marie Corelli.

Nagging is the repetition of unpalatable truths. Baroness Edith Summerskill.

If men can run the world, why can't they stop wearing neckties? How intelligent is it to start the day by tying a little noose around your neck. Linda Ellerbee.

I am a marvellous housekeeper. Every time I leave a man, I keep his house. Zsa Zsa Gabor

Finding A Suitable Mate

Mary had a final test she used to determine whether a man would be a successful partner. Even if they appeared to be well suited, this was still the decider on whether she continued with the relationship. If he left the toilet seat up - he was out of the picture. This would be especially true in North America where there is far more water in the toilet than in Australia for instance.

A woman often had a very rude, wet and sometimes painful awakening when she landed in or became wedged in the toilet when tending to nightly visits to the loo in the dark. Or she found that her partner had used the toilet before her and had left either puddles on the seat or on the floor under the toilet. Bloke's aim is especially bad when trying to aim at a toilet, in the dark, when they're half asleep. They need to know that there's no shame in sitting down, tucking Willy into the toilet and doing the job. That way the seat is left down and it's not piddled on.

If her fellow was married before, obviously his first wife or possibly even his mother before that, had not toilet trained him properly on how to use the bathroom and it was probably too late for her to start training him now. She determined that these males put their own comfort before that of their partners - so out they went.

Choose your man

A Chinese man had three daughters. He asked his eldest daughter what kind of man she would like to marry. *'I would like to marry a man with three dragons on his chest,'* said the oldest daughter.

He then asked his second daughter who she would like to marry. *'I would like to marry a man with two dragons on his chest,'* said the second daughter.

He finally asked his youngest daughter whom she would like to marry. *'I would like to marry a man with one draggin' on the ground,'* said the youngest daughter.

The Hearses

A woman notices two hearses going by very slowly. She also notices a lady walking behind the hearses with a pit bull on a leash and is followed by about two hundred women. Her curiosity gets the best of her and she says to the woman, *'This probably isn't the time to ask, but why are there two hearses?'*

The woman said, *'The first one is my husband. My pit bull killed him and the second one is my mother-in-law who tried to intervene. The pit bull killed her as well.'*

The lady thought for a minute and said, *'Would you let me borrow your dog?'* but of course the woman replied, *'Get in line.'*

The Bathing Suit

I have just been through the annual pilgrimage of torture and humiliation known as buying a bathing suit. When I was a child, the bathing suit for a woman with a mature figure was designed for a woman with a mature figure - boned, trussed and reinforced, not so much sewn - as engineered. They were built to hold back and uplift and they did a damned good job!

Today's stretch fabrics are designed for the pre-pubescent girl with a figure chipped from marble. The mature woman has a choice: she can either front up at the maternity department and try on a floral costume with a skirt, coming away looking like a hippopotamus escaped from Disney's Fantasia - or she can wander around every run-of-the-mill department store trying to make a sensible choice from what amounts to a designer range of flora rubber bands.

So what did I do? I wandered around, made my sensible choice and entered the chamber of horrors known as the fitting room. The first thing I noticed was the extraordinary tensile strength of the stretch material! The Lycra used in bathing suits was developed, I believe, by NASA to launch small rockets from a slingshot, which gives the added bonus that if you manage to actually lever yourself into one, you are protected from shark attacks. The reason for this is that a shark taking a swipe at your passing midriff would immediately suffer whiplash.

I fought my way into the bathing suit, but as I twanged the shoulder strap into place, I gasped in horror - my bosom had disappeared! Eventually, I found one bosom cowering under my left armpit. It took a while to find the other! At last I located it flattened beside my seventh rib. The problem is that modern bathing suits have no bra cups. The mature woman is meant to wear her bosom spread across the chest like a speed bump. I realigned my speed bump and lurched towards the mirror to take a full view assessment.

The bathing suit fit all right, but unfortunately it only fit those bits of me willing to stay inside it. The rest of me oozed out rebelliously from the top, bottom and sides. I looked like a lump of Play Dough wearing undersized cling wrap. As I tried to work out where all those extra bits had come from, the pre-pubescent salesgirl popped her head through the curtains and I could tell she was trying to suppress a smile. *'Did you find what you were looking for?'* she asked. I replied that I wasn't so sure and asked what else she could show me.

I tried on a cream crinkled one that made me look like a lump of masking tape and a floral two-piece which gave the appearance of an oversized napkin in a serviette ring. I struggled into a leopard skin with a ragged frill and came out looking like Tarzan's Jane on a bad day! I tried a black number with a midriff and looked like a jellyfish in mourning. I tried on a bright pink one with such a high cut leg; I thought I would have to wax my eyebrows to wear it.

Finally, I found one that fit – a two-piece affair with shorts-style bottoms and a halter-top. It was cheap, comfortable and bulge-friendly, so I bought it. When I got home, I read the label that said *'Material may become transparent in water,'* but I'm determined to wear it anyway. I just have to learn how to breaststroke in the sand.

Brain Surgery

In the hospital the relatives gathered in the waiting room, where their family member lay gravely ill. Finally, the doctor came in looking tired and sombre. *'I'm afraid I'm the bearer of bad news,'* he said as he surveyed the worried faces. *'The only hope left for your loved one at this time is a brain transplant. It's an experimental procedure, very risky but it is the only hope! Insurance will cover the procedure, but you will have to pay for the brain yourselves.'*

The family members sat silent as they absorbed the news. After a great length of time, someone asked, *'Well, how much does a brain cost?'*

The doctor quickly responded, *'$5,000 for a male brain and $200 for a female brain.'*

The moment turned awkward. Men in the room tried not to smile; avoiding eye contact with the women, but some actually smirked. A man unable to control his curiosity, blurted out the question everyone wanted to ask, *'Why is the male brain so much more?'*

The doctor smiled at the childish innocence and explained to the entire group, *'It's just standard pricing procedure. We have to mark down the price of the female brains, because they've actually been used.'*

Special Gift

Ladies, here are some tips on selecting that special gift for the man in your life:
1. When in doubt - buy him a cordless drill. It doesn't matter if he already has one. I have a friend who owns five of them and he still hasn't complained. As a man you can never have too many cordless drills. No one knows why.
2. If you cannot afford a cordless drill, buy him anything with the word ratchet or socket in it. Men love saying those two words. *'Hey George, can I borrow your ratchet? By-the-way, are you through with my 3/8 inch socket set yet?'* Again, no one knows why.
3. If you are really, really broke, buy him anything for his car. A 99-cent ice scraper, a small bottle of de-icer or something to hang from his rear view mirror. Men love gifts for their cars. No one knows why.
4. Do not buy a man any of those fancy liquors. If you do so, it will sit in a cupboard for 10 years.
5. Do not buy men socks. Do not buy men ties. And never buy men bathrobes. I was told that if God had wanted men to wear bathrobes, He wouldn't have invented Jockey shorts.
6. You can buy men new remote controls to replace the ones they have worn out. If you have a lot of money, buy your man a big screen TV with the little picture in the corner.
7. Do not buy any man industrial-sized canisters of after-shave or deodorant. I'm told they do not stink - they are earthy.
8. Buy men label makers. Almost as good as cordless drills. Within a couple of weeks, there will be labels absolutely everywhere. Socks, shorts, cups, saucers, door lock, sink. You get the idea. No one knows why.
9. Never buy a man anything that says, 'Some assembly required' on the box. It will ruin his Special Day and he will always have parts left over.
10. Good places to shop for men include Northwest Iron Works, Parr Lumber, Home Depot, John Deere, Valley RV Centre and Les Schwab Tire.

11. Men enjoy danger. That's why they never cook - but they will BBQ. Get him a monster barbecue with a 100-pound propane tank and keep your freezer supplied with hamburger, steak, sausages and hot dog makings.
12. Tickets to a footie or cricket game are always a sure bet. He will not appreciate tickets to 'A retrospective of 19th century quilts.' Everyone knows why.
13. Men love chainsaws. But never, ever, buy a man you love a chainsaw.
14. It's hard to beat a really good wheelbarrow or an aluminium extension ladder. Never buy a real man a step-ladder. It must be an extension ladder. No one knows why.

The Ranch Hand

A successful rancher died and left everything to his devoted wife. She was a very good-looking woman and determined to keep the ranch, but knew very little about ranching. So she decided to place an ad in the newspaper for a ranch hand. Two men applied for the job. One was homosexual and the other a drunk. She thought long and hard about it and when no one else applied she decided to hire the homosexual man, figuring it would be safer to have him around the house than the drunk.

He proved to be a hard worker who put in long hours every day and knew a lot about ranching. For weeks, the two of them worked hard and the ranch was doing very well. Then one day, the rancher's widow said to the hired hand, *'You have done a really good job and the ranch looks great! You should go into town and kick up your heels.'*

The hired hand readily agreed and went into town the following Saturday night. One o'clock came and he didn't return. Two o'clock and no hired hand. He returned around two-thirty and upon entering the house, he found the rancher's widow sitting by the fireplace with a glass of wine, waiting for him.

She quietly called him over to her. *'Unbutton my blouse and take it off,'* she said. Trembling, he did as she directed.

'Now take off my boots.' He did as she asked, ever so slowly. *'Now take off my stockings.'* He removed each gently and placed them neatly by her boots.

'Now take off my skirt.' He slowly unbuttoned it, constantly watching her eyes in the fire light.

'Now take off my bra.' Again, with trembling hands, he did as he was told and dropped it to the floor.

'Now,' she said, *'take off my panties.'* By the light of the fire, he slowly pulled them down and off. Then she looked at him and said, *'If you ever wear my clothes into town again, you're fired.'*

Mirror, Mirror

A young woman buys a mirror at an antique shop and hangs it on her bathroom door. One evening, while getting undressed, she playfully says, *'Mirror, mirror on my door, make my bust-line forty-four.'*

Instantly, there is a brilliant flash of light and her breasts grow to enormous proportions. Excited, she runs to tell her husband what happened. A few minutes later, they both return to the bathroom. This time the husband crosses his fingers and says, *'Mirror, mirror on the door, make my penis touch the floor!'*

Again, there is a bright flash and both his legs fell off.

Crossing the River

Three men were hiking through a forest when they came upon a large raging violent river. Needing to get to the other side, the first man prayed, *'God, please give me the strength to cross the river.'*

Poof! God gave him big arms and strong legs and he was able to swim across in about two hours – having almost drowned twice.

After witnessing that, the second man prayed, *'God, please give me strength and the tools to cross the river.'*

Poof! God gave him a rowboat and strong arms and strong legs and he was able to row across in about an hour after almost capsizing once.

Seeing what happened to the first two men, the third man prayed, *'God, please give me the strength, the tools and the intelligence to cross the river.'*

Poof! He was turned into a woman. She checked the map, hiked one hundred metres up stream and walked across the bridge.

Personal Trainer

For my fiftieth birthday, my husband (the dear) purchased a week of personal training at the local health club for me. Although I am still in great shape, I hadn't exercised since playing on my high school softball team, so I decided it would be a good idea to go ahead and give it a try. I called the club and made my reservations with a personal trainer I'll call Bruce, who identified himself as a 26-year-old aerobics instructor and model for athletic clothing and swim wear. My husband seemed pleased with my enthusiasm to get started. The club encouraged me to keep a diary to chart my progress.

Monday: Started my day at 6:00 am. Tough to get out of bed, but found it was well worth it when I arrived at the health club to find Bruce waiting for me. (He's something of a Greek God with blonde hair, dancing eyes and a dazzling white smile. Woo Hoo!!). Bruce gave me a tour and showed me the machines. He took my pulse after five minutes on the treadmill. He was alarmed that my pulse was so fast, but I attribute it to standing next to him in his Lycra aerobic outfit. (I enjoy watching the skilful way in which he conducted his aerobics class after my workout today. Very inspiring.) Bruce was encouraging as I did my sit-ups, although my gut was already aching from holding it in the whole time he was around. This is going to be a fantastic week!

Tuesday: I drank a whole pot of coffee, but finally made it out the door. Bruce made me lie on my back and push a heavy iron bar into the air – then he put weights on it! My legs were a little wobbly on the treadmill, but I made the full kilometre. Bruce's rewarding smile made it all worthwhile. I feel great! It's a whole new life for me.

Wednesday: The only way I can brush my teeth is by laying the toothbrush on the counter and moving my mouth back and forth over it. I believe I have a hernia in both pectorals. Driving was okay as long as I didn't try to steer or stop. I parked my Explorer on top of a GEO in the club lot. Bruce was impatient with me, insisting that my screams bothered other club members. (His voice is a little too perky for early in the morning and when he scolds, he gets this nasally whine that's very annoying). My chest hurt when I got on the treadmill, so Bruce put me on their stair monster. (Why the hell would anyone invent a machine to simulate an activity rendered obsolete by elevators?) Bruce told me it would help me get in shape and enjoy life. He said some other shit too.

Thursday: Bruce was waiting for me with his vampire-like teeth exposed as his thin, cruel lips were pulled back in a full snarl. (I couldn't help being a half hour late; it took me that long to tie my damned shoes!) Bruce took me to work out with dumbbells. When he was not looking, I ran and hid in the women's room. He sent Lars to find me, then, as punishment, put me on the rowing machine – which I sank.

Friday: I hate that bastard Bruce more than any human being has ever hated any other human being in the history of the world. (Stupid, skinny, anaemic little cheerleader wanna-be bastard). If there were a part of my body I could move without unbearable pain, I would beat him with it. Bruce wanted me to work on my triceps. I don't have any triceps! And if you don't want dents in the floor, don't hand me God damned barbells or anything that weighs more than a sandwich. (Which I am sure you learned at the sadist school you attended and graduated magna sans laude from, you Nazi Bastard). The treadmill flung me off and I landed on a health and nutrition teacher. Why couldn't it have been someone softer, like the drama coach or the choir director?

Saturday: Bruce left a message on my answering machine in his grating, shrilly voice wondering why I did not show up today. Just hearing him made me want to smash the machine with my day planner. However, I lacked the strength even to use the TV remote and ended up catching eleven straight hours of the son of a bitching weather channel.

Sunday: I'm having the church van pick me up for services today so I can go and thank God that this week is over. I will also pray that next year my husband (the bastard) will choose a gift for me that is fun – like a root canal or a hysterectomy.

I felt like my body had gotten totally out of shape, so I got my doctor's permission to join a fitness club and start exercising. I decided to take an aerobics class for seniors. I bent, twisted, gyrated, jumped up and down and perspired for an hour. But, by the time I got my leotards on, the class was over.

Ladies Washrooms

When you have to visit a public bathroom, you usually find a line of women, so you smile politely and take your place. Once it's your turn, you check for feet under the stall doors. Every stall is occupied.

Finally, a door opens and you dash in, nearly knocking down the woman leaving the stall. You get in to find the door won't latch. It doesn't matter. The dispenser for the modern 'seat covers' (invented by someone's mom, no doubt) is handy, but empty. You would hang your purse on the door hook, if there were one, but there isn't - so you carefully, but quickly, drape it around your neck, (Mom would turn over in her grave if you put it on the FLOOR!) yank down your pants and assume 'The Stance.'

In this position your aging, toneless thigh muscles begin to shake. You'd love to sit down, but you certainly hadn't taken time to wipe the seat or lay toilet paper on it, so you hold 'The Stance.'

To take your mind off your trembling thighs, you reach for what you discover to be the EMPTY toilet paper dispenser. In your mind, you can hear your mom's voice saying, *'Honey, if you had tried to clean the seat, you would have KNOWN there was no toilet paper!'* Your thighs shake more. You remember the tiny tissue that you blew your nose on yesterday - the one that's still in your purse. That would have to do.

You crumple it in the puffiest way possible. It is still smaller than your thumbnail. Someone pushes open your stall door because the latch doesn't work. The door hits your purse, which is hanging around your neck in front of your chest and you and your purse topple backward against the tank of the toilet. 'OCCUPIED!' you scream, as you reach for the door dropping your precious, tiny, crumpled tissue in a puddle on the floor, lose your footing altogether and slide down directly on the TOILET SEAT. It is wet of course.
You bolt up, knowing all too well that it's too late. Your bare bottom has made contact with every imaginable germ and life form on the uncovered seat because YOU never laid down toilet paper - not that there was any, even if you had taken time to try.

You know your mother would be utterly appalled if she knew, because, you're certain that her bare bottom never touched a public toilet seat because, frankly, dear, *'You just don't KNOW what kind of diseases you could get.'*

By this time, the automatic sensor on the back of the toilet is so confused that it flushes, propelling a stream of water like a fire hose that somehow sucks everything down with such force that you grab onto the toilet paper dispenser for fear of being dragged in too. At that point, you give up.

You are soaked by the spewing water and the wet toilet seat. You're exhausted. You try to wipe with a gum wrapper you found in your pocket and then slink out inconspicuously to the sinks.

Now, you can't figure out how to operate the faucets with the automatic sensors, so you wipe your hands with spit and a dry paper towel and walk past the line of women still waiting. You are no longer able to smile politely to them.

A kind soul at the very end of the line points out a piece of toilet paper trailing from your shoe. (Where was that when you NEEDED it?) You yank the paper from your shoe, plunk it into the woman's hand and tell her warmly, *'Here, you just might need this.'*
As you exit, you spot your hubby, who has long since entered, used and left the men's restroom. Annoyed, he asks, *'What took you so long and why is your purse hanging around your neck?'*

This is dedicated to women everywhere who deal with a public restroom (REST??? - You've got to be kidding!!). It finally explains to the men what really does take us so long. It also answers their other commonly asked question about why women go to the restroom in pairs. It's so the other gal can hold the door, hang onto your purse and hand you Kleenex under the door.

Why Women Are Crabby

We started to 'bud' in our blouses at 9 or 10 years old only to find that anything that came in contact with those tender, blooming buds hurt so bad it brought us to tears. Then came the ridiculously uncomfortable training bra contraption that the boys in school would snap until we had calluses on our backs.

Next, we get our periods in our early to mid-teens (or sooner). Along with those budding boobs, we bloated, we cramped, we got the hormone crankies, had to wear little mattresses between our legs or insert tubular, packed cotton rods in places we didn't even know we had.

Our next little rite of passage (premarital or not) was having sex for the first time which was about as much fun as having a ramrod push your uterus through your nostrils (IF he did it right and didn't end up with his little cart before his horse), leaving us to wonder what all the fuss was about.

Then it was off to Motherhood where we learned to live on dry crackers and water for a few months so we didn't spend the entire day leaning over Brother John. Of course, amazing creatures that we are (and we are) we learned to live with the growing little angels inside us steadily kicking our innards night and day making us wonder if we were preparing to have Rosemary's Baby.

Our once flat bellies looked like we swallowed a watermelon whole and we pee'd our pants every time we sneezed. When the big moment arrived, the dam in our blessed Nether Regions invariably burst right in the middle of the mall and we had to waddle, with our big cartoon feet, moaning in pain all the way to the ER.

Then it was huff and puff and beg to die while the OB says, *'Please stop screaming, Mrs. Hearmeroar. Calm down and push. Just one more good push (more like 10),'* warranting a strong, well-deserved impulse to punch the %*#!* (and hubby) square in the nose for making us cram a wiggling, mushroom-headed 10 pound bowling ball through a keyhole.

After that, it was time to raise those angels only to find that when all that 'cute' wears off, the beautiful little darlings morphed into walking, jabbering, wet, gooey, snot-blowing, life-sucking little poop machines.

Then came their 'Teen Years.' Need I say more?

When the kids are almost grown, we women hit our voracious sexual prime in our early 40's - while hubby had his somewhere around his 18th birthday.

So we progress into the grand finale: 'The Menopause,' the Grandmother of all womanhood. It's either take HRT and chance cancer in those now seasoned 'buds' or the aforementioned Nether Regions or sweat like a hog in July, wash your sheets and pillowcases daily and bite the head off anything that moves.

Now, you ask WHY women seem to be more spiteful than men, when men get off so easy, INCLUDING the icing on life's cake: Being able to pee in the woods without soaking their socks.

So, while I love being a woman, 'Womanhood' would make the Great Gandhi a tad crabby. Women are the 'weaker sex'? Yeah right.

A Woman's Poem

He didn't like the casserole,
And he didn't like my cake.
He said my biscuits were too hard,
Not like his mother used to make.
I didn't perk the coffee right
He didn't like the stew,
I didn't mend his socks
The way his mother used to do.
I pondered for an answer
I was looking for a clue.
Then I turned around and smacked the crap out of him,
Just like his mother used to do.

Expressions for a woman to use on high stress days

- You! Off my planet!
- Not the brightest crayon in the box now, are we?
- Well, this day was a total waste of makeup.
- Errors have been made. Others will be blamed.
- And your cry baby whiny-assed opinion would be?
- I'm not crazy. I've just been in a very bad mood for thirty years.
- Allow me to introduce myselves.
- Sarcasm is just one more service I offer.
- Whatever kind of look you were going for - you missed.
- Do you ever shut up on your planet?
- I'm just working here till a good fast-food job opens up.
- I'm trying to imagine you with a personality.
- Stress is when you wake up screaming and you haven't fallen asleep yet.
- I can't remember if I'm the good twin or the evil one.
- How many times do I have to flush before you go away?
- I just want revenge. Is that so wrong?

- You say I'm a bitch - like it's a bad thing.
- Can I trade you for what's behind door #2?
- Nice perfume. Must you marinate in it?
- Chaos, panic and disorder - my work here is done.
- Earth is full. Go home.
- Is it time for your medication or mine?
- Aw, did I step on your poor little bitty ego?
- How do I set the laser printer to stun?
- I'm not tense, just terribly, terribly alert.
- When I want your opinion, I'll give it to you!
- I'm out of estrogen and I have a gun.
- Warning: I have an attitude and I know how to use it.
- Do not start with me. You will NOT win.
- All stressed out and no one to choke.
- I can be one of those bad things that happens to bad people
- Don't upset me! I'm running out of places to hide the bodies.

Sick Baby

The young lady entered the doctor's office carrying an infant. *'Doctor,'* she explained, *'the baby seems to be ailing. Instead of gaining weight, he lost three ounces this week.'*

The medic examined the child and then started to squeeze the lady's breasts. Then he unbuttoned her blouse, removed her bra and began powerfully sucking on one nipple.

'Young lady,' he finally announced, *'No wonder the baby is losing weight, you haven't any milk!'*

'Of course not!' she shrieked. *'It's not my child - it's my sister's!'*

Giving up wine

I was walking down the street when I was accosted by a particularly dirty and shabby-looking homeless woman who asked me for a couple of dollars for dinner. I took out my wallet, got out ten dollars and asked, *'If I give you this money, will you buy wine with it instead of dinner?'*

'No I had to stop drinking years ago,' the homeless woman told me.

'Will you use it to go shopping instead of buying food?' I asked.

'No, I don't waste time shopping,' the homeless woman said. *'I need to spend all my time trying to stay alive.'*

'Will you spend this on a beauty salon instead of food?' I asked.

'Are you NUTS!' replied the homeless woman. *'I haven't had my hair done in 20 years!'*

'Well,' I said, *'I'm not going to give you the money. Instead, I'm going to take you out for dinner with my husband and me tonight.'*

The homeless woman was shocked. *'Won't your husband be furious with you for doing that? I know I'm dirty and I probably smell pretty disgusting.'*

I said, *'That's okay. It's important for him to see what a woman looks like after she has given up shopping, hair appointments and wine.'*

The Housewife

A woman, renewing her driver's license at the County Clerk's office, was asked by the woman recorder to state her occupation. She hesitated, uncertain how to classify herself.

'What I mean is,' explained the recorder, *'do you have a job or are you just a ...?'*

'Of course I have a job,' snapped the woman. *'I'm a Mom.'*

'We don't list 'Mom' as an occupation, 'housewife' covers it,' said the recorder emphatically.

I forgot all about her story until one day I found myself in the same situation, this time at our own Town Hall. The Clerk was obviously a career woman, poised, efficient and possessed of a high sounding title like, 'Official Interrogator' or 'Town Registrar.'

'What is your occupation?' she probed.

What made me say it? I do not know. The words simply popped out. *'I'm a Research Associate in the field of Child Development and Human Relations.'*

The clerk paused, ballpoint pen frozen in mid-air and looked up as though she had not heard right. I repeated the title slowly emphasising the most significant words. Then I stared with wonder as my pronouncement was written, in bold, black ink on the official questionnaire.

'Might I ask,' said the clerk with new interest, *'just what you do in your field?'*

Coolly, without any trace of fluster in my voice, I heard myself reply, *'I have a continuing program of research, (what mother doesn't). In the laboratory and in the field, (normally I would have said indoors and out). I'm working for my Masters (first the Lord and then the whole family) and already have four credits (all daughters). Of course, the job is one of the most demanding in the humanities. (Any mother care to disagree?) And I often work 14 hours a day, (24 is more like it).*

'But the job is more challenging than most run-of-the-mill careers and the rewards are more of a satisfaction rather than just money.'

There was an increasing note of respect in the clerk's voice as she completed the form, stood up and personally ushered me to the door.

As I drove into our driveway, buoyed up by my glamorous new career, I was greeted by my lab assistants - ages 13, 7 and 3. Upstairs I could hear our new experimental model, (a 6 month-old baby) in the child development program, testing out a new vocal pattern. I felt I had scored a beat on bureaucracy! And I had gone on the official records as someone more distinguished and indispensable to mankind than 'just another Mom.'

Motherhood! What a glorious career! Especially when there's a title on the door. Does this make Grandmothers: 'Senior Research Associates in the field of Child Development and Human Relations? And Great Grandmothers: 'Executive Senior Research Associates?' I think so!!! I also think it makes Aunts 'Associate Research Assistants.'

CHAPTER 4 - SINGLES

The Prize:

A guy meets a girl at a nightclub and she invites him back to her place for the night. Her parents are out of town and this is the perfect opportunity.

They got back to her house and go into her bedroom. When the guy walks in the door, he notices all the fluffy toys. There are hundreds of them. Fluffy toys on top of the wardrobe, fluffy toys on the bookshelf and windowsill and more on the floor - and of course fluffy toys all over the bed.

They clear off the bed and got at it. Later, after the sex, he turns to her and asks, *'Well, how was I?'*

She replies, *'Well, you can take anything from the bottom shelf.'*

10 Rules for Dating my Daughter

1. If you pull into my driveway and honk, you'd better be delivering a package, because you're sure not picking anything up.
2. You do not touch my daughter in front of me. You may glance at her, so long as you do not peer at anything below her neck. If you cannot keep your eyes or hands off of my daughter's body, I will remove them.
3. I am aware that it is considered fashionable for boys of your age to wear their trousers so loosely that they appear to be falling off their hips. Please don't take this as an insult, but you and all of your friends are complete idiots. Still, I want to be fair and open-minded about this issue, so I propose this compromise. You may come to the door with your underwear showing and your pants ten sizes too big and I will not object. However, in order to ensure that your clothes do not, in fact, come off during the course of your date with my daughter, I will take my electric nail gun and fasten your trousers securely in place to your waist.
4. I'm sure you've been told that in today's world, sex without utilising a 'barrier method' of some kind can kill you. Let me elaborate, when it comes to sex, I am the barrier and I will kill you.
5. It is usually understood that in order for us to get to know each other, we should talk about sports, politics and other issues of the day. Please do not do this. The only information I require

from you is an indication of when you expect to have my daughter safely back to my home and the only word I need from you on this subject is 'early.'

6. I have no doubt you are a popular fellow, with many opportunities to date other girls. This is fine with me as long as it's okay with my daughter. Otherwise, once you have gone out with my little girl, you will continue to date no one but her until she is finished with you. If you make her cry, I will make you cry.

7. If, by any chance, you decide to smoke in my daughter's presence or to try and entice her to try one - beware. If you think it's all right for either you or my daughter to even taste liquor - you will not live until the next morning.

8. The following places are not appropriate for a date with my daughter. Places where there are beds, sofas or anything softer than a wooden stool. Places where there are no parents, policemen or nuns within eyesight. Places where there is darkness. Places where there is dancing, holding hands or happiness. Places where the ambient temperature is warm enough to induce my daughter to wear shorts, tank tops, midriff T-shirts or anything other than overalls, a sweater and a goose down parka - zippered up to her throat. Movies with a strong romantic or sexual theme are to be avoided; movies that feature chainsaws are okay. Hockey games are okay. Old folk's homes are better.

9. Do not lie to me. I may appear to be a potbellied, balding, middle-aged dim-witted has-been. But on issues relating to my daughter, I am the all-knowing, merciless God of your universe. If I ask where you are going and with whom, you have one chance to tell me the truth, the whole truth and nothing but the truth. I have a shotgun, a shovel and five acres behind the house. Don't trifle with me.

10. Be afraid. Be very afraid. It takes very little for me to mistake the sound of your car in the driveway for a chopper coming over a rice paddy near Hanoi. When my Agent Orange starts acting up, the voices in my head frequently tell me to clean my guns as I wait for you to bring my daughter home. As soon as you pull into the driveway, you should exit your car with both hands in plain sight. Speak the perimeter password, announce in a clear voice that you have brought my daughter home safely and early and then return to your car. There is no need for you to come inside. The camouflaged face at the window is mine.

Woman's Poem

Before I lay me down to sleep,
I pray for a man, who's not a creep.
One who's handsome, smart and strong.
One who loves to listen long.
One who thinks before he speaks.
One who'll call, not wait for weeks.
I pray he's gainfully employed.
When I spend his cash, he won't be annoyed.
Pulls out my chair and opens my door.
Massages my back and begs to do more,
Oh! Send me a man who'll make love to my mind.
Knows what to answer to how big is my behind?
I pray that this man will love me to no end.
And always be my very best friend.

Man's Poem

I pray for a deaf-mute nymphomaniac with huge boobs who owns a boat, a liquor store and a golf course. This doesn't rhyme and I don't give a shit.

Different Perspectives on Life:

Her diary:

Tonight I thought my partner was acting weird. We had made plans to meet at a bar to have a drink. I was shopping with my friends all day long, so I thought he was upset at the fact that I was a bit late, but he made no comment.

Conversation wasn't flowing so I suggested that we go somewhere quiet so we could talk. He agreed but he kept quiet and absent. I asked him what was wrong. He said nothing.
I asked him if it was my fault that he was upset. He said it had nothing to do with me and not to worry.

On the way home I told him that I loved him, he simply smiled and kept driving. When we got home I felt as if I had lost him, as if he wanted nothing to do with me any more. He just sat there and watched T.V. Finally, I decided to go to bed. About ten minutes later he came to bed and to my surprise he responded to my caress and we made love, but I still felt that he was distracted and his thoughts were somewhere else. He fell asleep. I cried because I don't know what to do. I'm almost sure that his thoughts were with someone else. My life is a disaster.

His diary:

I shot the worst round of golf in my life today, but at least I got laid.

Which Movie star are you?

Ladies only. Ever wonder which movie star you are most like? Well, a team of researchers got together and analysed the personalities of movie stars and now that information has been incorporated into this quiz. Number your paper from 1 to 10. Answer each question with the choice that most describes you at this point in your life and then add up the points that correspond with your answers.

1. Which describes your perfect date?
    a) Candlelight dinner for two
    b) Amusement Park
    c) Rollerblading in the park
    d) Rock Concert
    e) Have dinner & see a movie
    f) Dinner at home with a loved one
    Points: a-4 b-2 c-5 d-1 e-3 f-6

2. What is your favourite type of music?
    a) Rock and Roll
    b) Alternative
    c) Soft Rock
    d) Classical
    e) Christian
    f) Jazz
    Points: a-2 b-1 c-4 d-5 e-3 f-6

4. What is your favourite type of movie?
    a) Comedy
    b) Horror
    c) Musical
    d) Romance
    e) Documentary
    f) Mystery
    Points: a-2 b-1 c-3 d-4 e-5 f-6

5. Which of the following jobs would you choose if you were given only these choices?
    a) Waiter/Waitress
    b) Sports Player
    c) Teacher
    d) Policeman
    e) Bartender
    f) Business person
    Points: a-4 b-5 c-3 d-2 e-1 f-6

6. Which would you rather do if you had an hour to waste?
   a) Work out
   b) Make out
   c) Watch TV
   d) Listen to the radio
   e) Sleep
   f) Read
   Points: a-5 b-4 c-2 d-1 e-3 f-6
7. Of the following colours, which do you like best
   a) Yellow
   b) White
   c) Sky blue
   d) Teal
   e) Gold
   f) Red
   Points: a-1 b-5 c-3 d-2 e-4 f-6
8. Which one of the following would you like to eat right now?
   a) Ice cream
   b) Pizza
   c) Sushi
   d) Pasta
   e) Salad
   f) Lobster Tail
   Points: a-3 b-2 c-1 d-4 e-5 f-6
9. Which is your favourite holiday?
   a) Halloween
   b) Christmas
   c) New Year's
   d) Valentine's Day
   e) Thanksgiving
   f) Fourth of July
   Points: a-1 b-3 c-2 d-4 e-5 f-6
10. If you could go to any of the following places, which would it be?
    a) Reno
    b) Spain
    c) Las Vegas
    d) Hawaii
    e) Hollywood
    f) British Columbia
    Points: a-4 b-5 c-1 d-4 e-3 f-6
11. Of the following, who would you rather spend time with?
    a) Someone who is smart
    b) Someone with good looks

     c) Someone who is a party animal
     d) Someone who has fun all the time
     e) Someone who is very emotional
     f) Someone who is fun to be with
Points: a -5 b-2 c-1 d-3 e-4 f-6

Now, take your total and find out which Movie Star you are:
     (10-17 points) You are MADONNA: You are wild and crazy and you know it. You know how to have fun, but you may take it to extremes. You know what you are doing though and are much in control of your own life. People don't always see things your way, but that doesn't mean that you should do away with your beliefs. Try to remember that your wild spirit can lead to hurting yourself and others.
     (18-26 points) You are DORIS DAY: You are fun, friendly and popular! You are a real crowd pleaser. You have probably been out on the town your share of times, yet you come home with the values that your mother taught you. Marriage and children are very important to you, but only after you have fun. Don't let the people you please influence you to stray.
     (27-34 points) You are DEBBIE REYNOLDS: You are cute and everyone loves you. You are a best friend that no one takes the chance of losing. You never hurt feelings and seldom have your own feelings hurt. Life is a breeze. You are witty and calm most of the time. Just keep clear of back stabbers and you are worry-free.
     (35-42 points) You are GRACE KELLY: You are a lover. Romance, flowers and wine are all you need to enjoy yourself. You are serious about all commitments and are a family person. You call your Mom every Sunday and never forget a birthday. Don't let your passion for romance get confused with the real thing.
     (43-50 points) You are KATHERINE HEPBURN: You are smart, a real thinker. Every situation is approached with a plan. You are very healthy in mind and body. You don't take crap from anyone! You have only a couple of individuals that you consider 'real friends.' You teach strong family values, keep your feet planted in them, but don't overlook a bad situation when it does happen.
     (51-60 points) You are ELIZABETH TAYLOR: Everyone is in awe of you. You know what you want and how to get it. You have more friends than you know what to do with. Your word is your bond. Everyone knows when you say something it is money in the bank. You attract the opposite sex. Your intelligence overwhelms most. Your memory is the next thing to photographic. Everyone admires you because you are so considerate and lovable. You know how to enjoy life and treat people right.

The ex-girlfriend

A man and his wife are dining at a table in a plush restaurant and the husband keeps staring at a drunken lady swigging her drink as she sat alone at a nearby table. The wife asks, *'Do you know her?'*

'Yes,' sighs the husband, *'She's my ex-girlfriend. I understand she took to drinking right after we split up seven years ago and I hear she hasn't been sober since.'*

'My God!' says the wife, *'Who would think a person could go on celebrating that long?'*

Dating manners

During one of her daily classes a teacher trying to teach good manners, asked her students the following question: *'Michael, if you were on a date having dinner with a nice young lady, how would you tell her that you have to go to the toilet?'*

Michael said, *'Just a minute I have to go pee.'*

The teacher responded by saying, *'That would be rude and impolite. What about you Peter. How would you say it?'*

Peter said, *'I am sorry, but I really need to go to the toilet. I'll be right back.'*

'That's better, but it's still not very nice to say the word toilet at the dinner table.'

'And you, little Johnny, can you use your brain for once and show us your good manners?'

'I would say: 'Darling, may I please be excused for a moment? I have to shake hands with a very dear friend of mine, whom I hope you'll get to meet after dinner.'

The teacher fainted.

Dinner with her folks

A girl asks her boyfriend to come over Friday night and have dinner with her parents. Since this is such a big event, the girl announces to her boyfriend that, after dinner, she would like to go out and make love for the first time. The boy is ecstatic, but he has never had sex before, so he takes a trip to the pharmacy to get some condoms. The pharmacist helps the boy for about an hour. He tells the boy everything there is to know about condoms and sex. At the register, the pharmacist asks the boy how many condoms he'd like to buy - a 3-pack, a 10-pack or a family pack. The boy insists on the family pack because he thinks he will be rather busy, it being his first time and all.

That night, the boy shows up at the girl's parent's house and meets his girlfriend at the door. *'I'm so excited for you to meet my parents, come on in!'*

The boy goes inside and is taken to the dinner table where the girl's parents are seated. The boy quickly offers to say grace and bows his head.

A minute passes and the boy is still deep in prayer, with his head sown. Five minutes pass and still no movement from the boy. Finally, after 10 minutes with his head down, the girlfriend leans over and whispers to the boyfriend. *'I had no idea you were this religious.'*

He turns and whispers back, *'I had no idea your father was a pharmacist.'*

Joe wanted to buy a motorbike. He doesn't have much luck until one day he comes across a Harley with a 'For Sale' sign on it. The bike seems even better than a new one, although it is 10 years old. It is shiny and in absolute mint condition. He immediately buys it and asks the seller how he kept it in such great condition for 10 years.

'Well, it's quite simple really' says the seller *'whenever the bike is outside and it's going to rain, rub Vaseline on the chrome. It protects it from the rain.'* And he hands Joe a jar of Vaseline.

That night his girlfriend Sandra invites him over to meet her parents. Naturally, they take the bike there. But just before they enter the house, Sandra stops him and says, *'I have to tell you something about my family before we go in.'*

'When we eat dinner, we don't talk. In fact, the first person who says anything during dinner has to do the dishes.'

'No problem,' he says and in they go.

Joe is shocked. Right smack in the middle of the living room is a huge stack of dirty dishes. In the kitchen is another huge stack of dishes. Piled up on the stairs, in the corridor, everywhere he looks, dirty dishes.

They sit down to dinner and, sure enough, no one says a word. As dinner progresses Joe decides to take advantage of the situation so he leans over and kisses Sandra. No one says a word. So he reaches over and fondles her breasts. Still, nobody says a word. So he stands up, grabs her, rips her clothes off, throws her on the table and screws her right there, in front of her parents.

His girlfriend is a little flustered, her dad is obviously livid and her mom horrified when he sits back down, but no one says a word. He looks at her mom. *'She's got a great body,'* he thinks. So he grabs the mom, bends her over the dinner table and has his way with her every which way right there on the table. Now his girlfriend is furious and her dad is boiling, but still, total silence.

All of a sudden there is a loud clap of thunder and it starts to rain. Joe remembers his bike, so he pulls the jar of Vaseline from his pocket. Suddenly the father backs away from the table and shouts, *'All right, that's enough. I'll do the damned dishes!'*

Revenge is Sweet

She spent the first day packing her belongings into boxes, crates and suitcases. On the second day, she sat down for the last time at their beautiful dining room table by candle-light, put on some soft background music and feasted on a pound of shrimp, a jar of caviar and a bottle of spring water. On the third day the movers came. When they finished, she went into each and every room and deposited a few half-eaten shrimp shells dipped in caviar into the hollow of the curtain rods, then left.

When the husband returned with his new girlfriend, all was bliss for the first few days. Then slowly, the house began to smell. They tried everything; cleaning, mopping and airing the place out. Vents were checked for dead rodents and carpets were steam cleaned. Air fresheners were hung everywhere. Exterminators were brought in to set off fumigation canisters, during which they had to move out for a few days and in the end they even paid to replace the expensive wool carpeting. Nothing worked. People stopped coming over to visit. Repairmen refused to work in the house. The maid quit.

Finally, they could not take the stench any longer and decided to move. One month later, even though they had cut their price in half, they could not find a buyer for their stinky house. Word got out and eventually even the local realtors refused to return their calls. Finally they had to borrow a huge sum of money from the bank to purchase a new place.

The ex-wife called the man and asked how things were going. He told her the saga of the rotting house. She listened politely and said that she missed her old home terribly and would be willing to reduce her divorce settlement in exchange for getting the house back. Knowing his ex-wife had no idea how bad the smell was, he agreed on a price that was about 1/10th of what the house had been worth, but only if she were to sign the papers that very day. She agreed and within the hour his lawyers delivered the paperwork.

A week later the man and his girlfriend stood smiling as they watched the moving company pack everything to take to their new home and to spite the ex-wife; they even took the curtain rods!!!
I just love a happy ending – don't you?

The Shoe

A young man is showing off his new sports car to his girlfriend. She was thrilled at the speed.

'If I do 200 kph, will you take off your clothes?' he asks.

'Yes!' said his adventurous girlfriend. And he gets up to 200 and she peeled off all her clothes. Unable to keep his eyes on the road, the car skidded onto some gravel and flipped over. The naked girl was thrown clear, but he was jammed beneath the steering wheel.

'Go and get help!' he cried.

'But I can't. I'm naked and my clothes are gone!'

'Take my shoe,' he said, *'and cover yourself.'*

Holding the shoe over her lower private area, the girl ran down the road and found a service station. Still holding the shoe between her legs, she pleaded to the service station proprietor, *'Please help me! My boyfriend's stuck!'*

The proprietor looked at the shoe and said, *'There's nothing I can do. He's in too far!'*

Train ride

A man and woman who had never met before found themselves in the same sleeping carriage of the train. After the initial embarrassment, they both manage to get to sleep; the man on the top bunk, the woman on the lower. In the middle of the night, the man leans down and says, *'I'm sorry to bother you, but I'm awfully cold and I was wondering if you could possibly pass me another blanket.'* The woman leans out and with a glint in her eye says, *'I've got a better idea . . . let's pretend we're married.'*

'Why not,' laughs the man.

'Good,' she replies. *'Get your own damned blanket.'*

David Letterman's Top Ten Reasons Why Golf Is Better Than Sex...

#10. A below par performance is considered damned good.
#9. You can stop in the middle and have a cheeseburger and a couple of beers.
#8. It's much easier to find the sweet spot.
#7. Foursomes are encouraged.
#6. You can still make money doing it as a senior.
#5. Three times a day is possible.
#4. Your partner doesn't hire a lawyer if you play with someone else.
#3. If you live in Florida, you can do it almost everyday.
#2. You don't have to cuddle with your partner when you're finished.

And the NUMBER ONE reason why golf is better than sex ...
#1. If your equipment gets old and rusty, you can replace it!

Hell explained by a chemistry student

The following is an actual question given on a chemistry mid-term exam. The answer by one student was so 'profound' that the professor shared it with his colleagues. The Question: Is Hell exothermic (gives off heat) or endothermic (absorbs heat)?

Most of the students wrote proofs of their beliefs using Boyle's Law (gas cools when it expands and heats when it is compressed) or some variant. One student, however, wrote the following:

First, we need to know how the mass of Hell is changing in time. So we need to know the rate at which souls are moving into Hell and the rate at which they are leaving. I think that we can safely assume that once a soul gets to Hell, it will not leave. Therefore, no souls are leaving. As for how many souls are entering Hell, let's look at the different religions that exist in the world today.

Most of these religions state that if you are not a member of their religion, you will go to Hell. Since there are more than one of these religions and since people do not normally belong to more than one religion, we can project that all souls will go to Hell. With birth and death rates as they are, we can expect the number of souls in Hell to increase exponentially.

Now, we look at the rate of change of volume in Hell because Boyle's Law states that in order for temperature and pressure in Hell to stay the same, the volume of Hell has to expand proportionately as souls are added. This gives two possibilities:

If Hell is expanding at a slower rate than the rate at which souls enter Hell, then the temperature and pressure in Hell will increase until all Hell breaks loose.

If Hell is expanding at a rate faster than the increase of souls in Hell, then the temperature and pressure will drop until Hell freezes over.

So which is it? If we accept the postulate given to me by Teresa during my Freshman year that, *'It will be a cold day in Hell before I sleep with you,'* and take into account the fact that I slept with her last night, then number two must be true and thus I am sure that Hell is exothermic and has already frozen over. The corollary of this theory is that since Hell has frozen over, it follows that it is not accepting any more souls and is therefore, extinct, leaving only Heaven, thereby proving the existence of a divine being which explains why, last night, Teresa kept shouting *'Oh my God.'*

Threesome

I met an older woman at a bar last night. She wasn't bad for 67. We drank and bullshitted a bit, then she asked if I'd ever had the 'sportsman's double,' a mother and daughter threesome? I said no.

We drank a bit more then she said that tonight was my lucky night. I went back to her place. She put the hall light on and shouted upstairs: *'Mom, you still awake?'*

The Black Panties

Anna had lost her husband almost four years ago. Her daughter was constantly calling her and urging her to get back into the world. Finally, Anna said she'd go out, but didn't know anyone. Her daughter immediately replied, *'Mom! I have someone for you to meet.'*

So they met and it was an immediate hit. They took to one another and after dating for six weeks, he asked her to join him for a weekend in a romantic motel. Their first night there, she undressed as he did. There she stood nude, except for a pair of black lacy panties; he was in his birthday suit. Looking her over, he asked, *'Why the black panties?'*

She replied: *'My breasts you can fondle, my body is yours to explore, but down there I am still in mourning.'*

He knew he was not getting lucky that night. The following night was the same - she stood there wearing the black panties and he was in his birthday suit - but now he was wearing a black condom.

She looked at him and asked: *'What's with the black condom?'*

He replied, *'I want to offer my deepest condolences.'*

The Spinster

My spinster aunt recently died and she had all women pallbearers. She had said about men, *'They didn't take me out when I was alive and they won't do it when I'm dead.'*

Great Ears

A young man moved into a new apartment of his own and went to the lobby to put his name on his mailbox. While there, an attractive young lady came out of the apartment next to the mailboxes, wearing a robe. The boy smiled at the young woman and she started a conversation with him.

As they talked, her robe slipped open and it was obvious that she had nothing else on. The poor kid broke into a sweat trying to maintain eye contact.

After a few minutes, she placed her hand on his arm and said, *'Let's go to my apartment, I hear someone coming.'*

He followed her into her apartment; she closed the door and leaned against it, allowing her robe to fall off completely. Now nude, she purred at him, *'What would you say is my best feature?'*
Flustered and embarrassed, he finally squeaked, *'It's got to be your ears.'*

Astounded and a little hurt she asked, *'My ears? Look at these breasts; they are full and 100% natural. I work out every day and my butt is firm and solid. Look at my skin - no blemishes anywhere. How can you think that the best part of my body is my ears?'*

Clearing his throat, he stammered ... *'Outside, when you said you heard someone coming ... .that was me.'*

CHAPTER 5 - LAWYERS

Trivia:

- What do you get when you have a hundred lawyers in your basement? A whine cellar.
- What's the different between God and a lawyer? God doesn't think he's a lawyer.
- How many lawyers does it take to shingle a roof? One, if you slice him real thin.
- Why did the lawyer cross the road? To get to the car accident on the other side.
- What do lawyers use for birth control? Their personalities.
- Did you hear about the terrorist that hijacked a 747 full of lawyers? He threatened to release one every hour if his demands weren't met.
- Why do lawyers never take their cats to the beach? Their cats keep trying to bury them with sand.
- What do a lawyer and a sperm have in common? Both have about a one in three million chance of becoming a human being.
- If a vampire bites a lawyer, isn't that cannibalism?
- Why did the post office recall the new lawyer stamps? Because people could not tell which side to spit on.
- Did you hear about the new microwave lawyer? You spend eight minutes in his office and get billed as if you'd been there eight hours.
- What is the ideal weight of a lawyer? About three pounds, including the urn.
- What do you call a lawyer with an IQ of 50? Your Honour.
- What do you call a lawyer who has gone bad? Senator.
- What is the difference between a tick and a lawyer? The tick stops draining you and drops off after you're dead.
- Why won't sharks attack lawyers? Professional courtesy.
- What do you have when a lawyer is buried up to his neck in sand? Not enough sand.
- How can you tell there's an afterlife for lawyers? Because after they die, they lie still.
- How do you get a lawyer out of a tree? Cut the rope.
- How do you stop a lawyer from drowning? Shoot him before he hits the water.

- How many lawyers does it take to stop a moving bus? Never enough.
- Have you heard about the lawyers' word processor? No matter what font you select, everything comes out in fine print.
- There's a blind rabbit and a blind snake that are friends. One day, the blind rabbit tells the blind snake that he doesn't know what he is, because he can't see. The blind snake takes hold of the rabbit and says, *'Well, you have long fur-covered ears and a short little tail. You must be a rabbit.'* The rabbit was happy to know what he was.
- He tells the blind snake, *'Come here and I will try to determine what you are.'* The blind rabbit feels the snake and finally says, *'You're cold and slimy and don't have any balls. You must be a lawyer.'*

Charity begins at home

George was a canvasser for the United Way, which had never received a donation from the most successful lawyer in town. He called on the attorney in an attempt to make him mend his ways. *'Our research shows that you made a profit of over $600,000 last year and yet you have not given a dime to the community charities! What do you have to say for yourself?'*

The lawyer replied, *'Do you know that my mother is dying of a long illness and has medical bills that are several times her annual income? Do you know about my brother, the disabled veteran, who is blind and in a wheelchair? Do you know about my sister, whose husband died in a traffic accident, leaving her with three children to raise?'*

George admitted that he had no knowledge of any of this. *'Well since I don't give any money to them, why should I give any to you?'*

That's the Law

A Houston corporate lawyer runs a stop sign and gets pulled over by a sheriff's deputy in rural West Texas. He thinks that he is smarter than the deputy because he is a lawyer educated in Massachusetts and is certain that he has a better grasp of the finer points of the law than any cop from Menard County. He decides to prove this to himself and have some fun at the deputy's expense.

Deputy says, *'License and registration, please.'*

Lawyer says, *'What for?'*

Deputy says, *'You didn't come to a complete stop at that FM highway stop sign.'*

Lawyer says, *'I slowed down and no one was coming.'*

Deputy says, *'Granted, but you still didn't come to a complete stop. License and registration, please.'*

Lawyer says, *'What's the difference?'*

Deputy says, *'The difference is, you have to come to a complete stop. That's the law. License and registration, please!'*

Lawyer says, *'If you can show me a legal difference between 'slow down' and 'stop' I'll gladly give you my license and registration; and you give me the ticket. If not, you let me go with just verbal warning and don't give me a ticket.'*

Deputy says, *'Sounds completely fair. Exit your vehicle, sir.'* At this point, the deputy takes out his Kubaton nightstick and starts beating the ever-loving crap out of the lawyer and says, *'Do you want me to stop or just slow down?'*

Telling it like it is

A man was sued by a woman for defamation of character. She charged that he had called her a pig. The man was found guilty and fined. After the trial he asked the judge, *'This means that I cannot call Mrs. Johnson a pig?'* The judge said that was true.

'Does that mean I can't call a pig Mrs. Johnson?' the man asked.

The judge replied that he could indeed call a pig Mrs. Johnson with no fear of legal action.

The man looked directly at Mrs. Johnson and said, *'Good afternoon, Mrs. Johnson.'*

Billing clients

A corporate executive received a monthly bill from the law firm that was handling a big case for his company. It included hourly billing for conferences, research, phone calls and everything but lunch hours. Unhappy as he was, the executive knew that the company would have to pay for each of these services. Then he noticed one item buried in the middle of the list: *'Crossing the street to talk to you - then discovering it wasn't you at all - $125.'*

Walking into a lawyer's office, a man asked what the barrister's rates were. *'Fifty dollars for three questions,'* the lawyer stated.

'Isn't that awfully expensive?' the man asked.

'Yes.' The lawyer replied. *'What's your third question?'*

Court Case

A lady about seven months pregnant got on a bus. She noticed the man opposite her was smiling at her and immediately moved to another seat. This time the smile turned into a grin, so she moved again. The man seemed even more amused. When on the fourth move, the man burst out laughing. She complained to the driver and had the man arrested.

The case came up in court. The judge asked the man what he had to say for himself. The man replied, *'Well your Honour, it was like this ... When the lady got on the bus, I couldn't help but notice her condition. She then sat under a sign that said, 'The Gold Dust Twins are Coming' and I had to smile. Then she moved and sat under a sign that said, 'Sloan's Liniment will reduce the swelling' and I had to grin. Then she placed herself under a sign that said, 'William's Big Stick Did the Trick' and I could hardly control myself.*

But, when she moved the fourth time and sat under the sign that said, 'Goodyear Rubber could have prevented this accident' I laughed out loud.'

'Case dismissed!' said the smiling judge.

Farmer Joe

Farmer Joe decided his injuries from the accident were serious enough to take the trucking company (responsible for the accident) to court. In the court, the trucking company's fancy lawyer was questioning farmer Joe. *'Didn't you say, at the scene of the accident, 'I'm fine?''* said the lawyer.

Farmer Joe responded, *'Well I'll tell you what happened. I had just loaded my favourite mule Bessie into the ...'*

'I didn't ask for any details,' the lawyer interrupted, *'just answer the question. Did you not say, at the scene of the accident, 'I'm fine!''*

Farmer Joe said, *'Well, I had just got Bessie into the trailer and I was driving down the road ...'*

The lawyer interrupted again and said, *'Judge, I'm trying to establish the fact that, at the scene of the accident, this man told the Highway Patrolman on the scene that he was 'just fine.' Now several weeks after the accident, he's trying to sue my client. I believe he's a fraud. Please tell him to simply answer the question.'*

By this time, the Judge was fairly interested in Farmer Joe's answer and said to the lawyer, *'I'd like to hear what he has to say about his favourite mule Bessie.'*

Joe thanked the Judge and proceeded, *'Well, as I was saying, I had just loaded Bessie, my favourite mule, into the trailer and was driving her down the highway when this huge semi-truck and trailer ran the stop sign and smacked my truck right on the side. I was thrown into one ditch and Bessie was thrown into the other. I was hurting real bad and didn't want to move. However, I could hear ole*

Bessie moaning and groaning. I knew she was in terrible shape just by her groans.

'Shortly after the accident a highway patrolman came on the scene. He could hear Bessie moaning and groaning, so he went over to her. After he looked at her, he took out his gun and shot her between the eyes. Then the patrolman came across the road with his gun in his hand and looked at me.'

He said, 'Your mule was in such bad shape I had to shoot her. How are you feeling?'

I had to answer, 'I'm fine.' Or he would have shot me too!'

Love letters

A guy walked into a post office one day and sees a middle-aged balding man standing at the counter methodically placing 'Love' stamps on bright pink envelopes with hearts all over them. He then took out a perfume bottle and sprayed scent on them.

His curiosity getting the better of him, so he goes up to the balding man and asks him what he's doing. The man replies, 'I'm sending out a thousand Valentine cards signed, 'Guess who?''

'But why?' the guy asked

'I'm a divorce lawyer,' the man replied.

Ten Husbands

A lawyer married a woman who had previously divorced ten husbands. On their wedding night, she told her new husband, 'Please be gentle; I'm still a virgin.'

'What?' said the puzzled groom. 'How can that be if you've been married ten times?'

'Well, Husband #1 was a Software Process Improvement Manager; he kept telling me how great it was going to be, but in the meantime nothing actually changed.

'Husband #2 was in Software Services; he said it was a hardware problem and was never really sure how it was supposed to function, but he said he'd look into it and get back to me.

'Husband #3 was from Field Services; he said everything checked out diagnostically but he just couldn't get the system up.

'Husband #4 was in Telemarketing; even though he knew he had the order, he didn't know when he would be able to deliver.

'Husband #5 was an Engineer; he understood the basic process but wanted three years to research, implement and design a new state-of-the-art method.

'Husband #6 was from Finance and Administration; he thought he knew how, but he wasn't sure whether it was his job or not.

'Husband #7 was in Marketing; although he had a nice product, he was never sure how to position it.

'Husband #8 was a psychiatrist. All he ever did was talk about it. 'Husband #9 was a gynaecologist; all he did was look at it.

'Husband #10 was a stamp collector; all he ever did as ... God! I miss him!!!!

'But now that I've married you, I'm really excited!'

'Good,' said the lawyer, 'but, why?'

'Duh! You're a lawyer. This time I know I'm gonna get screwed!'

The Cabin

A lawyer, who was quite wealthy, had a summer cabin to which he retreated for several weeks of the year. Each summer, the lawyer would invite a different friend of his to spend a week or two up at his place, which happened to be in a backwoods section of the country. On one particular occasion he invited a Czechoslovakian friend to stay with him and the friend, eager to get something free from a lawyer, agreed.

Early one morning the lawyer and his Czech companion went out to pick berries for their morning breakfast. As they went around the berry path, along came two huge bears - a male and a female. The lawyer, seeing the two bears, immediately dashed for cover. His friend, though, wasn't so lucky and the male bear reached him and swallowed him whole.

The lawyer ran back to his Mercedes, tore into town as fast as he could and got the local sheriff. The sheriff grabbed his rifle and dashed back to the berry patch with the lawyer. Sure enough, the two bears were still there.

'He's in that one!' cried the lawyer, pointing to the male, while visions of lawsuits from his friend's family danced in his head. He just had to save his friend.

The sheriff looked at the bears and without batting an eye, levelled his gun, took careful aim and shot the female!

'Why did you do that?' exclaimed the lawyer, 'I said he was in the other!'

'Exactly,' replied the sheriff, 'would you believe a lawyer who told you that the Czech was in the male?' (Ooh that one's awful!)

Pumpkin patch

Police arrested Malcolm Davidson, a 27 year-old white male, in a pumpkin patch at 11:38 pm last night. Davidson was charged with lewd and lascivious behaviour, public indecency and public intoxication. The suspect allegedly stated that as he was passing a pumpkin patch, he decided to stop.

'You know, a pumpkin is soft and squishy inside and there was no one around here for miles. At least I thought there wasn't.' he stated in a phone interview. Davidson went on to state that he pulled over to the side of the road, picked out a pumpkin that he felt was appropriate to his purpose, cut a hole in it and proceeded to satisfy his alleged 'need.' *'I guess I was just really into it, you know?'* he commented with evident embarrassment.

In the process, Davidson apparently failed to notice the police car approaching and was unaware of his audience until Officer Brenda Taylor approached him. *'It was an unusual situation, that's for sure.'* Said Officer Taylor. *'I walked up to (Davidson) and he's ... just working away at this pumpkin.'*

Taylor went on to describe what happened when she approached Davidson. *'I just went up and said, 'Excuse me sir, but do you realise that you're screwing a pumpkin?'* He got real surprised, as you'd expect and then looked me straight in the face and said, *'A pumpkin!! Damn ... is it midnight already?'*

The Picture

This guy was sitting in his attorney's office. *'Do you want the bad news first or the terrible news?'* the lawyer said.

'Give me the bad news first.'

'Your wife found a picture worth a half-million dollars.'

'That's the bad news?' asked the man incredulously. *'I can't wait to hear the terrible news.'*

'The terrible news is that it's of you and your secretary.'

The Spinster

An elderly spinster called the lawyer's office and told the receptionist she wanted to have a will prepared. The receptionist asked when they could set up an appointment at their office. The woman replied, *'You must understand, I've lived alone all my life. I rarely see anyone and I don't like to go out. Would it be possible for the lawyer to come to my home?'*

The lawyer agreed to come to her home and they discussed her assets. She said, *'Besides the furniture and accessories you see here, I have $40,000 in my savings account at the bank.'*

'How would you like the $40,000 to be distributed?'

The spinster said, *'Well, as I told you, I've lived a reclusive life. People have hardly ever noticed me, so I'd like them to notice when I pass on. I'd like to provide $35,000 for my funeral.'*

The lawyer remarked, *'Well, for $35,000 you will be able to have a funeral that will certainly be noticed and will leave a lasting impression on anyone who may not have taken much note of you! What would you like to do with the remaining $5,000?'*

The spinster replied, *'As you know, I've never married. I've lived alone almost my entire life and in fact, I've never slept with a man. I'd like you to use the $5,000 to arrange for a man to sleep with me.'*

'This is a very unusual request,' the lawyer said, adding, *'but I'll see what I can do to arrange it and get back to you.'*

That evening, the lawyer told his wife about the eccentric spinster and her weird request. After thinking about how much she could do around the house with $5000 and with a bit of coaxing, she got her husband to agree to provide the service himself. She said, *'I'll drive you over tomorrow morning and wait in the car till you're finished.'*

The next morning, she drove him to the spinster's home and waited for over an hour, but her husband didn't come out. So she blew the car horn. Shortly, the upstairs bedroom window opened and the lawyer stuck his head out. He yelled, *'Pick me up tomorrow, she's going to let the County bury her!'*

Divorce Proceeding

A Polish man moved to the USA and married an American girl. Although his English was far from perfect, they got along very well until one day he rushed into a lawyer's office and asked him if he could arrange a divorce for him.

The lawyer said that getting a divorce would depend on the circumstances and asked him the following questions:

Lawyer: *'Have you any grounds?'*
Answer: *'Yes, an acre and a half and nice little home.'*
Lawyer: *'No, I meant what is the foundation of this case?'*
Answer: *'It made of concrete.'*
Lawyer: *'I don't think you understand. Does either of you have a real grudge?'*
Answer: *'No, we have a carport and not need one.'*
Lawyer: *'I mean. What are your relations like?'*
Answer: *'All my relations still in Poland.'*
Lawyer: *'Is there infidelity in your marriage?'*
Reply: *'We have hi-fidelity stereo and good DVD player.'*
Lawyer: *'Does your wife beat you up.'*
Reply: *'No I always up before her.'*

Lawyer: *'Is your wife a nagger?'*
Reply: *'No, she white.'*
Lawyer: *'Why do you want a divorce?'*
Reply: *'She going to kill me'*
Lawyer: *'What makes you think that?'*
Reply: *'I got proof.'*
Lawyer: *'What kind of proof?'*
Reply: *'She going to poison me. She buy a bottle at drugstore and put on shelf in bathroom. I can read and it say, 'Polish Remover.''*

Don't Mess With a Newfie (from Newfoundland, Canada)

A lawyer and a Newfie are sitting next to each other on a long flight. The lawyer asks if the Newfie would like to play a fun game. The Newfie is tired and just wants to take a nap, so he politely declines and tries to catch a few winks.

The lawyer persists, that the game is a lot of fun. *'I ask you a question and if you don't know the answer, you pay me only $5; you ask me one and if I don't know the answer, I will pay you $500.'*

This catches the Newfie's attention and to keep the lawyer quiet, agrees to play the game.

The lawyer asks the first question. *'What's the distance from the earth to the moon?'* The Newfie doesn't say a word, reaches in his pocket pulls out a five-dollar bill and hands it to the lawyer.

Now, it's the Newfie's turn. He asks the lawyer, *'What goes up a hill with three legs and comes down with four?'* The lawyer uses his laptop, searches all references. He uses the Air phone: he searches the Net and even the Library of Congress. He sends e-mails to all the smart friends he knows, all to no avail.

After one hour of searching he finally gives up. He wakes the Newfie and hands him $500. The Newfie pockets the $500 goes right back to sleep.

The lawyer is going nuts not knowing the answer. He wakes the Newfie and asks, *'Well, so what goes up a hill with three legs and comes down with four?'*

The Newfie reaches in his pocket, hands the lawyer $5 and goes back to sleep.

Subject: Lawyers

These are from a book called Disorder in the American Courts and are things people actually said in court, word for word, taken down and published by court stenographers who had the torment of staying calm while these exchanges were actually taking place. (From the desk of Dr. James Basterdsen.)

Question: Are you sexually active?
Response: No, I just lie there.
Question: What is your date of birth?
Response: July 15th.
Question: What year?
Response: Every year.
Question: What gear were you in at the moment of the impact?
Response: Gucci sweats and Reeboks.
Question: This myasthenia gravis, does it affect your memory at all?
Response: Yes.
Question: And in what ways does it affect your memory?
Response: I forget.
Question: You forget? Can you give us an example of something that you've forgotten?
Question: How old is your son, the one living with you?
Response: Thirty-eight or thirty-five, I can't remember which.
Question: How long has he lived with you?
Response: Forty-five years.
Question: What was the first thing your husband said to you when he woke up that morning?
Response: He said, 'Where am I Doris?'
Question: And why did that upset you?
Response: My name is Susan.
Question: Do you know if your daughter has ever been involved in voodoo or the occult?
Response: We both do.
Question: Voodoo?
Response: We do.
Question: You do?
Response: Yes, voodoo.
Question: Now doctor, isn't it true that when a person dies in his sleep, he doesn't know about it until the next morning?
Response: Did you actually pass the bar exam?
Question: The youngest son, the twenty-year-old, how old is he?
Response: He's twenty.
Question: Were you present when your picture was taken?
Question: So the date of conception (of the baby) was August 8th?
Response: Yes.
Question: And what were you doing at that time?
Answer: I'd like you to guess.
Question: She had three children, right?
Response: Yes.
Question: How many were boys?

Response: None.
Question: Were there any girls?
Question: How was your first marriage terminated?
Response: By death.
Question: And by whose death was it terminated?
Question: Can you describe the individual?
Response: He was about medium height and had a beard.
Question: Was this a male or a female?
Question: Is your appearance here this morning pursuant to a deposition notice, which I sent to your attorney?
Response: No, this is how I dress when I go to work.
Question: Doctor, how many autopsies have you performed on dead people?
Response: All my autopsies are performed on dead people.
Question: All your responses must be oral, okay? What school did you go to?
Response: Oral.
Question: Do you recall the time that you examined the body?
Response: The autopsy started around 8:30 pm.
Question: And Mr. Dennington was dead at the time?
Response: No, he was sitting on the table wondering why I was doing an autopsy.
Question: Are you qualified to give a urine sample?
And to save the best for last!!!!!!
Question: Doctor, before you performed the autopsy, did you check for a pulse?
Response: No.
Question: Did you check for blood pressure?
Response: No.
Question: Did you check for breathing?
Response: No.
Question: So, then it is possible that the patient was alive when you began the autopsy?
Response: No.
Question: How can you be so sure, Doctor?
Response: Because his brain was sitting on my desk in a jar.
Question: But could the patient have still been alive, nevertheless?
Response: Yes, it is possible that he could have been alive and practicing law somewhere.

Best lawyer Joke

One afternoon a lawyer was riding in his limousine when he saw two men along the roadside eating grass. Disturbed, he ordered his driver to stop and he got out to investigate.

He asked one man, *'Why are you eating grass?'*

'We don't have any money for food,' the poor man replied. *'We have to eat grass.'*

'Well, then, you can come with me to my house and I'll feed you,' the lawyer said.

'But sir, I have a wife and two children with me. They are over there, under that tree.'

'Bring them along,' the lawyer replied. Turning to the other poor man he stated, *'You come with us, too.'*

The second man, in a pitiful voice, then said, *'But sir, I also have a wife and SIX children with me!'*

'Bring them all, as well,' the lawyer answered.

They all entered the car, which was no easy task, even for a car as large as the limousine was.

Once underway, one of the poor fellows turned to the lawyer and said, *'Sir, you are too kind. Thank you for taking all of us with you.'*

The lawyer replied, *'Glad to do it. You'll really love my place. The grass is almost a foot high.'*

The Duck and the Lawyer

A big city lawyer went duck hunting in rural North Cowra. He shot and dropped a bird, but it fell into a farmer's field on the other side of a fence. As the lawyer climbed over the fence, an elderly farmer drove up on his tractor and asked him what he was doing. The litigator responded, *'I shot a duck and it fell in this field and now I'm going to retrieve it.'*

The old farmer Peter replied, *'This is my property and you are not coming over here.'*

The indignant lawyer said, *'I am one of the best trial lawyers in Australia and, if you don't let me get that duck, I'll sue you and take everything you own.'*

The old farmer smiled and said, *'Apparently, you don't know how we settle disputes in North Cowra. We settle small disagreements like this with the 'Three Kick Rule.''*

The lawyer asked, *'What is the 'Three Kick Rule'?'*

The Farmer replied, *'Well, because the dispute occurs on my land, I get to go first. I kick you three times and then you kick me three times and so on back and forth until someone gives up.'*

The lawyer quickly thought about the proposed contest and decided that he could easily take the old codger. He agreed to abide by the local custom. The old farmer slowly climbed down from the tractor and walked up to the attorney. His first kick planted the toe of his heavy steel-toed work boot into the lawyer's groin and dropped him to his knees!

His second kick to the midriff sent the lawyer's last meal gushing from his mouth. The lawyer was on all fours when the farmer's third kick to his rear end, sent him face-first into a fresh cow pie.

Summoning every bit of his will and remaining strength the lawyer very slowly managed to get to his feet. Wiping his face with the arm of his jacket, he said, *'Okay, you old fart. Now it's my turn.'*

The old farmer smiled and said, *'Nah, I give up. You can have the duck.'*

CHAPTER 6 - DOCTORS

Insane Asylum

A doctor at an insane asylum decided to take his inmates to a baseball game. For weeks in advance, he coached his patients to respond to his commands. When the day of the game arrived, everything seemed to be going well. As the national anthem started, the doctor yelled, *'Up nuts!'* And the inmates complied by standing up. After the anthem he yelled, *'Down nuts!'* And they all sat.

After a home run, he yelled, *'Cheer nuts!'* And they all broke into applause and cheers. Thinking things were going very well, he decided to go get a beer and a hot dog, leaving his assistant in charge.

When he returned there was a riot in progress. Finding his assistant, he asked what happened. The assistant replied, *'Well ...everything was fine until some guy walked by and yelled, 'peanuts!'*

How to avoid the flu shot

- Eat right!
- Make sure you get your daily dose of fruits and veggies.
- Take your vitamins and bump up your vitamin C.
- Get plenty of exercise because exercise helps build your immune system. Walk for at least an hour a day, go for a swim, take the stairs instead of the elevator, etc.
- Wash your hands often. If you can't wash them, keep a bottle of antibacterial stuff around.
- Get lots of fresh air. Open doors and windows whenever possible.
- Try to eliminate as much stress from your life as you can.
- Get plenty of rest.

OR

Take the doctor's approach. Think about it ... When you go for a shot, what do they do first? They clean your arm with alcohol ... Why? Because alcohol KILLS GERMS. So ...

- I walk to the liquor store ... (exercise)
- I put lime in my Corona ... (fruit)
- Celery in my Bloody Mary ... (veggies)
- Drink outdoors on the bar patio ... (fresh air)
- Tell jokes, laugh ... (eliminate stress)
- Then pass out ... (rest)

The way I see it.... If you keep your alcohol levels up, flu germs can't get you! My grandmother always said, *'A shot in the glass is better than one in the ass! Live well, laugh often and love much.'*

'Hey Doc! I'm cured! I'm free!'

John and Bill were in a mental institution. This place had an annual contest picking two of the best patients and giving them two questions. If they got them correct, they're deemed cured and were free to go. John was called into the doctor's office first and asked if he understood that he'd be free if he answered the questions correctly. John nodded yes. The doctor asked, *'John, what would happen if I poked out one of your eyes?'*
'I'd be half blind.'
'That's correct. What would happen if I poked out both eyes?'
'I'd be completely blind.'
The doctor stood up, shook John's hand and told him he was free. On his way out, as the doctor filled out the paperwork, John mentioned the exam to Bill. He told him what questions were going to be asked and gave him the answers.
So Bill came in. The doctor went through the formalities and asked, *'What would happen if I cut off one ear?'*
Bill remembering what John had said was the correct answer said, *'I'd be half blind.'*
The doctor looked a little puzzled, but went on. *'What if I cut off the other ear?'*
'I'd be completely blind,' Bill replied.
'Bill, can you explain how you'd be blind?'
'My hat would fall down over my eyes,' was the answer. He was allowed to go.

Jim and Edna were both patients in a mental hospital. One day while they were walking past the hospital swimming pool, Jim suddenly jumped into the deep end. He sank to the bottom of the pool and stayed there. Edna promptly jumped in to save him. She swam to the bottom and pulled Jim out.
When the Director of Nursing became aware of Edna's heroic act, she immediately ordered her to be discharged from the hospital, as she now considered her to be mentally stable. When she went to tell Edna the news she said, *'Edna, I have good news and bad news. The good news is you're being discharged; since you were able to rationally respond to a crisis by jumping in and saving the life of another patient, I have concluded that your act displays soundness of mind. The bad news is that Jim, the patient you saved, hanged*

himself in his bathroom with the belt to his robe right after you saved him. I am so sorry, but he's dead.'

Edna replied, *'He didn't hang himself, I put him there to dry. How soon can I go home?'*

Paddy

Paddy was working at the fish plant in Cork when he accidentally cut off all 10 of his fingers. He went to the emergency room in Cork's hospital. The doctor looked at Paddy and said, *'Let's be avin' da fingers and I'll see what oi can do.'*

Paddy said, *'Oi haven't got da fingers.'*

'Whadda ya mean you haven't got da fingers? Lord Tunderin' Jesus, it's 2013! We's got microsurgery and all kinds of incredible techniques. I could have put dem back on and made you like new! Why didn't ya bring da fingers?'

And Paddy said, *'And how was I 'spose to pick dem up?'*

Sore Elbow

One day, in line at the works cafeteria, Jack says to Mike behind him, *'My elbow hurts like hell. I suppose I'd better see a doctor!'*

'Listen; don't waste your time down at the surgery,' Mike replies. *'There's a diagnostic computer at Tesco. Just give it a urine sample and the computer will tell you what's wrong and what to do about it. It takes ten seconds and only costs five quid ... a lot quicker and better than a doctor and you get Club card points.'*

So Jack collects a urine sample in a small jar and takes it to Tesco. He deposits Five pounds and the computer lights up and asks for the urine sample. He pours the sample into the slot and waits. Ten seconds later, the computer ejects a printout: *'You have tennis elbow. Soak your arm in warm water and avoid heavy activity. It will improve in two weeks.'*

That evening while thinking how amazing this new technology was, Jack began wondering if the computer could be fooled. He mixed some tap water, a stool sample from his dog, urine samples from his wife and daughter and 'pleasured himself' into the mixture for good measure. Jack hurried back to Tesco, eager to check what would happen. He deposits five pounds, pours in his concoction and awaits the results. The computer prints the following:

Your tap water is too hard. Get a water softener.

Your dog has ringworm. Bathe him with anti-fungal shampoo.

Your daughter has a cocaine habit. Get her into rehab.

Your wife is pregnant. Twins. They aren't yours. Get a lawyer.

And if you don't stop playing with yourself, your elbow will never get better!

Thank you for shopping at Tesco.

New Hospital Wing

When a panel of doctors was asked to vote on adding a new wing to their hospital, the Allergists voted to scratch it; the Dermatologists advised no rash moves; the Gastroenterologists had a gut feeling about it; but the Neurologists thought the administration had a lot of nerve and the Obstetricians stated they were all labouring under a misconception.

The Ophthalmologists considered the idea short-sighted; the Pathologists yelled, *'Over my dead body!'* The Paediatricians said, *'Grow up!'* The Psychiatrists thought the whole idea was madness; the Surgeons decided to wash their hands of the whole thing and the Radiologists could see right through it!

The Internists thought it was a bitter pill to swallow; the Plastic Surgeons said, *'This puts a whole new face on the matter.'* The Podiatrists thought it was a step forward, but the Urologists felt the scheme wouldn't hold water. The Anaesthesiologists thought the whole idea was a gas and the Cardiologists didn't have the heart to say no. And in the end, the Proctologists left the decision up to some asshole.

I've got what, doctor?

A man went to his doctor to find out why he'd been having such severe headaches. The doctor ran some tests and after a few hours called the man into his office. *'I have terrible news,'* he told his patient. *'Your condition is terminal.'*

'Oh no!' the man wailed. *'How long do I have?'*

'Ten ...' began the doctor.

'Ten what?' the patient interrupted. *'Days, months, years?'*

'Nine,' said the doctor, *'eight, seven, six, five ...'*

A doctor made it his regular habit to stop off at a bar for a hazelnut daiquiri on his way home. The bartender knew of his habit and would always have the drink waiting at precisely 5:03 pm. One afternoon, as the end of the workday approaches, the bartender was dismayed to find that he was out of hazelnut extract.

Thinking quickly, he threw together a daiquiri made with hickory nuts and set it on the bar. The doctor came in at his regular time, took one sip of the drink and exclaimed, *'This isn't a hazelnut daiquiri!'*

'No, I'm sorry,' replied the bartender, *'It's a hickory daiquiri, Doc.'* (groan)

Dinner Club

A group of country neighbours wanted to get together on a regular basis and socialise. As a result, about ten couples formed a dinner club and agreed to meet for dinner at a different neighbours' house each month. Of course, the lady of the house was to prepare the meal. When it came time for Jimmy and Susie Brown to have the dinner at their house, like most women, Susie wanted to outdo all the others and prepare a meal that was the best that any of them had ever lapped a lip over.

A few days before the big event, Susie got out her cookbook and decided to have mushroom smothered steak. When she went to the store to buy some mushrooms, she found the price for a small can was more than she wanted to pay. She then told her husband, *'We aren't going to have mushrooms because they are too expensive.'*

He said, *'Why don't you go down in the pasture and pick some of those mushrooms? There are plenty of them right in the creek bed.'*

She said, *'No, I don't want to do that, because I have heard that wild mushrooms are poison.'*

He then said, *'I don't think so. I see the varmints eating them all the time and it never has affected them.'*

After thinking about this, Susie decided to give this a try and got in the pickup and went down in the pasture and picked some. She brought the wild mushrooms back home and washed them, sliced and diced them to get them ready to go over her smothered steak. Then she went out on the back porch and got Ol' Spot's (the yard dog) bowl and gave him a double handful. She even put some bacon grease on them to make them tasty. Ol' Spot didn't slow down until he had eaten every bite.

All morning long, Susie watched him and the wild mushrooms didn't seem to affect him, so she decided to use them.

The meal was a great success and Susie even hired a lady from town to come out and help her serve. She had on a white apron and a little cap on her head. It was first class. After everyone had finished, they all began to kick back and relax and socialise. The men were visiting and the women started to gossip a bit. About this time, the lady from town came in from the kitchen and whispered in Susie's ear. She said, *'Mrs. Brown, Spot just died.'*

With this news, Susie went into hysterics. After she finally calmed down, she called the doctor and told him what had happened. The doctor said, *'It's bad, but I think we can take care of it. I will call for an ambulance and I will be there as quick as I can get there.*

We'll give everyone enemas and we will pump out everyone's stomach. Everything will be fine. Just keep them all there and keep them calm.'

It wasn't long until they could hear the wail of the siren as the ambulance was coming down the road. When they got there, the EMTs got out with their suitcases, syringes and a stomach pump. The doctor arrived shortly thereafter. One by one, they took each person into the master bathroom, gave them an enema and pumped out their stomach. After the last one was finished, the doctor came out and said, 'I think everything will be fine now and he left.'

They were all looking pretty peaked sitting around the living room and about this time, the town lady came in and said, 'You know, that fellow that ran over Ol' Spot never even stopped!!'

The End is near!

Reverend Ole was the pastor of the local Norwegian Lutheran Church and Pastor Sven was the minister of the Swedish Covenant Church across the road. One day they were seen pounding a sign into the ground, that said:

'DA END ISS NEAR! TURN YERSELF AROUND NOW BEFORE IT'S TOO LATE'

As a car sped past them, the driver leaned out his window and yelled, 'Leave us alone, you religious nuts!'

From the curve we heard screeching tires and a big splash ... Rev. Ole turns to Pastor Sven and asks, 'Do ya tink maybe da sign should yust say 'Bridge Out'?'

Shingles

A fella walked into a doctor's office and the receptionist asked him what he had. He replied, 'Shingles.'

So she took down his name, address and medical insurance number and told him to have a seat. Fifteen minutes later a nurse's aid came out and asked him what he had. He said, 'Shingles.'

So she took down his height, weight, a complete medical history and told him to wait in the examining room. A half-hour later, a nurse came in and asked him what he had. Rather exasperated, he replied, 'Shingles.'

So she gave him a blood test, a blood pressure test, an electrocardiogram. She told him to take off all his clothes and wait for the doctor. An hour later the doctor came in and asked him what he had. 'Shingles.'

'Where,' asked the doctor.

'Outside in the truck. Where do you want me to put them?'

'Will I live to be 80?'

I recently chose a new primary care physician. After two visits and exhaustive lab tests, he said I was doing 'fairly well' for my age. A little concerned about that comment, I couldn't resist asking him, *'Do you think I'll live to be 80?'*

He asked, *'Do you smoke tobacco or drink alcoholic beverages?'*

'No,' I replied. *'I don't do drugs, either.'*

Then he asked, *'Do you eat rib-eye steaks and barbecued ribs?'*

I said, *'No, my other doctor said that all red meat is unhealthy!'*

'Do you spend a lot of time in the sun, like playing golf, boating, fishing or relaxing in the beach?'

'No, I don't,' I said.

He asked, *'Do you gamble, drive fast cars or have a lot of sex?'*

'No,' I said. *'I don't do any of those things.'*

Then he looked at me and asked, *'Then why do you give a shit?'*

Obsessions

A psychiatrist was conducting a group therapy session with four young mothers and their small children. *'You all have obsessions,'* he observed. To the first mother, he said, *'You are obsessed with eating. You've even named your daughter Candy.'*

He turned to the second Mom. *'Your obsession is with money. Again, it manifests itself in your child's name, Penny.'*

He turns to the third Mom. *'Your obsession is alcohol. This too manifests itself in your child's name, Brandy.'*

At this point, the fourth mother gets up, takes her little boy by the hand and whispers. *'Come on, Dick, we're leaving.'*

Doctor Dave

Doctor Dave had slept with one of his patients and felt guilty all day long. No matter how much he tried to forget about it, he couldn't. The guilt and sense of betrayal were overwhelming. But every now and then he'd hear an internal reassuring voice in his head that said: *'Dave, don't worry about it. You aren't the first medical practitioner to sleep with one of their patients and you won't be the last. And you're single. Just let it go.'*

But invariably another voice in his head would bring him back to reality whispering, *'Dave ... Dave ... Dave ... you're a vet!'*

Should you be institutionalised?

It doesn't hurt to take a hard look at yourself from time to time. This little test should get you started.

During a visit to the mental asylum, a visitor asked the Director what the criteria was that defined a patient that required institutionalisation.

'Well,' said the Director, 'we fill up a bathtub with water, then we offer a teaspoon, a teacup and a bucket to the patient and ask him or her to empty the bathtub.'

Okay, here's your test:
Would you use the teaspoon?
Would you use the teacup?
Would you use the bucket?

'Oh, I understand,' said the visitor. 'A normal person would use the bucket because it's bigger than the spoon or teacup.'

'No!' said the Director. 'A normal person would pull the plug! Do you want a room with or without a view?'

Cure for Sunburn

A guy falls asleep on the beach for several hours and gets a horrible sunburn. He goes to the hospital and is promptly admitted after being diagnosed with second-degree burns. He was already starting to blister and in agony. The doctor prescribed continuous intravenous feeding with saline and electrolytes, a sedative and a Viagra pill every four hours.

The nurse, rather astounded, said, 'What good will the Viagra do him?'

The doctor smiled, 'It'll help keep the sheets off his legs.

Everywhere it hurts!

A man went to the doctor and said, 'Doc, I ache all over. Everywhere I touch it hurts.'

The doctor said, 'Okay, touch your elbow.'

He touches his elbow and winces in genuine pain. The doctor surprised, said, 'Touch your head.'

He touches his head and jumps in agony. The doctor asks him to touch his knee and the same thing happens. Everywhere the guy touches, he hurts like hell. The doctor is stumped and orders a complete examination with X-rays, etc and tells him to come back in three hours.

Three hours later he comes back and the doctor said, 'We've found your problem.'

'Oh yeah? What is it?'

'You've broken your finger!'

Longevity

People in Louisiana know that Cajun Indians live longer. A Cajun went to the doctor for a check up. The doctor came with the results and said, *'You're in excellent shape for a 55 year-old man.'*

'Did I say I was 55?' said the Cajun.

'You mean you're not 55?' said the doctor.

'No. I'm 75,' said the Cajun.

'Good heavens. You are in remarkable shape. You must have incredible genes. Let me ask you this. How old was your father when he died?'

'Did I say my father was dead?' said the Cajun.

'You don't mean he's alive too?'

'He sure is. He is 98 and still dancing,' said the Cajun.

'How old was your grandfather when he died?'

'Did I say my grandfather was dead?'

'You mean he's alive too?'

'Why he sure is. In fact, he is 127 and getting married tomorrow.'

'Getting married! Why in the world would a 127 year-old man want to get married?'

'Did I say he wanted to get married?'

Cardiologist's funeral

Twisted, but funny!

A cardiologist died and was given an elaborate funeral. A huge heart covered in flowers stood behind the casket during the service. Following the eulogy, the heart opened and the casket rolled inside. The heart then closed, sealing the doctor in the beautiful heart forever.

At that point, one of the mourners burst into laughter. When all eyes stared at him, he said, *'I'm sorry, I was just thinking of my own funeral .... I'm a gynecologist.'*

That's when the proctologist fainted.

The Painter

There was this world famous painter. In the prime of her career, she started losing her eyesight. Fearful that she might lose her life as a painter, she went to see the best eye surgeon in the world. After several weeks of delicate surgery and therapy, her eyesight was restored. The painter was so grateful that she decided to show her gratitude by repainting the doctor's office.

Part of her work included painting a gigantic eye on one wall. When she had finished her work, she held a press conference to unveil her latest work of art: the doctor's office.

During the press conference, one reporter noticed the eye on the wall and asked the doctor, *'What was your first reaction upon seeing your newly painted office, especially that large eye on the wall?'*

To this, the eye doctor responded, *'I said to myself, 'Thank God I'm not a gynaecologist.''*

This is a good and simple reasoning!!

A mechanic was removing a cylinder head from the motor of a Harley Motorcycle when he spotted a well-known cardiologist in his shop. The cardiologist was there waiting for the service manager to come and take a look at his bike, when the mechanic shouted across the garage, *'Hey Doc, want to take a look at this?'*

The cardiologist, a bit surprised, walked over to where the mechanic was working on the motorcycle. The mechanic straightened up, wiped his hands on a rag and asked, *'So Doc, look at this engine. I open its heart, take the valves out, repair any damage and then put them back in and when I finish, it works just like new. So how come I make $39,675 a year and you get the really big bucks ($1,695,759) when you and I are doing basically the same work?'*

The cardiologist paused, smiled and leaned over, then whispered to the mechanic. *'Try doing it with the engine running.'*

Bank Robbery

A pregnant woman walked into a bank and lined up at the first available teller. Just at that moment, the bank was robbed and she was shot three times in the stomach. She was rushed to the hospital where she was fixed up. As she left she asked the doctor about her baby. The doctor says, *'You're going to have triplets. They're fine but each one has a bullet lodged in its stomach. Don't worry though. The bullets will pass through their system through normal metabolism.'*

As time goes on the woman has three children - two girls and a boy. Twelve years later, one of the girls came up to her mother and said, *'Mommy, I've done a very weird thing!'* Her mother asked what happened and her daughter replied, *'I passed a bullet into the toilet.'* The woman comforted her and explained all about the incident at the bank.

A few weeks later, her other daughter comes up to her with tears streaming from her eyes. *'Mommy, I've done a very bad thing!'*

The mother said, *'Let me guess. You passed a bullet into the toilet, right?'*

The daughter looks up from her teary eyes and said, *'Yes, how did you know?'* The mother comforted her child and explained about the incident at the bank.

A month later the boy came up and said, *'Mommy, I've done a very bad thing!'*

'You passed a bullet into the toilet, right?'

'No, I was masturbating and I shot the dog!'

Ants

Some people do goofy things. I'm a medical student currently doing a rotation in toxicology at the poison control centre. Today, a woman called in very upset because she caught her little daughter eating ants. I quickly reassured her that the ants are not harmful and there would be no need to bring her daughter into the hospital. She calmed down and at the end of the conversation happened to mention that she had given her daughter some ant poison to eat in order to kill the ants.

I told her she'd better bring her daughter into the Emergency room right away ...

Medical Terminology:

(Best if said out loud)
- Barium - what doctors do when treatment fails.
- Bowel - letter like a.e.i.o.u.
- Caesarean section - district in Rome.
- Cat scan - searching for kitty.
- Cauterise - make eye contact with her.
- Colic - sheep dog.
- Coma - a punctuation mark.
- Congenital - friendly.
- D&C - where Washington is.
- Diarrhoea - journal of daily events.
- Dilate - to live long.
- Enema - not a friend.
- Fester – quicker.
- Fibula - a small lie.
- Genital - not Jewish.
- G.I series - soldier's ball game.
- Grippe - suitcase.
- Hangnail - coat hook.
- Impotent - distinguished, well-known.

- Intense pain - torture in a tepee.
- Labour pain - got hurt at work.
- Medical staff - doctor's cane.
- Morbid - higher offer.
- Nitrate - cheaper than day rate.
- Node - was aware of.
- Outpatient - person who had fainted.
- Pap smear - fatherhood test.
- Pelvis - cousin of Elvis.
- Post operative - letter carrier.
- Protein - favouring young people.
- Rectum - damn near killed 'em.
- Recovery room - place to do upholstery.
- Rheumatic - amorous.
- Secretion - hiding anything.
- Seizure - Roman emperor.
- Serology - study of knighthood.
- Tablet - small table.
- Terminal illness - sickness at airport.
- Tibia - country in North Africa.
- Tumour - an extra pair.
- Urine - opposite of you're out.
- Varicose - located nearby.
- Vein - conceited.

Trivia

Did you hear about the guy that lost his left arm and leg in a car crash? He's all right now.

Doctor to patient: I have good news and bad news: The good news is that you're not a hypochondriac ...

I pointed out to my doctor that I have done the right thing by not following his advice a number of times. He said medicine is more of an art than a science. So I'm thinking about getting him a paint-by-numbers set for Christmas.

How do crazy people go through the forest? They take the psycho path.

Radio Station

A radio station paid $100 - $500 for people to tell their most embarrassing stories. This one won $300:

'I was due for an appointment with the gynaecologist when early one morning I received a call from his office that I had been

rescheduled for early that morning at 9:30 am. I had only just packed everyone off to work and school and it was around 8:45 am already. The trip to his office would take about 35 minutes, so I didn't have any time to spare.

As most women do, I like to take a little extra effort over hygiene when making such visits, but this time I wasn't going to be able to make the full effort. So I rushed upstairs and threw off my dressing gown, wet the washcloth and gave myself a wash in 'that area' in front of the sink, taking care to ensure that I was presentable. I threw the washcloth into the clothesbasket, donned some clothes, hopped in my car and raced for my appointment.

I was in the waiting room only a few minutes when he called me in. Knowing the procedure, I hopped on the table, looked over the side of the room and pretended I was in Hawaii or some other place a million miles away from there. I was a little surprised when he said, 'My ... we have taken a little extra effort this morning, haven't we?' but I didn't respond. The appointment over, I heaved a sigh of relief and went home. The rest of the day went normal - some shopping, cleaning, preparing the evening meal etc.

About 8:30 that evening, my 18-year-old daughter was fixing to go to a school dance, when she called down from the bathroom, 'Mom, where is my washcloth?'

I called back for her to get another one from the cabinet. She called back, 'No I need the one that was here by the sink. It had all my glitter and sparkles in it.''

Personal Questions

They always ask at the doctor's office why you are there and you have to answer in front of others what's wrong and sometimes it is embarrassing. There's nothing worse than a Doctor's receptionist who insists you tell her what is wrong with you in a room full of other patients. I know most of us have experienced this and I love the way this old guy handled it.

An 86-year-old man walked into a crowded waiting room and approached the desk. The receptionist said, *'Yes sir, what are you seeing the Doctor for today?'*

'There's something wrong with my dick,' he replied.

The receptionist became irritated and said, *'You shouldn't come into a crowded waiting room and say things like that.'*

'Why not? You asked me what was wrong and I told you,' he said.

The receptionist replied; *'Now you've caused some embarrassment in this room full of people. You should have said there is something wrong with your ear or something and discussed the problem further with the Doctor in private.'*

The man replied, *'You shouldn't ask people questions in a room full strangers, especially if the answer could embarrass anyone.'* The man walked out, waited several minutes and then re-entered.

The Receptionist smiled smugly and asked, *'Yes??'*

'There's something wrong with my ear', he stated.

The Receptionist nodded approvingly and smiled, knowing he had taken her advice. *'And what is wrong with your ear, Sir?'*

'I can't piss out of it,' he replied.

The waiting room erupted in laughter.

Observation

A lecturer teaching medicine was tutoring a class on 'Observation.' He took out a jar of yellow-coloured liquid. *'This,'* he explained, *'is urine. To be a doctor, you have to be observant to colour, smell, sight and taste.'*

After saying this, he dipped his finger into the jar and put it into his mouth. His class watched on in amazement, most, in disgust. But being the good students that they were, the jar was passed and one by one, they dipped one finger into the jar and then put it into their mouth.

After the last student was done, the lecturer shook his head. *'If any of you had been observant, you would have noticed that I put my second finger into the jar and my third finger into my mouth.'*

There was a mass exodus from the lecture hall.

The Cure

A man goes to the doctor and tells him that he hasn't been feeling well. The doctor examines him, leaves the room and comes back with three different bottles of pills.

The doctor says, *'Take the green pill with a big glass of water when you get up. Take the blue pill with a big glass of water after lunch. Then just before going to bed, take the red pill with another big glass of water.'*

Startled to be put on so much medicine, the man stammers, *'Cheesh Doc, exactly what's my problem?'*

Doctor replies, *'You're not drinking enough water.'*

Won't Laugh

'Of course I won't laugh,' the doctor said. *'I'm a professional. In over twenty years I've never laughed at a patient.'*

'Okay then,' Fred said and proceeded to drop his trousers, revealing the tiniest penis the doctor had ever seen. It couldn't have

been the size of a peanut. Unable to control himself, the doctor started giggling and then fell laughing to the floor.

Ten minutes later he was able to struggle to his feet and regain his composure. *'I'm so sorry,'* said the doctor, *'I really am ... I don't know what came over me. On my honour as a doctor and a gentleman, I promise it won't happen again. Now what seems to be the problem?'*

'It's swollen,' Fred replied

The Surgeons

Five surgeons are discussing who makes the best patients to operate on. The first surgeon says, *'I like to see accountants on my operating table, because when you open them up, everything inside is numbered.'*

The second responds, *'Yeah, but you should try electricians! Everything inside them is colour coded.'*

The third surgeon says, *'No, I really think librarians are the best; everything inside them is in alphabetical order.'*

The fourth surgeon chimes in: *'You know, I like engineers ... those guys always understand when you have a few parts left over in the end and when the job takes longer than you said it would.'*

But the fifth surgeon shut them all up when he observed: *'You're all wrong. Politicians are the easiest to operate on. There's no guts, no heart and no spine and the head and butt are interchangeable.'*

Following Orders

Helen accompanied Art to the doctor's office for his check-up. Afterwards, the doctor took Helen aside and said, *'Unless you do the following things, Art will surely die.'*

The doctor went on to say, *'Here's what you need to do. Every morning, make sure you serve him a good healthy breakfast. Meet him at home each day for lunch so that you can serve him a well-balanced meal. Make sure that you feed him a good hot meal each evening and don't overburden him with any stressful conversation, nor ask him to perform any household chores. Also, keep the house spotless and clean so that he doesn't get exposed to any threatening germs'*

On the way home, Art asked Helen what the doctor said. She replied, *'He said you're going to die.'*

Country Doctor

An old country doctor went way out to the boondocks to deliver a baby. It was so far out, there was no electricity. When the doctor arrived, no one was at home except for the labouring mother and her five-year-old child.

The doctor instructed the child to hold a lantern high so he could see while he helped the woman deliver the baby. The child did so, the mother pushed and after a little while, the doctor lifted the newborn baby by the feet and spanked him on the bottom to get him to take his first breath. The doctor then asked the five-year-old what he thought of the baby.

'Hit him again,' the five-year-old said. 'He shouldn't have crawled up there in the first place!'

Doctor's Own Stories

A man comes into the ER and yells, *'My wife's going to have her baby in the taxi!'* I grabbed my stuff, rushed out to the taxi, lifted the lady's dress and began to take off her underwear. Suddenly I noticed that there were several taxis - and I was in the wrong one.

Submitted by Dr. Mark MacDonald, San Antonio, TX.

At the beginning of my shift I placed a stethoscope on an elderly and slightly deaf female patient's anterior chest wall. *'Big breaths,'* I instructed. *'Yes, they used to be,'* replied the patient.

Submitted by Dr. Richard Byrnes, Seattle, WA.

One day I had to be the bearer of bad news when I told a wife that her husband had died of a massive myocardial infarct. Not more than five minutes later, I heard her reporting to the rest of the family that he had died of *a 'massive internal fart.'*

Submitted by Dr. Susan Steinberg, Manitoba, Canada

During a patient's two-week follow-up appointment with his cardiologist, he informed me, his doctor, that he was having trouble with one of his medications. *'Which one?'* I asked. *'The patch. The nurse told me to put on a new one every six hours and now I'm running out of places to put it!'* I had him quickly undress and discovered what I hoped I wouldn't see. Yes, the man had over fifty patches on his body! Now, the instructions include removal of the old patch before applying a new one.

Submitted by Dr. Rebecca St. Clair, Norfolk, VA.

While acquainting myself with a new elderly patient, I asked, *'How long have you been bedridden?'* After a look of complete confusion she answered... *'Why, not for about twenty years - when my husband was alive.'*

Submitted by Dr. Steven Swanson, Corvallis or.

I was caring for a woman and asked, *'So how's your breakfast this morning?'* *'It's very good, except for the Kentucky Jelly. I can't seem to get used to the taste'* the patient replied. I then asked to see the jelly and the woman produced a foil packet labelled *'KY Jelly.'*

Submitted by Dr. Leonard Kransdorf, Detroit, MI.

A nurse was on duty in the Emergency Room, when a young woman with purple hair styled into a punk rocker Mohawk, sporting a variety of tattoos and wearing strange clothing, entered. It was quickly determined that the patient had acute appendicitis, so she was scheduled for immediate surgery. When she was completely disrobed on the operating table, the staff noticed that her pubic hair had been dyed green and above it there was a tattoo that read, *'Keep off the grass.'* Once the surgery was completed, the surgeon wrote a short note on the patient's dressing, which said, *'Sorry, had to mow the lawn.'*

Submitted by RN no name

A Professor was giving a lecture on 'Involuntary Muscular Contractions' to his first year medical students. Realising that this was not the most riveting subject, the Professor decided to lighten the mood slightly. He pointed to a young woman in the front row and said, *'Do you know what your arse hole is doing while you're having an orgasm?'*

She replied, *'Probably fishing and drinking beer with his mates.'*

The professor laughed so much he could not continue with the lecture.

And finally!!!

As a new, young MD doing his residency in OB, I was quite embarrassed when performing female pelvic exams. To cover my embarrassment I had unconsciously formed a habit of whistling softly. The middle-aged lady upon whom I was performing this exam suddenly burst out laughing and further embarrassing me. I looked up from my work and sheepishly said, *'I'm sorry. Was I tickling you?'* She replied, *'No doctor, but the song you were whistling was, 'I wish I was an Oscar Meyer Wiener.''*

Dr. wouldn't submit his name

Knowledge Pills

A somewhat advanced society has figured how to package basic knowledge in pill form. A student, needing some of this advanced learning, goes to the pharmacy and asks what kind of knowledge pills are available. The pharmacist says, *'Here's a pill for English literature.'* The student takes the pill and swallows it and has new knowledge about English literature!

'What else do you have?' asks the student.

'Well, I have pills for art, history, biology and world history,' replies the pharmacist.

The student asks for these and swallows them and has new knowledge about these subjects.

Then the student asks, *'Do you have a pill for math?'*

The pharmacist says, *'Wait just a moment,'* and goes back into the storeroom and brings back a whopper of a pill and plunks it on the counter.

'I have to take that huge pill for math?' inquires the student.

The pharmacist replied, *'Well, you know math always was a little hard to swallow.'*

Near Death Experience

A middle-aged woman has a heart attack and is taken to the hospital. While on the operating table, she has a near-death experience. During that experience she sees God and asks if this is it. God says no and explains that she has another 30 years to live. Upon her recovery, she decides to stay in the hospital and have a face-lift, liposuction, breast augmentation, tummy tuck, etc. She figures since she's got another 30 years, she might as well make the most of it.

She walks out of the hospital after the last operation and is killed by an ambulance speeding to the hospital. She arrives in front of God and complains: *'I thought you said I had another 30 years.'*

God replies, *'I didn't recognise you.'*

The Colorectal Surgeon's Sing-a-long

We praise the colorectal surgeon
Misunderstood and much maligned
Slaving away in the heart of darkness
Working where the sun don't shine
Respect the colorectal surgeon
It's a calling few would crave
Lift up your hands and join us
Let's all do the finger wave
When it comes to spreading joy
There are many techniques
Some spread joy to the world
And others just spread cheeks
Some may think the cardiologist
Is their best friend
But the colorectal surgeon knows ...
He'll get you in the end!
Why the colorectal surgeon?
It's one of those mysterious things.
Is it because in that profession
There are always openings?

When I first met a colorectal surgeon
He did not quite understand;
I said, 'Hey nice to meet you
But do you mind? We don't shake hands.'
He sailed right through medical school
Because he was a whiz
Oh but he never thought of psychology
Though he read passages
A doctor he wanted to be
For golf he loved to play
But this is not quite what he meant ...
By eighteen holes a day!
Praise the colorectal surgeon
Misunderstood and much maligned
Slaving away in the heart of darkness
Working where the sun don't shine!

Ed Zachary Disease

A woman was very distraught because she hadn't had a date or sex in quite some time. Concerned that she may have something wrong with her, she decided to employ the medical expertise of a sex therapist. Her family doctor recommended Dr. Chang, a well-known Chinese sex therapist.

The next day, the woman entered the examination room and Dr. Chang said, *'Okay, take off all your crose.'*

The woman thinks nothing of the doctor's request considering she is in a doctor's office, after all. Then Dr. Chang said, *'Now, get down and crawl reery fass to the other side of room.'*

The reluctant woman complied. She got down onto the floor and crawled to the other side of the room. The doctor held back a smirk, slowly shook his head and said, *'Your problem vewy bad. You haf Ed Zachary Disease. Worse case I ever see. That why you not haf sex or dates.'*

Confused, the woman asks, *'What in the world is this Ed Zachary Disease?'*

Dr. Chang replies, *'It when your face rook Ed Zachary rike your ass.'*

The Midget

The testicles of a midget hurt and ached almost all the time. The midget went to the doctor and told him about his problem. The doctor told him to drop his pants and he would have a look. The midget dropped his pants. The doctor stood him up onto the examining table and started to examine him. The doctor put one finger under his left testicle and told the midget to turn his head and cough, the usual method to check for a hernia.

'*Aha!*' mumbled the doctor and as he put his finger under the right testicle, he asked the midget to cough again. '*Aha!*' said the doctor once more and reached for his surgical scissors.

Snip-snip-snip-snip on the right side ... then snip-snip-snip-snip on the left side. The midget was so scared he was afraid to look, but noted with amazement that the snipping did not hurt. The doctor then told the midget to walk around the examining room to see if his testicles still hurt. The midget was absolutely delighted as he walked around and discovered his boys were no longer aching.

The doctor said, *'How does that feel now?'*

The midget replied, *'Perfect Doc and I didn't even feel it. What did you do?'*

The doctor replied, *'I cut two inches off the top of your cowboy boots.'*

Medical Advice

My philosophy is: No Pain - No Pain.

Q: I've heard that cardiovascular exercise can prolong life. Is this true?
A: Your heart is only good for so many beats and that's it. Everything wears out eventually. Speeding up your heart will not make you live longer; that's like saying you can extend the life of your car by driving it faster. Want to live longer? Take a nap.

Q: Should I cut down on meat and eat more fruit and vegetables?
A: You must grasp logistical efficiencies. What does a cow eat? Hay and corn. And what are these? Vegetables. So a steak is nothing more than an efficient mechanism of delivering vegetables to your system. Need grain? Eat chicken. Beef is also a good source of field grass (green leafy vegetable). And pork chops can give you 100% of your recommended daily allowance of vegetable slop.

Q: Is beer or wine bad for me?
A: Look, it goes to the earlier point about fruit and vegetables. As we all know, scientists divide everything in the world into three categories: animal, mineral and vegetable. We all know that beer and wine are not animal and they're not on the periodic table of elements, so that only leaves one thing, right? Our advice: Have a burger and a beer and enjoy your liquid vegetables.

Q: At the gym, a guy asked me to 'spot' for him while he did the bench press. What did he mean?

A: 'Spotting' for someone means you stand over him while he blows air up your shorts. It's an accepted practice at health clubs; though if you find that it becomes the only reason why you're going in, you probably ought to re-evaluate your exercise programme.

Q: What are some advantages of participating in a regular exercise programme?
A: Sorry - can't think of a single one.

Q: Will sit-ups help prevent me from getting a little soft around the middle?
A: Definitely not! When you exercise a muscle, it gets bigger. You should only be doing sit-ups if you want a bigger stomach.

New Name

In Pharmacology, all drugs have two names, a trade name and generic name. For example, the trade name of Tylenol also has a generic name of Acetaminophen. Aleve is also called Naproxen. Amoxil is also called Amoxicillin and Advil is also called Ibuprofen.

The FDA has been looking for a generic name for Viagra. After careful consideration by a team of government experts, it recently announced that it has settled on the generic name of Mycoxafloppin. Also considered were Mycoxafailin, Mydixadrupin, Mydixarizin, Dixafix and of course, Ibepokin.

Pfizer Corporation announced today that Viagra will soon be available in liquid form and will be marketed by Pepsi Cola as a power beverage suitable for use as a mixer. It will now be possible for a man to literally pour himself a stiff one. Obviously we can no longer call this a soft drink and it gives new meaning to the names of 'cocktails,' 'highballs' and just a good old-fashioned 'stiff drink.' Pepsi will market the new concoction by the name of: 'mount & do'

CHAPTER 7 - POLICE

The Trooper:

Two men were driving through Texas when they were pulled over by a state trooper. The trooper walked up, tapped on the window with his nightstick, the driver rolled down the window and the trooper smacked him in the head with the stick.

The driver, rubbing his head said, *'Why'd you do that?'*

The trouper said, *'You're in Texas, son. When I pull you over, you'll have your license ready.'*

The driver said, *'I'm sorry, officer, I'm not from around here.'*

The trouper ran a check on the guy's license and found he was clean. He gave the guy his license back and walked around to the passenger side and tapped on the window. The passenger rolled his window down and the trouper smacked him with the nightstick.

The passenger said, *'What'd you do that for?'*

The cop said, *'Just making your wishes come true.'*

The passenger said, *'Huh?'*

The cop said, *'I know that two miles down the road you're gonna say, 'I wish that mother would've tried that shit with me!''*

Never say this to a cop

- I can't reach my license unless you hold my beer. (Okay in Texas)
- Sorry, Officer, I didn't realise my radar detector wasn't plugged in.
- Aren't you the guy from the Village People?
- Hey, you must've been doin' about 125 mph to keep up with me. Good job!
- You're not gonna check the trunk, are you?
- Are you Andy or Barney?
- I thought you had to be in relatively good physical condition to be a police officer.
- I pay your salary!
- Gee, Officer! That's terrific. The last officer only gave me a warning, too!
- Do you know why you pulled me over? Okay, just so one of us does.
- I was trying to keep up with traffic. Yes, I know there are no other cars around. That's how far ahead of me they are.
- When the Officer says *'Gee Son. Your eyes look red, have you been drinking?'* You probably shouldn't respond with, *'Gee*

Officer your eyes look glazed, have you been eating doughnuts?'

Smart Answer

Craig drove his brand new BMW Z3 convertible out of the car salesroom. Taking off down the motorway, he floored it to 120kph; enjoying the wind blowing through what little hair he had left. *'Amazing!'* he thought as he flew down the road, enjoying pushing the pedal to the metal even more. Looking in his rear view mirror, he saw a police car behind him, blue lights flashing and siren blaring. *'I can get away from him - no problem!'* thought Craig as he floored it.

To 130kph, then 140, then 150kph. Suddenly, he thought, *'What on earth am I doing? I'm too honest for this nonsense!'* So he pulled over to the side of the road and waited for the police car to catch up with him.

Pulling in behind him, the police officer walked up to the driver's side of the BMW, looked at his watch and said, *'Sir, my shift ends in 10 minutes. Today is Friday and I'm taking off for the weekend. If you give me a reason why you were speeding that I've never heard before, I'll let you go.'*

Craig looked very seriously at the policeman and replied, *'Years ago, my wife ran off with a policeman. I thought you were bringing her back.'*

'Have a good day, sir,' said the policeman.

Radar

A police officer had a perfect hiding place for watching for speeders. But one day, when everyone was under the speed limit, the officer found the problem: a ten-year-old boy was standing on the side of the road with a huge hand-painted sign that said, *'Radar Trap Ahead.'*

A little more investigative work led the officer to the boy's accomplice, another boy about 100 yards beyond the radar trap with a sign reading, *'Tips'* and a bucket at his feet, full of change.

A motorist was unknowingly caught in an automated speed trap that measured his speed using radar and photographed his car. He later received in the mail, a ticket for $40 and a photo of his car. Instead of sending a payment, he sent the police department a photograph of $40. Several days letter, he received a letter from the police that contained another picture - this one of handcuffs.

Having the right equipment

One morning at the lake I decided to take the neighbour's boat out that was full of fishing equipment. I motored out a short distance, anchored and was reading my book.

Along came a Game Warden in his boat. He pulled up alongside me and said, *'Good morning, Ma'am. What are you doing?'*

'Reading a book,' I said, (thinking, *'Isn't that obvious?'*)

'You're in a restricted fishing area,' he informed me.

'I'm sorry, officer, but I'm not fishing. I'm reading.'

'Yes, but you have all the equipment. For all I know you could start at any moment. I'll have to take you in and write you up.'

'If you do that, I'll have to charge you with sexual assault,' said the woman.

'But I haven't even touched you,' said the game warden.

'That's true, but you have all the equipment. For all I know you could start at any moment.'

'Have a nice day ma'am,' and he left.

The Bulge

A drug possession man on trial said he had been searched without a warrant. The prosecutor said the officer didn't need a warrant because of the 'bulge' in his jacket could have been a gun.

'Nonsense,' said the defendant who happened to be wearing the same jacket that day in court. He handed it over so the judge could see it. The judge discovered a packet of cocaine in the pocket and laughed so hard he required a five-minute recess to compose himself.

The Robber

A man, wanting to rob a downtown bank. walked into the branch and wrote, *'This iz a stickup. Put all your muny in this bag.'* While standing in line, waiting to give his note to the teller, he began to worry that someone had seen him write the note and might call the police before he reached the teller window. So he left the bank and crossed the street to another bank.

After waiting a few minutes in line, he handed his note to the teller. She read it and, surmising from the spelling errors that he wasn't the brightest light in the harbour, told him that she could not accept this stickup note because it was written on the other bank's deposit slip and he would either have to fill our their deposit slip or go back to the other bank.

Looking somewhat defeated, the man said, *'Okay,'* and left. The teller then called the police who arrested the man a few minutes later as he was waiting in line back at the original bank.

A woman reported her car as stolen and mentioned that there was a car phone in it. The policeman taking the report called the phone and told the guy that he had read the ad in the newspaper and wanted to buy the car. They arranged to meet and the thief was arrested.

A man walked into a little corner store with a shotgun and demanded all the cash from the cash drawer. After the cashier put the cash in the bag, the robber saw a bottle of scotch that he wanted. He told the cashier to put it in the bag as well, but he refused and said, *'Because I don't believe you are over twenty-one.'*

The robber said he was, but the clerk still refused to give it to him because he didn't believe him. At this point the robber took his driver's license out of his wallet and gave it to the clerk. The clerk looked it over and agreed that the man was in fact over twenty-one and put the scotch in the bag. The robber then ran from the store with his loot. The cashier promptly called the police and gave the name and address of the robber that he got off the license. They arrested him two hours later.

A pair of robbers entered a record shop nervously waving revolvers. The first one shouted, *'Nobody move!'* When his partner moved, the startled bandit shot him.

The Wife

A police officer pulls over a speeding car. The officer says, *'I clocked you at 80 miles per hour, sir.'*

The driver says, *'Gee, officer I had it on cruise control at 60, perhaps your radar gun needs calibrating.'*

Not looking up from her knitting the wife says: *'Now don't be silly dear, you know that this car doesn't have cruise control.'*

As the officer writes out the ticket, the driver looks over at his wife and growls, *'Can't you please keep your mouth shut for once?'*

The wife smiles demurely and says, *'You should be thankful your radar detector went off when it did'*

As the officer makes out the second ticket for the illegal radar detector unit, the man glowers at his wife and says through clenched teeth, *'Damit, woman, can't you keep your mouth shut?'*

The officer frowns and says, *'And I notice that you're not wearing your seat belt, sir. That's an automatic $75 fine.'*

The driver says, *'Yeah, well, you see officer, I had it on, but took it off when you pulled me over so that I could get my license out of my back pocket.'*

The wife says, *'Now, dear, you know very well that you didn't have your seat belt on. You never wear your seat belt when you're driving.'*

And as the police officer is writing out the third ticket the driver turns to his wife and barks, *'WHY DON'T YOU PLEASE SHUT UP??'*

The officer looks over at the woman and asks, *'Does your husband always talk to you this way, Ma'am?'*

I love this part ... *'Only when he's been drinking.'*

Bike ride

A man decided that he was going to ride a 10-speed bike to a nearby city. On the way he had to climb a mountain and it just became too much and he could go no further.

He stuck his thumb out, but after three hours not a single person stopped for him. Finally a Corvette pulled over and the driver offered him a ride. Of course, the bike wouldn't fit into the car. The owner found a piece of rope lying by the highway and tied it to his bumper and the other end to the bike. He told the man that if he was going too fast, to honk the horn on his bike and he would slow down.

Everything went fine for the first thirty kilometres. Suddenly, another Corvette blew past them. Not to be outdone, the Corvette pulling the bike took off after the other one. A short distance down the road, the Corvettes, both doing well over 190 kph, blew through a speed trap.

The police officer noted the speeds from his radar gun and radioed to the other officer that he had two Corvettes headed his way at over 190 kph. He then relayed, *'And you're not going to believe this, but there's a guy on a 10-speed bike honking to pass.'*

Not There

A man was on trial for the armed robbery of a convenience store in a district court when he fired his lawyer. The Assistant District Attorney said the man, 47, was doing a fair job of defending himself until the store manager testified that he was the robber. The man jumped up, accused the woman of lying and then said, *'I should have blown your (expletive) head off.'* The defendant paused, then quickly added, *'If I'd been the one that was there.'*

The jury took twenty minutes to convict him and recommended a thirty-year sentence.

Caughtcha

A man, twenty-one, walked up to two patrol officers who were showing their squad car computer equipment to children in a neighbourhood. When he asked how the system worked, the officer asked him for identification. He gave them is driver's license, they entered it into the computer and moments later, arrested him because information on the screen showed he was wanted for a two-year-old armed robbery charge.

The Jerk

A motorcycle officer stops a man for running a red light. The guy is a real jerk and comes running back to the motor officer. The violator demands to know why he is being harassed by the Gestapo! The officer calmly tells him of the red light violation. The motorist instantly goes on a tirade questioning the officer's ancestry, sexual orientation, etc. in rather explicit terms.

The officer, being a professional, takes it all in stride, figuring, 'Alligator mouth and hummingbird ass.'

The tirade goes on without the cop saying anything. When he gets done with writing the citation, he puts an 'AH' in the lower right corner of the narrative portion of the citation. He then hands it to the violator for his signature. The guy signs the citation angrily tearing the paper and, when presented his copy, points to the 'AH' and demands to know what it stands for. The officer then removes his mirrored sunglasses, gets in the middle of the guy's face and says, *'That's so when we go to court, I'll remember that you're an asshole!'*

Three months later they are in court. Loud mouth has such a bad record he is about to lose his license and has hired an attorney to represent him. On the stand the officer testifies to seeing the man run the red light.

On cross-examination the defence attorney asks, *'Officer, is this a reasonable facsimile of the citation you issued my client?'*

Officer responds, *'Yes sir, this is the defendant's copy, his signature and mine, same number at the top.'*

The attorney continued, *'Officer, is there any particular marking or notation on this citation you don't normally make?'*

The officer replied, *'Yes sir, in the lower right corner of the narrative there is an 'AH' underlined.'*

'What does the 'AH' stand for, officer?'

'Aggressive and Hostile, Sir.'

'Aggressive and hostile?'

'Yes, Sir?'

'Officer, are you sure it doesn't stand for Asshole?'

'Well, sir, you know your client better than I do!'

Speeding

Ron, a lawyer, was driving home after spending a great day out on the ocean fishing. His catch, cleaned and filleted, was wrapped in newspaper on the passenger side floor. He was late getting home and was speeding. Wouldn't you know, a cop jumped out, radar gun in hand, motioned him to the side of a bridge. Ron pulled over like a good citizen. The cop walked up to the window and said, *'You know how fast you were going, BOY?'*

Ron thought for a second and said, *'Uhh, 60?'*

'67 mph, son! 67 in a 55 mph zone!' exclaimed the cop.

'But if you already knew, officer,' replied Ron, *'Why did you ask me?'*

Fuming over Ron's answer, the cop growled, in his normal sarcastic fashion, *'That's speeding and you're getting a ticket and a fine!'* The cop took a good close look at Ron, in his stained fishing attire and said, *'You don't even look like you have a job! I've never seen anyone so scruffy in my entire life!'*

Ron answered, *'I've got a job! I have a good, well-paying job!'*

The cop leaned in the window, smelling Ron's fish catch and said, *'What kind of a job would a bum like you have?'*

'I'm a rectum stretcher!' replied Ron.

'What did you say, BOY?' asked the cop.

'I'm a rectum stretcher!'

The cop, scratching his head, asked, *'What does a rectum stretcher do?'*

Ron explained, *'People call me up and say they need to be stretched, so I go over to their house. I start with a couple of fingers, then a couple more and then one whole hand, then two. Then I slowly pull them farther and farther apart until it's a full six feet across.'*

The cop, absorbed with these bizarre images in his mind, asked, *'What the hell do you do with a six foot asshole?'*

Ron nonchalantly answered, *'You give it a badge, a radar gun and stick it at the end of a bridge.'*

Purse Snatcher

As a female shopper exited a convenience store, a man grabbed her purse and ran. The clerk called the police immediately and the woman was able to give them a detailed description of the snatcher. Within minutes, the police had apprehended the snatcher. They put him in the car and drove back to the store. The thief was then taken out of the car and told to stand there for a positive ID. To which he replied, *'Yes Officer. That's her. That's the lady I stole the purse from.'*

Petrol Thief

A man attempted to siphon petrol from a parked motor home and got much more than he bargained for. Police arrived at the scene to find an ill man curled up next to a motor home near spilled sewage. The police spokesman said that the man admitted to trying to steal petrol and plugged his hose into the motor home's sewage tank by mistake. The owner of the vehicle declined to press charges, saying that it was the best laugh he'd ever had.

Cash Machine

Two men tried to pull the front off a cash machine by running a chain from the machine to the bumper of their truck. Instead of pulling the front panel off the machine - they pulled the bumper off their truck. Scared, they left the scene and drove home - with the chain still attached to the machine; with their bumper still attached to the chain; and with their vehicle's licence plate still attached to the bumper!

Liquor Store

Seems a fellow wanted some beer quite badly. He decided that he'd just throw a cinder block through a liquor store window, grab some booze and run. So he lifted the block and heaved it over his head at the window. The block bounced back and hit the would-be thief on the head, knocking him unconscious. Seems the liquor store window was made of Plexi-Glass. The whole event was caught on videotape.

Armed Robbery

A man walked into a convenience store, put a $20 bill on the counter and asked for change. When the clerk opened the cash drawer, the man pulled a gun and asked for all the cash in the register, which the clerk promptly provided. The man took the cash from the clerk and fled, leaving the $20 bill on the counter. The total amount of cash he got from the drawer? Fifteen dollars. (If someone points a gun at you and gives you money, was a crime committed?)

CHAPTER 8 - AIRPLANE JOKES

West Jet

West Jet is an airline with head office situated in Calgary, Alberta, Canada. West Jet airline attendants make an effort to make the in-flight 'safety lecture' and announcements a bit more interesting. Here are some real examples that have been heard or reported:

There is no assigned seating - you just sit where you want. Passengers were having a hard time choosing a seat, when the flight attendant announced, *'People, people, we're not picking out furniture here - find a seat and get in it!'*

On another flight with a very 'senior' flight attendant crew, the pilot said, *'Ladies and gentlemen, we've reached cruising altitude and will be turning down the cabin lights. This is for your comfort and to enhance the appearance of your flight attendants.'*

On landing, the flight attendant said, *'Please be sure to take all of your belongings. If you're going to leave anything, please make sure it's something we'd like to have.'*

As we waited just off the runway for another airliner to cross in front of us, some of the passengers were beginning to retrieve luggage from the overhead bins. The head attendant announced on the intercom, *'This aircraft is equipped with a video surveillance system that monitors the cabin during taxiing. Any passengers not remaining in their seats until the aircraft comes to a full and complete stop at the gate will be strip-searched as they leave the aircraft.'*

'There may be 50 ways to leave your lover, but there are only 4 ways out of this airplane.'

The pilot said, *'We've reached our cruising altitude now and I'm turning off the seat belt sign. I'm switching to autopilot too so I can come back there and visit with all of you for the rest of the flight.'*

'Last one off the plane must clean it.'

'Thank you for flying West Jet Express. We hope you enjoyed giving us the business as much as we enjoyed taking you for a ride.'

As the plane landed and was coming to a stop at the Vancouver airport, a lone voice came over the loudspeaker, *'Whoa, big fella. whoa!'*

After a particularly rough landing during a thunderstorm in Ontario, a flight attendant announced, *'Please take care when opening the overhead compartments because, after a landing like that, sure as hell everything has shifted.'*

From one of their employees, *'Welcome aboard West Jet Flight 245 to Calgary. To operate your seat belt, insert the metal tab into the buckle and pull tight. It works just like every other seat belt; and, if you don't know how to operate one, you probably shouldn't be out in public unsupervised.'*

'In the event of a sudden loss of cabin pressure, masks will descend from the ceiling. Stop screaming, grab the mask and pull it over your face. If you have a small child travelling with you, secure your mask before assisting others. If you are travelling with more than one small child, pick your favourite.'

'Weather at our destination is 50 degrees with some broken clouds, but we'll try to have them fixed before we arrive.'

'Thank you and remember; nobody loves you or your money more than West Jet Airlines.'

'Your seat cushions can be used for flotation; and in the event of an emergency water landing, please paddle to shore and take them with our compliments.'

'As you exit the plane, make sure to gather all your belongings. Anything left behind will be distributed evenly among the flight attendants. Please do not leave children or spouses.'

And from the pilot during his welcome message, *'West Jet Airlines is pleased to announce that we have some of the best flight attendants in the industry. Unfortunately, none of them are on this flight!'*

Just after a very hard landing in Edmonton, the flight attendant said, *'That was quite a bump and I know what y'all are thinking. I'm here to tell you it wasn't the airline's fault, it wasn't the pilot's fault, it wasn't the flight attendant's fault - it was the asphalt.'*

Overheard on flight to Regina on a particularly windy and bumpy day when the captain was really having an extremely hard landing, the Flight Attendant said, *'Ladies and Gentlemen, welcome to Regina. Please remain in your seats with your seat belts fastened while the Captain taxis what's left of our airplane to the gate.'*

Another flight attendant's comment on a less-than-perfect landing, *'We ask you to please remain seated as Captain Kangaroo bounces us to the terminal.'*

An airline pilot wrote that on this particular flight he had hammered his ship into the runway really hard. The airline had a policy, which required the first officer to stand at the door while the passengers exited - smile and give them a *'Thanks for flying with our airline.'* He said that, in light of the bad landing, he had a hard time looking the passengers in the eye, thinking that someone would have a smart comment. Finally everyone had left the plane except for a little old lady walking with a cane. She said, *'Sir do you mind if*

I ask you a question?' 'Why no Ma'am,' said the pilot. *'What is it?'* The little old lady said, *'Did we land or were we shot down?'*

After a real crusher of a landing in Halifax, the attendant came on with, *'Ladies and Gentlemen; please remain in your seats until Captain Crash and the Crew have brought the aircraft to a screeching halt at the gate. And once the tire smoke has cleared and the warning bells are silenced, we will open the door and you can pick your way through the wreckage to the terminal.'*

Part of a flight attendant's arrival announcement, *'We'd like to thank you folks for flying with us today. And, the next time you get the insane urge to go blasting through the skies in a pressurised metal tube, we hope you'll think of West Jet Airways!'*

'Ladies and Gentlemen, if you wish to smoke, the smoking section on this airplane is on the wing. If you can light 'em, you can smoke 'em.'

'Smoking in the lavatories is prohibited. Any person caught smoking in the lavatories will be asked to leave the plane immediately.'

Pilot: *'Folks, we have reached our cruising altitude now, so I am going to switch the seat belt sign off. Feel free to move about as you wish, but please stay inside the plane till we land. It's a bit cold outside and if you walk on the wings it affects the flight pattern.'*

The plane was taking off from the Winnipeg airport. After it reached a comfortable cruising altitude, the captain made an announcement, *'Ladies and gentlemen, this is your captain speaking. Welcome to flight 293, non-stop from Winnipeg to Montreal. The weather ahead is good and therefore, we should have a smooth and uneventful flight. Now sit back and relax. Oh, my God!'*

Silence followed and after a few minutes, the captain came back on the intercom and said, *'Ladies and gentlemen, I'm so sorry if I scared you earlier. While I was talking to you, the flight attendant accidentally spilled a cup of hot coffee on my lap. You should see the front of my pants!'*

A passenger in economy yelled, *'That's nothing. You should see the back of mine!'*

A friend of mine is blind and travels with her guide dog that sits with her on the front row of the airplane. The plane was making a short stop, but the passengers were encouraged to disembark for the half-hour turnaround. So it wouldn't be an ordeal for my friend, the co-pilot offered to take the dog to a grassy area around the airport to do his business. Can you imagine what the passengers thought when they saw the co-pilot walking through the area, wearing sunglasses and walking her guide dog!

Free Round of Drinks

An elderly doctor and a Baptist minister were seated next to each other on the plane. The plane was delayed at the start due to some technical problems. Just after taking off, the pilot offered his apologies to the passengers and announced that a round of free drinks would be served.

When the charming hostess came around with the trolley, the doctor ordered a gin and tonic for himself. The hostess then asked the minister whether he wanted anything. He replied, *'Oh no, thank you. I would rather commit adultery than drink alcohol.'*

The elderly doctor promptly handed back his gin and tonic to the air hostess and said, *'Miss, I didn't know there was a choice.'*

Extra passenger

When preparing to return home from an out-of-town trip, a man got a small puppy as a present for his son. Not having time to get the paperwork done to take the puppy on board, the man just hid the pup down the front of his pants and snuck him on board the airplane.

About 30 minutes into the trip, a flight attendant noticed the man shaking and quivering. *'Are you okay, sir?'* she asked.

'Yes, I'm fine,' said the man.

Later, the attendant noticed the man moaning and shaking again. *'Are you sure you're all right sir?'*

'Yes,' said the man, *'but I have a confession to make. I didn't have time to get the paperwork to bring a puppy on board, so I hid him down the front of my pants.'*

'What's wrong?' asked the attendant. *'Isn't he housebroken?'*

'No, that's not the problem. The problem is he's not weaned yet!'

Real Woman

On a trans-Atlantic flight, a plane passes through a severe storm. The turbulence is awful and things go from bad to worse when one wing is struck by lightening. One woman in particular loses it. Screaming, she stands up in the front of the plane. *'I'm too young to die!'* she wails. Then she yells, *'Well, if I'm going to die, I want my last minutes on Earth to be memorable! I've had plenty of sex in my life, but no one has ever made me really feel like a woman! Well, I've had it! Is there anyone on this plane who can make me feel like a woman??'*

For a moment there is silence. Everyone has forgotten their own peril and they all stare, riveted at the desperate woman at the front of the plane. Then a man stands up near the rear of the plane. *'I can make you feel like a woman,'* he says. He's gorgeous. Tall, built, with long flowing black hair and jet black eyes, he starts to walk slowly up the aisle, unbuttoning his shirt one button at a time.

Nobody moves.

The woman is breathing heavily in anticipation as the stranger approaches. He removes his shirt. Muscles ripple across his chest as he reaches her and extends the arm holding his shirt to the trembling woman and whispers, *'Iron this.'*

Help Line

Ever tried to get help from a 'Help Line?' A helicopter was flying around Seattle yesterday when an electrical malfunction disabled all of the aircraft's electronic navigation and communications equipment. Due to the clouds and haze, the pilot could not determine the helicopter's position and course to steer to the airport. The pilot saw a tall building, flew towards it, circled, drew a handwritten sign and held it in the helicopter's window. The pilot's sign said, *'WHERE AM I?'* in large letters.

People in the tall building quickly responded to the aircraft, drew a large sign and held in a building window. Their sign said, *'YOU ARE IN A HELICOPTER.'* The pilot smiled, waved, looked at his map, determined the course to steer to SEATAC airport and landed safely.

After they were on the ground, the co-pilot asked the pilot how the, *'YOU ARE IN A HELICOPTER'* sign helped determine their position. The pilot responded, *'I knew that had to be the Microsoft building because, similar to their help-lines, they gave me a technically correct but completely useless answer.'*

Have you ever wondered ...

Why are there flotation devices under plane seats instead of parachutes?

Why infants and small children are not made to sit in car seats while travelling on a plane?

Superman

One day flying home after a long hard day of catching bad guys, Superman wanted to relax, get a drink and maybe get laid. So while he's flying over Gotham City, he figures he'll get Batman and they'll go out. Superman gets to the Bat cave, but Batman's busy and can't go right then.

Superman understands and just flies around for a while. Travelling over Atlantis, he figures he'd see if Aquaman can go out for a bit, but he's busy too.

Disgruntled, Superman starts flying home so he can just go to sleep. As he's flying to his house, he sees Wonder Woman sun bathing nude on the top of a building. He does a couple of fly bys to check things out. Wonder Woman being a babe and all, gets Superman pretty horned up. He gets the idea that, with his super speed, he can go in there, get the job done and get outta there before she even notices anything. So with that, he swoops down there, gets the job done and gets out.

Shocked, Wonder Woman says, *'What the hell was that??'*

The Invisible Man replies, *'I don't know, but my ass is killing me!'*

Doesn't Know Shit

A stranger was seated next to a little girl on the airplane when the stranger turned to her and said, *'Let's talk. I've heard that flights go quicker if you strike up a conversation with your fellow passenger.'*

The little girl, who had just opened her book, closed it slowly and said to the stranger, *'What would you like to talk about?'*

'Oh, I don't know,' said the stranger. *'How about nuclear power?'* and he smiles.

'OK,' she said. *'That could be an interesting topic. But let me ask you a question first. A horse, a cow and a deer all eat the same stuff - grass. Yet a deer excretes little pellets, while a cow turns out a flat patty and a horse produces clumps of dried grass. Why do you suppose that is?'*

The stranger, visibly surprised by the little girl's intelligence, thinks about it and says, *'Hmmm, I have no idea.'*

To which the little girl replies, *'Do you really feel qualified to discuss nuclear power when you don't know shit?'*

Cancelled Flight

An award should go to the Virgin Airlines gate attendant in Sydney some weeks ago for being smart and funny, while making her point, when confronted with a passenger who probably deserved to fly as cargo. A crowded Virgin flight was cancelled after Virgin's 767s had been withdrawn from service. A single attendant was re-booking a long line of inconvenienced travellers. Suddenly an angry passenger pushed his way to the desk. He slapped his ticket down on the counter and said, *'I have to be on this flight and it has to be first class'.*

The attendant replied, *'I'm sorry, sir. I'll be happy to try to help you, but I've got to help these people first and I'm sure we'll be able to work something out.'*

The passenger was unimpressed. He asked loudly, so that the passengers behind him could hear, *'Do you have any idea who I am?'*

Without hesitating, the attendant smiled and grabbed her public address microphone: *'May I have your attention please. May I have your attention please,'* she began - her voice heard clearly throughout the terminal. *'We have a passenger here at Gate 14 who does not know who he is. If anyone can help him find his identity, please come to Gate 14.'*

With the folks behind him in line laughing hysterically, the man glared at the Virgin attendant, gritted his teeth and said, *'F... You!'*

Without flinching, she smiled and said, *'I'm sorry sir, but you'll have to fly Qantas for that service.'*

The Elk

Two hunters got a pilot to fly them into the far north of Canada for elk hunting. They were quite successful in their venture and bagged six big bucks. The pilot came back as arranged to pick them up. They started loading their gear into the plane, including the six elk. But the pilot objected, saying, *'The plane can take out only four of your elk; you'll have to leave two behind.'*

They argued with him indicating that the year before they had shot six and that pilot had allowed them to put all on board and the plane was the same model and capacity as his. Reluctantly the pilot finally permitted them to put all six aboard.

But when they attempted to take off and leave the valley where they were, the little plane could not make it and they crashed in the wilderness. Climbing out of the wreckage, one hunter said to the other, *'Do you know where we are?'*

'I think so,' replied the other hunter. *'I think this is about the same place where the plane crashed last year.'*

Flying Nympho

A man boards an airplane and takes his seat. As he settles in, he glances up and sees the most beautiful woman boarding the plane. He soon realises she is heading straight towards his seat. A wave of nervous anticipation washes over him. Lo and behold, she takes the seat right beside his. Anxious to strike up a conversation, he blurts out, *'So where are you flying to today?'*

She turns and smiles and says, *'To at the annual Nymphomaniac Convention in Chicago.'*

He swallows hard and is instantly crazed with excitement. Here's the most gorgeous woman he has ever seen, sitting right next to him and she's going to a meeting of nymphomaniacs. Struggling to maintain his outward cool, he calmly asks, *'And what's your role at the convention?'*

She flips her hair back, turns to him, locks onto his eyes and says, *'Well, I try to debunk some of the popular myths about sexuality.'*

'Really,' he says, swallowing hard. *'And what myths are those?'*

She explains: *'Well, one popular myth is that African American men are the most well-endowed; when in fact it is the Native American Indian who is most likely to possess that trait. Another popular myth is that Frenchmen are the best lovers, when actually it is men of Jewish descent who romance best on average.'*

'How very interesting,' the man responds.

Suddenly, the woman becomes embarrassed and blushes, *'I'm sorry,'* she says, *'I feel so awkward discussing this with you and I don't even know your name.'*

The man extends his hand and replies, *'Tonto. Tonto Goldstein.'*

Seatmate

The following scene took place on a BA flight between Johannesburg and London and is a true story.

A white woman, about 50 years old, was seated next to a black man. Obviously disturbed by this, she called the air hostess.

'Madam, what is the matter,' the hostess asked.

'You obviously do not see it then?' she responded. *'You placed me next to a Black man. I did not agree to sit next to someone from such a repugnant group. Give me an alternative seat.'*

'Be calm please,' the hostess replied. *'Almost all the places on this flight are taken. I will go to see if another seat is available.'*

The hostess went away and then came back a few minutes later. *'Madam, just as I thought, there are no other available seats in the Economy class. I spoke to the Captain and he informed me that there are also no seats in the Business class. All the same, we still have one seat in the First class.'*

Before the woman could say anything, the hostess continued: *'It is not usual for our company to permit someone from the economy class to sit in the First class. However, given the circumstances, the Captain feels that it would be scandalous to make someone sit next to someone so disgusting.'*

She turned to the black guy and said, *'Therefore, sir, if you would like to, please collect your hand luggage, a seat awaits you in first class.'*

At that moment, the other passengers who were shocked by what they had just witnessed stood up and applauded.

Jet Propelled

Bud and Jim were a couple of drinking buddies who worked as airplane mechanics in Atlanta. One day the airport was fogged in and they were stuck in the hangar with nothing to do. Bud said, *'Man, I wish we had something to drink!'*

Jim says, *'Me too. Y'know, I've heard you can drink jet fuel and get a buzz. You wanna try it?'*

So they pour themselves a couple of glasses of high-octane hooch and get completely smashed.

The next morning Bud wakes up and is surprised at how good he feels. In fact he feels GREAT! NO hangover! NO bad side effects. Nothing! Then the phone rings. ... It's Jim.

Jim says, *'Hey, how do you feel this morning?'*

Bud says, *'I feel great. How about you?'*

Jim says, *'I feel great, too. You don't have a hangover?'*

Bud says, *'No, that jet fuel is great stuff - no hangover; nothing. We ought to do this more often.'*

'Yeah, well there's just one thing ...'

'What's that?'

'Have you farted yet?'

'No ...'

'Well, DON'T, 'cause I'm in PHOENIX!!!'

CHAPTER 9 - CHILDREN

Deep Thoughts:

Below are comments from entrants to a newspaper contest (aged 4 - 15) who were asked to submit their beliefs about deep thoughts:

I believe you should live each day as if it was your last, which is why I don't have any clean laundry because, come on, who wants to wash clothes on the last day of their life - Aged 15.

Give me strength to change the things I can, the grace to accept the things I cannot and a great big bag of money - Aged 13.

democracy is a beautiful thing, except for the part about letting just any old yokel vote -Aged 10.

Home is where the house is - Aged 6.

I bet living in a nudist colony takes all the fun out of Halloween - Aged 13.

For centuries, people thought the moon was made of green cheese. Then the astronauts found that the moon is really a big hard rock. That's what happens to cheese when you leave it out - Aged 6.

When I go to heaven, I want to see my grandfather again. But he better have lost the nose hair and the old-man smell - Aged 5.

I once heard the voice of God. It said, 'Vrrrrmmmmm.' Unless it was just a lawn mower - Aged 11.

As you make your way through this hectic world of ours, set aside a few minutes each day. At the end of the year, you'll have a couple of days saved up - Aged 7.

Often, when I'm reading a good book, I stop and thank my teacher. That is, I used to, until she got an unlisted number - Aged 15.

It would be terrible if the Red Cross Bloodmobile got into an accident. No wait. That would be good, because if anyone needed it, the blood would be right there - Aged 5.

Think of the biggest number you can. Now add five. Then, imagine if you had that many Twinkies. Wow, that's five more than the biggest number you could come up with - Aged 6.

The only stupid question is the one that is never asked, except maybe, *'Don't you think it's about time you audited my return?'* or, *'Isn't it morally wrong to give a warning when, in fact, I was speeding?'* - Aged 15.

Once I wept for I had no shoes, then I came upon a man who had no feet, so I took his shoes. I mean, it's not like he needed them right? - Aged 15.

What does Love mean?

A group of professional people posed this question to a group of 4 to 8 year-olds, *'What does love mean?'* The answers they got were broader and deeper than anyone could have imagined. See what you think:

'When my grandmother got arthritis, she couldn't bend over and paint her toenails anymore. So my grandfather does it for her all the time, even when his hands got arthritis too. That's love.' - Rebecca- age 8.

'When someone loves you, the way they say your name is different. You just know that your name is safe in their mouth.' - Billy - age 4.

'Love is when a girl puts on perfume and a boy puts on shaving cologne and they go out and smell each other.' - Karl - age 5.

'Love is when you go out to eat and give somebody most of your French fries without making them give you any of theirs.' - Chrissy - age 6.

'Love is what makes you smile when you're tired.' - Terri - age 4.

'Love is when my mommy makes coffee for my daddy and she takes a sip before giving it to him, to make sure the taste is okay.' - Danny - age 7.

'Love is when you kiss all the time. Then when you get tired of kissing, you still want to be together and you talk more. My Mommy and Daddy are like that. They look gross when they kiss' - Emily - age 8.

'Love is what's in the room with you at Christmas if you stop opening presents and listen.' - Bobby - age 7 (Wow!)

'If you want to learn to love better, you should start with a friend who you hate.' - Nikka - age 6. (We need a few million more Nikka's on this planet.)

'Love is when you tell a guy you like his shirt, then he wears it everyday.' - Noelle - age 7.

'During my piano recital, I was on a stage and I was scared. I looked at all the people watching me and saw my daddy waving and smiling. He was the only one doing that. I wasn't scared any more.' - Cindy - age 8.

'Love is like a little old woman and a little old man who are still friends even after they know each other so well.' - Tommy - age 6.

'My mommy loves me more than anybody. You don't see anyone else kissing me to sleep at night.' - Clare - age 6.

'Love is when Mommy gives Daddy the best piece of chicken.' - Elaine-age 5.

'Love is when Mommy sees Daddy smelly and sweaty and still says he is handsomer than Robert Redford.' - Chris - age 7.

'Love is when your puppy licks your face even after you left him alone all day.' - Mary Ann - age 4.

'When you love somebody, your eyelashes go up and down and little stars come out of you.' (What an image!) - Karen - age 7.

'Love is when Mommy sees Daddy on the toilet and she doesn't think it's gross.' - Mark - age 6.

'You really shouldn't say 'I love you' unless you mean it. But if you mean it, you should say it a lot. People forget.' - Jessica - age 8.

And the final one –

Author and lecturer Leo Buscaglia once talked about a contest he was asked to judge. The purpose of the contest was to find the most caring child. The winner was a four-year-old child whose next door neighbour was an elderly gentleman who had recently lost his wife. Upon seeing the man cry, the little boy went into the old gentleman's yard, climbed onto his lap and just sat there.

When his Mother asked what he had said to the neighbour, the little boy said, *'Nothing, I just helped him cry.'*

Taking Belle for a walk

A little girl asked her Mom, *'Mom, may I take the dog for a walk around the block?'*

Mom replies, *'No, because she's in heat.'*

'What's that mean?' asked the child.

'Go ask your father. I think he's in the garage.'

The little girl goes to the garage and says, *'Dad, may I take Belle for a walk around the block? I asked Mom, but she said the dog was in heat and to see dad'*

Dad said, *'Bring Belle over here.'*

He took a rag, soaked it with petrol and scrubbed the dog's backside with it to disguise the scent and said, *'Okay, you can go now. Keep Belle on the leash and only go around the block once.'*

The little girl left and returned a few minutes later with no dog on the leash. Surprised, Dad asked, *'Where's Belle?'*
(You're going to love this!!!!!!)

The little girl said, *'She ran out of petrol about halfway down the block, so another dog is pushing her home.'*

The Bath

A three-year-old boy was examining his testicles while taking a bath.
'Mum,' he asked, *'are these my brains?'*
'Not yet,' she replied.

How children see life at sea

1. This is a picture of an octopus. It has eight testicles. (Kelly age 6)
2. Oysters' balls are called pearls. (James age 6)
3. If you are surrounded by sea you are an Island. If you don't have sea all round you, you are in continent. (Wayne age 7)
4. Sharks are ugly and mean and have big teeth, just like Emily Richardson. She's not my friend no more. (Kylie age 6)
5. A dolphin breaths through an ass hole on the top of its head. (Billy age 8)
6. My uncle goes out in his boat with pots and comes back with crabs. (Millie age 6)
7. When ships had sails, they used to use the trade winds to cross the Ocean. Sometimes, when the wind didn't blow, the sailors would whistle to make the wind come. My brother said they would be better off eating beans. (William age 7)
8. I like mermaids. They are beautiful and I like their shiny tails. How do Mermaids get pregnant? (Helen age 6)
9. I'm not going to write about the sea. My baby brother is always screaming and being sick, my Dad keeps shouting at my Mom and my big sister has just got pregnant, so I can't think what to write. (Amy age 6
10. Some fish are dangerous. Jellyfish can sting. Electric eels can give you a shock. They have to live in caves under the sea where I think they have to plug themselves into chargers. (Christopher age 7)
11. When you go swimming in the sea, it is very cold and it makes my willy small. (Kevin age 6)
12. Divers have to be safe when they go under the water. Two divers can't go down alone, so they have to go down on each other. (Becky age 8)
13. On holiday my Mom went water skiing. She fell off when she was going very fast. She says she won't do it again because water shot up her fanny. (Julie age 7)

The powder room

A little boy and girl are playing in a sandbox. The little boy has to take a pee and he was told by his mother to always be polite and don't talk about private matters in public. At first he holds it in for a little while because he does not know what to say to the little girl to excuse himself. Then he remembers what his Mom had said at the restaurant to excuse herself from the table.

So he turns to the little girl and says *'Will you excuse me I have to go powder my nose.'* And saying that he leaps out of the sandbox and runs to the washroom.

When he comes back the little girl looks up at him and asks, *'Did you powder your nose?'*

'Yes' said the little boy stepping back into the sandbox.

'Well then' said the little girl, *'You'd better close your purse because your lipstick is hanging out.'*

Being A Mom

We are sitting at lunch one day when my daughter casually mentions that she and her husband are thinking of 'starting a family.'

'We're taking a survey,' she says half-joking. *'Do you think I should have a baby?'*

'It will change your life,' I say, carefully keeping my tone neutral.

'I know,' she says, *'no more sleeping in on weekends, no more spontaneous vacations.'*

But that is not what I meant at all. I look at my daughter, trying to decide what to tell her. I want her to know what she will never learn in childbirth classes. I want to tell her that the physical wounds of child bearing will heal, but becoming a mother will leave her with an emotional wound so raw that she will forever be vulnerable.

I consider warning her that she will never again read a newspaper without asking, *'What if that had been MY child? That every plane crash, every house fire will haunt her. That when she sees pictures of starving children, she will wonder if anything could be worse than watching your child die.'*

I look at her carefully manicured nails and stylish suit and think that no matter how sophisticated she is, becoming a mother will reduce her to the primitive level of a bear protecting her cub. That an urgent call of *'Mom!'* will cause her to drop a soufflé or her best crystal without a moment's hesitation.

I feel that I should warn her that no matter how many years she has invested in her career, she will be professionally derailed by motherhood. She might arrange for childcare, but one day she will be going into an important business meeting and she will think of her baby's sweet smell. She will have to use every ounce of discipline to keep from running home, just to make sure her baby is all right.

I want my daughter to know that every day decisions will no longer be routine. That a five year old boy's desire to go to the men's room rather than the women's at McDonald's will become a major dilemma. That right there, in the midst of clattering trays and screaming children, issues of independence and gender identity will be weighed against the prospect that a child molester may be lurking in that restroom.

However decisive she may be at the office, she will second-guess herself constantly as a mother.

Looking at my attractive daughter, I want to assure her that eventually she will shed the pounds of pregnancy, but she will never feel the same about herself. That her life, now so important, will be of less value to her once she has a child. That she would give herself up in a moment to save her offspring, but will also begin to hope for more years, not to accomplish her own dreams, but to watch her children accomplish theirs.

I want her to know that a cesarean scar or shiny stretch marks will become badges of honour. My daughter's relationship with her husband will change, but not in the way she thinks.

I wish she could understand how much more you can love a man who is careful to powder the baby or who never hesitates to play with his child. I think she should know that she will fall in love with him again for reasons she would now find very unromantic.

I wish my daughter could sense the bond she will feel with women throughout history who have tried to stop war, prejudice and drunk driving. I want to describe to my daughter the exhilaration of seeing your child learn to ride a bike. I want to capture for her the belly laugh of a baby who is touching the soft fur of a dog or cat for the first time. I want her to taste the joy that is so real it actually hurts.

My daughter's quizzical look makes me realise that tears have formed in my eyes. *'You'll never regret it,'* I finally say. Then I reached across the table, squeezed my daughter's hand and offered a silent prayer for her and for me and for all the mere mortal women who stumble their way into this most wonderful of callings.

The 'Middle Wife' by an anonymous 2nd grade teacher

I've been teaching now for about fifteen years. I have two kids myself, but the best birth story I know is the one I saw in my own second grade classroom a few years back.

When I was a kid, I loved show-and-tell. So I always have a few sessions with my students. It helps them get over shyness and usually, show-and-tell is pretty tame. Kids bring in pet turtles, model airplanes, pictures of fish they catch, stuff like that. And I never, ever place any boundaries or limitations on them. If they want to lug it in to school and talk about it, they're welcome.

Well, one day this little girl, Erica, a very bright, very outgoing kid, takes her turn and waddles up to the front of the class with a pillow stuffed under her sweater.

She holds up a snapshot of an infant. *'This is Luke, my baby brother and I'm going to tell you about his birthday. First, Mom and Dad made him as a symbol of their love and then Dad put a seed in my Mom's stomach and Luke grew in there. He ate for nine months through an umbrella cord.'*

She's standing there with her hands on the pillow and I'm trying not to laugh and wishing I had my camcorder with me. The kids are watching her in amazement. *'Then, about two Saturdays ago, my Mom starts saying and going, 'Oh, Oh, Oh, Oh!'* Erica puts a hand behind her back and groans. *'She walked around the house for, like an hour, 'Oh, oh, oh!'* (Now this kid is doing a hysterical duck walk and groaning.)

'My Dad called the middle wife. She delivers babies, but she doesn't have a sign on the car like the Domino's man. They got my Mom to lie down in bed like this.' (Then Erica lies down with her back against the wall.)

'And then, pop! My Mom had this bag of water she kept in there in case he got thirsty and it just blew up and spilled all over the bed, like psshhheew!' (This kid has her legs spread with her little hands miming water flowing away. It was too much!)

'Then the middle wife starts saying 'push, push,' and 'breathe, breathe and they started counting, but never even got past ten. Then, all of a sudden, out comes my brother. He was covered in yucky stuff that they all said it was from Mom's play-centre, so there must be a lot of toys inside there.'

Then Erica stood up, took a big theatrical bow and returned to her seat. I'm sure I applauded the loudest. Ever since then, when it's show-and-tell day, I bring my camcorder, just in case another 'Middle Wife' comes along.

And the moral of the story is ...?

A little boy comes home from school and is greeted by his mother. The little boy said, *'As I was leaving school today I saw Daddy driving into the forest with Auntie Mary. I went into the forest and saw Daddy kissing Auntie Mary.'*

Mummy says, *'That sounds a very interesting story. Why don't you save it for when daddy comes home?'*

When they were having their evening meal the boy's mother encourages him to retell his story. The little boy said, *'As I was leaving school today I saw Daddy driving into the forest with Auntie Mary.'*

Daddy goes pink.

'I went into the forest and saw Daddy kissing Auntie Mary.'

Daddy goes bright Red.

'Then I saw daddy doing to Auntie Mary what Uncle George did to Mummy while Daddy was away in the army.'

Mummy faints.

Moral: Make sure you have the whole story before you react.

The teacher gave her class an assignment to go home and get their parents to tell them a story with a moral at the end of it. The next day the kids came back and one by one began to tell their stories:

Kathy said, *'My father's a farmer and we have a lot of egg-laying hens. One time we were taking our eggs to market in a basket on the front seat of the pickup when we hit a bump in the road and all the eggs went flying and broke and made a mess.'*

The teacher asked, *'And what was the moral of the story?'*

'Don't put all your eggs in one basket!' replied Kathy.

Lucy said, *'Our family are farmers too. But we raise chickens for the meat market. One time we had a dozen eggs that a hen was hatching, but when the eggs hatched, we only got ten live chicks. And the moral to this story is 'Don't count your chickens until they're hatched.''*

Johnny said, *'My dad told me this story about my uncle Bob. My uncle Bob was a pilot in Vietnam and a SAM missile hit his plane. He had to bail out over enemy territory and all he had was a bottle of whisky, a machine gun and a machete. He drank the whisky on the way down and then landed in the middle of one hundred enemy troops. He killed seventy of them with the machine gun but the machine gun ran out of bullets. Then he killed twenty more with the machete until the blade broke and then he killed the last ten with his bare hands.'*

'My goodness,' said the horrified teacher, *'What kind of moral did your father give you from that horrible story?'*

Johnny smiled brightly and replied *'Don't mess with Uncle Bob when he's been drinking.'*

Jonah

A little girl was talking to her teacher about whales. The teacher said it was physically impossible for a whale to swallow a human because even though it was a very large mammal its throat was very small.

The little girl stated that Jonah was swallowed by a whale.

Irritated, the teacher reiterated that a whale could not swallow a human; it was physically impossible.

The little girl said, *'When I get to heaven I will ask Jonah.'*

The teacher asked, *'What if Jonah went to hell?'*

Without batting an eye, the little girl replied, *'Then you ask him.'*

Marriage Advice (Written by kids)

How do you decide whom to marry?
- *'You got to find somebody who likes the same stuff. Like, if you like sports, she should like it that you like sports and she should keep the chips and dip coming.'* - Alan, aged 10
- *'No person really decides who they're going to marry before they grow up. God decides it all way before and you get to find out later who you're stuck with.'* -- Kristen, aged 10

When is it okay to kiss someone?
- *'When they're rich.'* - Pam, aged 7
- *'The law says you have to be eighteen, so I wouldn't want to mess with that.'* - Curt, aged 7
- *'The rule goes like this: If you kiss someone, then you should marry them and have kids with them. It's the right thing to do.'* - Howard, aged 8

What is the right age to get married?
- *'Twenty-three is the best age because you know the person FOREVER by then.'* - Camille, aged 10

How can a stranger tell if two people are married?
- *'You might have to guess, based on whether they seem to be yelling at the same kids.'* - Derrick, aged 8
- What do you think your mom and dad have in common?
- *'Both don't want any more kids.'* - Lori, aged 8

What do most people do on a date?
- *'Dates are for having fun and people should use them to get to know each other. Even boys have something to say if you listen long enough.'* - Lynnette, aged 8

- *'On the first date, they just tell each other lies and that usually gets them interested enough to go for a second date.'* - Martin, aged 10

What would you do on a first date that was turning sour?
- *'I'd run home and play dead. The next day I would call all the newspapers and make sure they wrote about me in all the dead columns.'* - Craig, aged 9

Is it better to be single or married?
- *'It's better for girls to be single but not for boys. Boys need someone to clean up after them.'* - Anita, aged 9

How would the world be different if people didn't get married?
- *'There sure would be a lot of kids to explain, wouldn't there?'* - Kelvin, aged 8

And the #1 Favourite is
How would you make a marriage work?
- *'Tell your wife that she looks pretty, even if she looks like a truck.'* - Ricky, aged 10

Retarded grandparents

After Christmas, a teacher asked her young pupils how they spent their holiday away from school. One child wrote the following:

'We always used to spend the holidays with Grandma and Grandpa. They used to live in a big brick house but Grandpa got retarded and they moved to Florida. Now they live in a tin box and have rocks painted green to look like grass. They ride around on their bicycles and wear nametags because they don't know who they are anymore. They go to a building called a wrecked centre, but they must have got it fixed because it is all okay now and do exercises there, but they don't do them very well. There is a swimming pool too, but in it, they all jump up and down with hats on.

At their gate, there is a doll house with a little old man sitting in it. He watches all day so nobody can escape. Sometimes they sneak out! They go cruising in their golf carts.

Nobody there cooks, they just eat out. And, they eat the same thing every night ... early birds. Some of the people can't get out past the man in the doll house. Those who do get out bring food back to the wrecked centre and call it pot luck.

My Grandma says that Grandpa worked all his life to earn his retardment and says I should work hard so I can be retarded someday too. When I earn my retardment, I want to be the man in the doll house. Then I will let people out so they can visit their grandchildren.'

'Rules Kids Won't Learn in School.'

This list is the work of Charles J. Sykes, author of the book Dumbing down our kids: Why American children feel good about themselves but can't read, write or add although Bill Gates has often been credited with authoring the following list:

Rule No. 1: Life is not fair. Get used to it. The average teen-ager uses the phrase *'It's not fair'* 8.6 times a day. You got it from your parents, who said it so often you decided they must be the most idealistic generation ever. When they started hearing it from their own kids, they realised Rule No. 1.

Rule No. 2: The real world won't care as much about your self-esteem as much as your school does. It'll expect you to accomplish something before you feel good about yourself. This may come as a shock. Usually, when inflated self-esteem meets reality, kids complain that it's not fair. (See Rule No. 1)

Rule No. 3: Sorry, you won't make $40,000 a year right out of high school. And you won't be a vice president or have a car phone either. You may even have to wear a uniform that doesn't have a Gap label.

Rule No. 4: If you think your teacher is tough, wait 'til you get a boss. He doesn't have tenure, so he tends to be a bit edgier. When you screw up, he's not going to ask you how you feel about it.

Rule No. 5: Flipping burgers is not beneath your dignity. Your grandparents had a different word for burger flipping. They called it opportunity. They weren't embarrassed making minimum wage either. They would have been embarrassed to sit around talking about Kurt Cobain all weekend.

Rule No. 6: It's not your parents' fault. If you screw up, you are responsible. This is the flip side of *'It's my life,'* and 'You're not the boss of me,' and other eloquent proclamations of your generation. When you turn 18, it's on your dime. Don't whine about it or you'll sound like a baby boomer.

Rule No. 7: Before you were born your parents weren't as boring as they are now. They got that way paying your bills, cleaning up your room and listening to you tell them how idealistic you are. And by the way, before you save the rain forest from the blood-sucking parasites of your parents' generation, try delousing the closet in your bedroom.

Rule No. 8: Your school may have done away with winners and losers. Life hasn't. In some schools, they'll give you as many times as you want to get the right answer. Failing grades have been abolished and class valedictorians scrapped, lest anyone's feelings be hurt. Effort is as important as results. This, of course, bears not the slightest resemblance to anything in real life. (See Rule No. 1, Rule No. 2 and Rule No. 4.)

Rule No. 9: Life is not divided into semesters and you don't get summers off. Not even Easter break. They expect you to show up every day. For eight hours. And you don't get a new life every 10 weeks. It just goes on and on. While we're at it, very few jobs are interested in Aniston.

Rule No. 10: Television is not real life. Your life is not a sitcom. Your problems will not all be solved in 30 minutes, minus time for commercials. In real life, people actually have to leave the coffee shop to go to jobs. Your friends will not be as perky or pliable as Jennifer Aniston.

Rule No. 11: Be nice to nerds. You may end up working for them. We all could.

Rule No. 12: Smoking does not make you look cool. It makes you look moronic. Next time you're out cruising, watch an 11-year-old with a butt in his mouth. That's what you look like to anyone over 20. Ditto for 'expressing yourself' with purple hair and/or pierced body parts.

Rule No. 13: You are not immortal. (See Rule No. 12.) If you are under the impression that living fast, dying young and leaving a beautiful corpse is romantic, you obviously haven't seen one of your peers at room temperature lately.

Rule No. 14: Enjoy this while you can. Sure parents are a pain, school's a bother and life is depressing. But someday you'll realise how wonderful it was to be a kid. Maybe you should start now. You're welcome.

Car Deal

A fifteen year-old boy came home with a new Chevrolet Avalanche and his parents began to yell and scream, *'Where did you get that truck?!'*

He calmly told them, *'I bought it today.'*

'With what money?' demanded his parents. They knew what a Chevrolet Avalanche cost.

'Well,' said the boy, *'this one cost me fifteen dollars.'* So the parents began to yell even louder. *'Who would sell a truck like that for fifteen dollars?'* they said.

'It was the lady up the street,' said the boy. *'I don't know her name - they just moved in. She saw me ride past on my bike and asked me if I wanted to buy a Chevrolet Avalanche for fifteen dollars.'*

'Oh my Goodness!' moaned the mother, 'she must be a child abuser. Who knows what she will do next? John, you go right up there and see what's going on.'

So the boy's father walked up the street to the house where the lady lived and found her out in the yard calmly planting petunias! He introduced himself as the father of the boy to whom she had sold a new Chevrolet Avalanche for fifteen dollars and demanded to know why she did it.

'Well,' she said, 'This morning I got a phone call from my husband. I thought he was on a coffee break, but learned from a friend he had run off to Hawaii with his mistress and really doesn't intend to come back. He claimed he was stranded and asked me to sell his new Chevrolet Avalanche and send him the money. So I did.'

[Are women good or what?]

Nursery School

A nursery school teacher asked her students to use the word 'Definitely' in a sentence:

A little girl says, 'The sky is definitely blue.'

Teacher says, 'Sorry Amy, but the sky can be grey or orange.'

Little boy says, 'Trees are definitely green.'

Teacher says, 'Sorry Tommy, trees can be brown, red orange or yellow as well as green'

Little Johnny from the back of the class stands up and asks: 'Does a fart have lumps?'

The teacher (looking horrified) says, 'Johnny! Of course not!!!'

'Okay then. I definitely pooped my pants!'

A teacher was trying to broaden the student's horizons through sensory exploration. With their eyes closed they would feel objects from pumice stones to pine cones and smell aromatic herbs and exotic fruits. Then one day, the teacher brought in a great variety of lifesavers, more flavours than the children ever imagined.

She said, 'Children, I'd like you to close your eyes and taste these.'

Without difficulty, they managed to identify the taste of cherries, lemons and mint, but when the teacher had them put honey-flavoured lifesavers in their mouths; every one of the children was stumped.

'I'll give you a hint,' said the teacher. 'It's something your Mommy probably calls your Daddy all the time.'

Instantly, one of the children spat the lifesaver out of his mouth and shouted, 'Spit them out you guys! They're assholes!!!'

A kindergarten pupil told his teacher he'd found a cat, but it was dead.

'How did you know the cat was dead?' she asked.

'Because I pissed in its ear and it didn't move,' answered the child innocently.

'You did what?' the teacher exclaimed in surprise.

'You know,' explained the boy, 'I leaned over and went 'Pssst!' and it didn't move.'

Horsie ride

Little Johnny is passing his parents' bedroom in the middle of the night, in search of a glass of water. Hearing a lot of moaning and thumping, he peeks in and catches his folks in 'the act'. Before dad can even react, Little Johnny exclaims *'Oh, boy! horsie ride! Daddy, can I ride on your back?'*

Daddy agrees, relieved that Johnny's not asking more uncomfortable questions and seeing the opportunity not to break his stride. Johnny hops on and daddy starts going to town. Pretty soon mommy starts moaning and gasping.

Johnny cries out *'Hang on tight, Daddy! This is the part where me and the milkman usually get bucked off!'*

Cleaning Chickens

'*Late again,*' the third-grade teacher said to little Sammy.

'*It ain't my fault, Miss Crabtree. You can blame this on my Daddy. The reason I'm three hours late is Daddy sleeps naked!*'

Now Miss Crabtree had taught grammar school for thirty-some-odd years. So she asked little Sammy what he meant by that, despite her mounting fears. Full of grins and mischief and in the flower of his youth, little Sammy and trouble were old friends, but he always told the truth.

'*You see, Miss Crabtree, at the ranch we got this here low-down coyote. The last few nights he done et six hens and killed Ma's best milk goat. And last night, when Daddy heard a noise out in the chicken pen, he grabbed his gun and said to Ma, 'That coyote's back again, I'm a gonna git him!'*'

'*Stay back,' he yelled to all us kids! He was naked as a jaybird, no boots, no pants and no shirt! To the hen house he crawled, just like an Injun on the snoop. Then he stuck that double barrel through the window of the coop. As he stared into the darkness, with coyotes on his mind, our old hound dog Zeke done woke up and come a sneakin' up behind Daddy. Then we all looked on plumb helpless as old Zeke stuck that cold nose in Daddy's crack! Miss Crabtree, we been cleanin' chickens since three o'clock this mornin'!*'

End of school year

It was the end of the school year and a kindergarten teacher was receiving gifts from her pupils. The florist's son handed her a gift. She shook it, held it overhead and said, *'I'll bet I know what is it - flowers?'*

'That's right,' the boy said, *'but how did you know?'*

'Oh, just a wild guess,' she replied.

The next pupil was the sweet shop owner's daughter. The teacher held her gift overhead, shook it and said, *'I'll bet I can guess what it is - a box of sweets?'*

'That's right, but how did you know?' asked the girl.

'Oh, just a wild guess,' said the teacher.

The next gift was from the son of the liquor store owner. The teacher held the package overhead, but it was leaking. She touched a drop of the leakage with her finger and put it to her tongue. *'Is it wine?'* she asked.

'No,' replied the boy with more excitement.

The teacher took one more big taste before declaring, *'I give up - what is it?'*

With great glee, the boy replied, *'It's a puppy!'*

The difference between potentially and realistically:

A young boy went up to his father and asked him, *'Dad, what is the difference between potentially and realistically?'*

The father thought for a moment, then answered, *'Go ask your mother if she would sleep with Brad Pitt for a million dollars. Then ask your sister if she would sleep with Brad Pitt for a million dollars and then, ask your brother if he'd sleep with Brad Pitt for a million dollars. Come back and tell me what you learn from that.'*

So the boy went to his mother and asked, *'Would you sleep with Brad Pitt for a million dollars?'*

The mother replied, *'Of course I would! We could really use that money to fix up the house and send you kids to a great university!'*

The boy then went to his sister and asked, *'Would you sleep with Brad Pitt for a million dollars?'*

The girl replied, *'Oh my God! I LOVE Brad Pitt. I would sleep with him in a heartbeat, are you nuts?'*

The boy then went to his brother and asked, *'Would you sleep with Brad Pitt for a million dollars?'*

'Of course,' the brother replied. *'Do you know how much a million bucks would buy?'*

The boy pondered the answers for a few days then went back to his dad. His father asked him, *'Did you find out the difference between potentially and realistically?'*

The boy replied, *'Yes ... potentially, you and I are sitting on three million dollars, but realistically, we're living with two loose women and a queer.'*

First day of school

Johnny was excited about his first day at school. So excited in fact, that only a few minutes after class had started, he realised that he desperately needed to go to the bathroom. So he raised his hand politely to ask if he could be excused. Of course the teacher said, *'Yes,'* but asked Johnny to be quick.

Five minutes later Johnny returned, looking more desperate and embarrassed. *'I can't find it,'* he admitted.

The teacher sat Johnny down and drew him a little diagram to where he should go and asked him if he would be able to find it. Johnny looked at the diagram and said, *'Yes'* and went on his way.

Five minutes later he returns to the classroom and announces, *'I can't find it.'*

Frustrated, the teacher asks Tommy, a boy who had been at the school for a while to help him find the bathroom. They go together and return five minutes later and sit down at their seats. The teacher asks Tommy, *'Well did you find it?'*

Tommy is quick with his reply, *'Oh sure, he just had his boxer shorts on backwards.'*

A group of former kindergartners were trying to become accustomed to the first grade. The biggest hurdle they faced was that the teacher insisted on no baby talk. She would always remind them, *'You need to use 'big people' words.'*

She asked Wendy what she had done over the weekend. Wendy replied, *'I went to visit my Nana.'*

The teacher replied, *'No, you went to visit your grandmother. Use big people words!'*

The teacher then asked Joey what he had done. *'I took a ride on a choo-choo,'* he said.

The teacher corrected him, *'No you took a ride on a train - use big people words!'*

She asked Eddie what he had done. *'I read a book,'* he replied.

'That's wonderful,' his teacher said. *'What book did you read?'*

Eddie thought about it, then puffed out his chest with great pride and said, *'Winnie The Shit!'*

Third Graders

Three third graders, Angus, John and Geordie are in the playground at recess. One of them suggests that they play a new game. *'Let's see who has the largest weenie,'* he says.

'Okay.' They all agree.

The Angus pulls down his zipper and whips it out. *'That's nothing,'* says John. He whips his out. His is a couple of inches longer.

Not to be outdone, Geordie whips his out. It is by far the biggest.

That night, eating dinner at home, Geordie's mother asks him what he did at school today. *'Oh, we worked on a science project, had a math test and read out loud from a new book ... and during recess, my friends and I played 'Let's see who has the largest weenie.''*

'What kind of game is that, honey?' asks the mother.

'Well, me, Angus and John each pulled out our weenies and I had the biggest! The other kids say it's because I'm from New Zealand. Is that true, Mum?'

Mom replies, *'No, Honey. It's because you're fourteen.'*

Something Exciting

The kindergarten class had a homework assignment to find out about something exciting and relate it to the class the next day. When the time came for the children to give their reports, the teacher asked everyone, but was reluctant to call on little Johnnie, knowing that he sometimes could be a bit crude. But, eventually, his turn came.

Little Johnny walked up to the front of the class and with a piece of chalk, made a small white dot on the blackboard, then sat back down. The teacher couldn't figure out what Johnny had in mind for his report on something exciting, so she asked him what it was.

'It's a period,' reported Johnny.

'Well, I can see that,' she said, *'but what is so exciting about a period?'*

'Damned if I know,' Johnny replied, *'but, this morning my sister said she had missed one. My Dad had a heart attack, Mom fainted and the man next door shot himself.'*

Squirmy Boy

A teacher noticed that a little boy at the back of the class was squirming around, scratching his crotch and not paying attention. She went back to find out what was going on. He was quite embarrassed and whispered that he had just recently been circumcised and was quite itchy. The teacher told him to go down to the principal's office. He was to telephone his mother and ask her what he should do about it.

He did this and returned to class. Suddenly there was a commotion at the back of the room. She went back to investigate only to find him sitting at his desk with his penis hanging out.

'I thought I told you to call your Mom!' she said.

'I did' he said, *'and she told me that if I could stick it out until lunchtime, she'd come and pick me up from school.'*

Sex Education

A little boy goes to his father and asks, *'Daddy, how was I born?'*
The father answers: *'Well son, I guess one day you will need to find out anyway! Your Mom and I first got together in a chat room on Yahoo. Then I set up a date via e-mail with your Mom and we met at a cyber-cafe. We sneaked into a secluded room, where your mother agreed to a download from my hard drive. As soon as I was ready to upload, we discovered that neither one of us had used a firewall. Since it was too late to hit the delete button, nine months later a little Pop-Up appeared that said: 'You got Male.'*

Too smart

Johnny said, *'I'm too smart for the first grade. My sister's in the third grade and I'm smarter than she is! I think I should be in the third grade!'*

The teacher had had enough. As a result she took Johnny to the principal's office and explained Johnny's request. While Johnny waited in the outer office, the teacher explained the situation to the principal. The principal told Johnny's teacher that he would give the boy a test and if Johnny failed to answer any of the special questions, he was to go back to the first grade and behave.

The teacher agreed. Johnny was brought into the room. The principal told Johnny his terms and Johnny agreed.

Principal: *'What is 3 x 3?'*
Johnny: *'9.'*
Principal: *'What is 6 x 6?'*
Johnny: *'36.'*
Principal: *'What is 9 x 9.'*
Johnny: *'81.'*

And so it went with every question the principal thought a third grader should know. Johnny appeared to have a strong case. The principal looked at the teacher and told her, *'I think Johnny can go on to the third grade.'*

The teacher, knowing Little Johnny's tendency toward sexual wisecracks, said to the principal, *'Let me ask him some questions before we make that decision.'*

The principal and Johnny both agreed, Johnny with a sly look on his face. The teacher began by asking, *'What does a cow have 4 of that I have only 2 of?'*

Johnny: *'Legs.'*

Teacher: *'What is in your pants that you have but I do not have?'*

The principal's eyes opened wide! Before he could stop Johnny's expected answer, Johnny said, *'Pockets.'*

The principal breathed a sigh of relief and told the teacher, *'I think we should put Johnny in the fifth grade. I missed the last two questions myself!'*

Free Kittens

Little Suzy had a box of very small kittens that she was trying to give away, so she had them out on the street corner with a sign 'FREE KITTENS' next to them. Suddenly a long line of big black cars came up with a policeman on a motorcycle in front. The cars all stopped and a tall man stepped out from the biggest car. *'Hi, little girl, what do you have there in the box?'* he asked.

'Kittens' Little Suzy replied. *'They're so small; their eyes are not even open yet.'*

'What kind of kittens are they?' he asked.

'Democrats' says Little Suzy.

The tall man smiled, returned to his car and they drove away. Sensing a good photo opportunity, Sen. Obama called his campaign manager and told him about the little girl and the kittens. It was planned that they would return the next day, have all the media there and tell everyone about these great kittens.

The next day Little Suzy is standing out on the corner with her box of kittens with the 'FREE KITTENS' sign and the big motorcade of black cars pulled up with all the vans and trucks from ABC, NBC, CBS and CNN.

Everyone had their cameras ready and then, Senator Obama got out of his limo and walked up to Little Suzy. *'Now, don't be frightened,'* he said, *'I just want you to tell all these nice news people what kind of kittens you're giving away today.'*

'Yes sir,' Suzy said, *'These are all REPUBLICAN kittens.'*

Taken by surprise, Senator Obama said, *'But yesterday you told me that they were DEMOCRATS.'*

Little Suzy says, *'Yes, I know. But today they have their eyes open.'*

Bed Time

His father sends a small boy to bed. Five minutes later. *'Da-ad.'*
'What?'
'I'm thirsty. Can you bring a drink of water?'
'No. You had your chance. Lights out.'
Five minutes later: *'Da-aaaad.'*
'WHAT?'
'I'm thirsty. Can I have a drink of water?'
'I told you NO! If you ask again, I'll have to spank you!'
Five minutes later. *'Daaa-aaaad.'*
'WHAT?'
'When you come in to spank me, can you bring a drink of water?'

When I was six months pregnant with my third child, my three-year-old came into the room when I was just getting ready to get into the shower. She said, *'Mommy, you're getting fat!'*

I replied, *'Yes honey, remember Mommy has a baby growing in her tummy.'*

'I know,' she replied, *'but what's growing in your behind?'*

A little boy was doing his math homework. He said to himself, *'Two plus five, that son of a bitch is seven. Three plus six, that son of a bitch is nine.'*

His mother heard what he was saying and gasped, *'What are you doing?'*

The little boy answered, *'I'm doing my math homework, Mom.'*
'And is that how your teacher taught you to do it?' the mother asked.

'Yes,' he answered.

Infuriated, the mother asked the teacher the next day, *'What are you teaching my son in math?'*

The teacher replied, *'Right now, we're learning addition.'*

The mother asked, *'And are you teaching them to say two plus two, that son of a bitch is four?'*

After the teacher stopped laughing, she answered, *'What I taught them was two plus, the sum of which is four.'*

One day the first grade teacher was reading the story of Chicken Little to her class. She came to the part of the story where Chicken Little tried to warn the farmer. She read, *'... and so Chicken Little went up to the farmer and said, 'The sky is falling, the sky is falling!''*

The teacher paused then asked the class, *'And what do you think the farmer said?'*

One little girl raised her hand and said, *'I think he said: 'Holy Shit! A talking chicken!''*

The teacher was unable to teach for the next ten minutes.

A little girl when asked her name, would reply, *'I'm Mr. Sugarbrown's daughter.'*

Her mother told her this was wrong, she must say, *'I'm Jane Sugarbrown.'*

The Vicar spoke to her in Sunday school and said, *'Aren't you Mr. Sugarbrown's daughter?'*

She replied, *'I thought I was, but Mother says I'm not.'*

A little girl asked her mother, *'Can I go outside and play with the boys?'*

Her mother replied, *'No, you can't play with the boys, they're too rough.'*

The little girl thought about it for a few moments and asked, *'If I find a smooth one, can I play with him?'*

A little girl goes to the barbershop with her father. She stands next to the barber chair while her dad gets his hair cut, eating a snack cake. The barber says to her, *'Sweetheart, you're goona get hair on your Twinkie.'*

She replied, *'Yes, I know and I'm gonna get boobs too.'*

Mom's Logic

My Mom taught me:

To appreciate a job well done: *'If you're going to kill each other, do it outside. I just finished cleaning!'*

Religion: *'You'd better pray that will come out of the carpet.'*

About time travel: *'If you don't straighten up, I'm going to knock you into the middle of next week!'*

Logic: *'Because I said so, that's why.'*

Foresight: *'Make sure you wear clean underwear in case you're in an accident.'*

Irony: *'Keep laughing and I'll give you something to cry about.'*

The science of osmosis: *'Shut your mouth and eat your supper!'*

Contortionism: *'Will you look at the dirt on the back of your neck!'*

Weather: *'It looks as if a tornado swept through your room.'*

Physics problems: *'If I yelled because I saw a meteor coming towards you, would you listen then?'*

Hypocrisy: *'If I've told you once, I've told you a million times. Don't Exaggerate!!!'*

The Circle of Life: *'I brought you into this world and I can take you out.'*

Humour: *'If I cut off your foot with the lawn mower, don't come running to me.'*

Stamina: *'You'll sit there 'til all that spinach is finished.'*

Envy: *'There are millions of less fortunate children in this world who don't have wonderful parents like you do!'*

Behaviour Modification: *'Stop acting like your father.'*

Train Schedule

A mother was working in the kitchen listening to her son playing with his new electric train in the living room. She heard the train stop and her son saying, *'This is the last stop - so everyone get the hell out.'*

The mother went into the living room and told her son, *'We don't use that kind of language in this house. Now go to your room and stay there for two hours. When you come out, you may go back and play with your train, but only if you use nice language.'*

Two hours later the boy resumed playing with his train. Soon the train stopped and the mother heard her son say, *'All passengers who are disembarking the train; please remember to take all your belongings with you. We thank you for riding with us today and hope your trip was a pleasant one.'* He continued, *'For those of you who are just boarding, we ask you to stow all your hand luggage under the seat.'* Then he added, *'Those of you who are pissed off about the two hour delay - please address your questions to the grumpy woman in the kitchen.'*

Teen Aged Sex

The mother of a 17-year-old girl was concerned that her daughter was having sex. Worried the girl might become pregnant and adversely impact the family's status, she consulted the family doctor. The doctor told her that teenagers today were very wilful and any attempt to stop the girl would probably result in rebellion. He then told her to arrange for her daughter to be put on birth control and until then, talk to her and give her a box of condoms.

Later that evening, as her daughter was preparing for a date, the woman told her about the situation and handed her a box of condoms. The girl burst out laughing and reached over to hug her mother saying: *'Oh Mom! You don't have to worry about that! I'm dating Susan!'*

Neighbour's kid

An old man was sitting on his front porch watching the sunrise. He sees the neighbour's kid walking by carrying something big under his arm and yells out, *'Hey boy, whatcha got there?'*

The boy yells back, *'Roll of chicken wire.'*

The old man says, *'Whatcha gonna do with that?'*

The boy says, *'Gonna catch some chickens.'*

The old man yells, *'You damn fool, you can't catch chickens with chicken wire!'*

The boy just laughs and keeps walking. That evening at sunset, the boy comes walking by and to the old man's surprise; he's dragging behind him the chicken wire and about thirty chickens caught in it.

Same time next morning the old man sees the boy walk by carrying something round in his hand. He yells out, *'Hey boy, whatcha got there?'*

The boy replies, *'Gonna catch me some ducks.'*

The old man says, *'What with?'*

The boy says, *'A roll of duck tape.'*

'You damn fool. You can't catch ducks with duck tape!'

The boy just laughs and keeps walking. That night around sunset he walks by coming home and to the old man's amazement, he's trailing behind him the unrolled roll of duck tape with about thirty-five ducks caught in it.

Same time the next morning he sees the boy walking by carrying what looks like a long reed with something fuzzy on the end and asks, *'Hey boy, whatcha got there?'*

The boy replies, *'It's a pussy willow.'*

The old man says, *'Wait up ... I'll get my hat.'*

The Wedding

Attending a wedding for the first time, a little girl whispered to her mother, *'Why is the bride dressed in white?'*

'Because white is the colour of happiness and today is the happiest day of her life,' her mother tried to explain, keeping it simple.

The child thought about this for a moment, then said, *'So why's the groom wearing black?'*

Kid's Talk

A new neighbour asked the little girl next door if she had any brothers and sisters. She replied, *'No, I'm a lonely child.'*

A little girl was diligently pounding away at her father's word processor. She told him she was writing a story.
 'What about?' he asked.
 'I don't know,' she replied, *'I can't read.'*

I didn't know if my granddaughter had learned her colours yet, so I decided to test her. I would point out something and ask what colour it was. She would tell me and was always correct. But it was fun for me, so I continued. At last, she headed for the door, saying sagely, *'Grandma, I think you should try to figure out some of these yourself?'*

It was March 17th (St. Patrick's Day) and the supermarket was bustling as normal. Mom was busy loading groceries onto the conveyor belt with her one-year-old in the cart and four-year-old son Reece nearby. An older, grandpa type, pinches Reece and tells him he's not wearing green! Reece, a bit stunned, quickly returns the pinch with a kick to the shin of the elderly man and says, *'Well you're not wearing blue!'*

After putting her children to bed, a mother changed into old slacks and a droopy blouse and proceeded to use a facial mud pack. As she heard the children getting more and more rambunctious, her patience grew thin. At last she stormed into the room, putting them back to bed with stern warnings. As she left the room, she heard her three-year-old say with a trembling voice, *'Who was that?'*

A mother was telling her little girl what her own childhood was like. *'We used to skate outside on a pond. I had a swing made from a tire. It hung from a tree in our front yard and we rode our pony. We picked wild raspberries in the woods.'*
 The little girl was wide-eyed, taking this in. At last she said, *'I sure wish I'd gotten to know you sooner!'*

Grandpa's Medicine

A thirteen year-old boy had been rushed to hospital. Apparently he had taken two of his grandpa's Viagra pills and had to be treated for third degree burns on both of his hands.

Two little boys were visiting their grandfather and he took them to a restaurant for lunch. They couldn't make up their minds about what they wanted to eat. Finally the grandfather grinned at the server and said, *'Just bring them bread and water.'*

One of the little boys looked up and quavered, *'Can I have ketchup on it?'*

There is a family gathering, with all the generations around the table. The teenagers smuggle in a Viagra tablet and put it in Grandpa's drink.

After a while, Grandpa excused himself because he has to go to the bathroom. When he returned, however, his trousers were wet all over.

'What happened, Grandpa,' asked his concerned children?

'Well,' he answered, *'I had to go to the bathroom. So I took it out, but then I saw that it wasn't mine, so I put it back.'*

The Bath

A young boy, about eight years old, was at the corner 'Mom and Pop' grocery store picking out a large-sized box of laundry detergent. The grocer walked over and, trying to be friendly, asked the boy if he had a lot of laundry to do.

'Oh, no laundry,' replied the boy, *'I'm going to wash my dog.'*

'But you shouldn't use this to wash your dog! It's very powerful and if you wash your dog in this, he'll get sick. In fact it might even kill him.'

But the boy was not to be stopped and carried the detergent to the counter and paid for it, even as the grocer still tried to talk him out of washing his dog.

About a week later the boy was back in the store to buy some candy. The grocer asked the boy how his dog was doing.

'Oh, he died,' the boy said.

The grocer, trying not to be an I-told-you-so, said he was sorry the dog died, but added, *'I tried to tell you not to use that detergent on your dog.'*

'Well,' the boy replied, *'I don't think it was the detergent that killed him. I think it was the spin cycle!'*

One day, a little girl was watching her mother do the dishes at the kitchen sink. She suddenly noticed that her mother had several strands of white hair sticking out in contrast to her brunette head. She inquisitively asked, *'Why are some of your hairs white, Mom?'*

Her mother replied, *'Well, every time that you do something wrong and make me cry or unhappy, one of my hairs turns white.'*

The little girl thought about this revelation for a while and then said, *'Momma, how come all of Grandma's hairs are white?'*

A kid was playing with himself in his room when all of a sudden his father walked into the room and said, *'Son, stop playing with that. It will make you go blind.'* The child replied, *'But, Dad, I'm over here.'*

Reindeer

According to the Alaska Department of Fish and Game, while both male and female reindeer grow antlers in the summer each year, male reindeer drop their antlers at the beginning of winter, usually late November to mid-December.

Female reindeer retain their antlers till after they give birth in the spring. Therefore, according to every historical rendition depicting Santa's reindeer, every single one of them, from Rudolph to Blitzen - had to be a female reindeer.

We should have known. Only women, while pregnant, would be able to drag a fat man in a red velvet suit all around the world in one night and not get lost!

Day Care

A little girl and a little boy were at day care one day. The girl approaches the boy and said, *'Hey Tommy, do you want to play house?'*

He replied, *'Sure! What do you want me to do?'*

'I want you to communicate your feelings,' she replies.

'Communicate my feelings?' said the bewildered Tommy. *'I have no idea what that means.'*

The little girl smirks and says, *'Perfect. You can be the husband.'*

The Trick

The little boy greeted his grandmother with a hug and said, *'I'm so happy to see you grandma. Now maybe daddy will do the trick he has been promising us.'*

The grandmother was curious, *'What trick is that my dear,'* she asked.

The little boy replied, *'I heard daddy tell mommy that he would climb the walls if you came to visit us again.'*

Little Leroy

Little Leroy went to his mother demanding a new bicycle. His mother decided that he should take a look at himself and the way he acted. She said, *'Well, Leroy, it isn't Christmas and I don't have the money to just go out and buy you anything you want. So why don't you write a letter to Jesus and pray for one instead.'*

After his temper tantrum, his mother sent him to his room. He finally sat down to write a letter to Jesus. *'Dear Jesus, I've been a good boy this year and would appreciate a new bicycle. Your friend Leroy.'*

Now Leroy knew that Jesus really knew what kind of boy he was (a brat). So he ripped up the letter and decided to give it another try. *'Dear Jesus, I've been an okay boy this year and want a new bicycle. Yours truly, Leroy.'*

Well, Leroy knew this wasn't totally honest so he tore it up and tried again: *'Dear Jesus, I've thought about being a good boy this year and can I have a bicycle? Leroy.'*

Well, Leroy looked deep down in his heart, which by the way was what his mother really wanted. He knew he had been terrible and was deserving of almost nothing. He crumpled up the letter, threw it in the garbage and ran outside. He wandered aimlessly about, thinking of the way he treated his parents and really considering his actions.

He finally found himself in front of a Catholic Church. Leroy went inside and knelt down, looked around not knowing what he should really do. Leroy finally got up and began to walk out the door and noticed all the statues. He grabbed a small one and ran out the door. He went home, hid it under his bed then wrote this letter: *'Jesus, I've got your mama. If you ever want to see her again, give me a bike. You know who.'*

Marriage

The child was a typical four-year-old girl - cute, inquisitive and bright as a new penny. When she expressed difficulty in grasping the concept of marriage, her father decided to pull out his wedding photo album, thinking visual images would help. One page after another, he pointed out the bride arriving at the church, the entrance, the wedding ceremony, the reception, etc. *'Now do you understand?'* he asked.

'I think so,' she said, *'Is that when mommy came to work for us?'*

The Sissy

One summer evening during a violent thunderstorm a mother was tucking her son into bed. She was about to turn off the light when he asked with a tremor in his voice, *'Mommy will you sleep with me tonight?'*

The mother smiled and gave him a reassuring hug. *'I can't dear,'* she said, *'I have to sleep in Daddy's room.'*

A long silence was broken at last by his shaky little voice: *'The big sissy.'*

Where is God?

Two little boys, ages eight and ten, were excessively mischievous. They were always getting into trouble and their parents knew all about it. If any mischief occurred in their town, the two boys are probably involved.

The boys' mother heard that a preacher in town had been successful in disciplining children, so she asked if he would speak with her boys. The preacher agreed, but he asked to see them individually. So the mother sent the eight-year-old first, in the morning, with the older boy to see the preacher in the afternoon.

The preacher, a huge man with a booming voice, sat the younger boy down and asked him sternly, *'Do you know where God is, son?'*

The boy's mouth dropped open, but he made no response, sitting there wide-eyed with his mouth hanging open. So the preacher repeated the question in an even sterner tone, *'Where is God?'*

Again, the boy made no attempt to answer. The preacher raised his voice even more and shook his finger in the boy's face and bellowed, *'Where is God?'*

The boy screamed and bolted from the room, ran directly home and dove into his closet, slamming the door behind him. When his older brother found him in the closet, he asked, *'What happened?'* the younger brother, gasping for breath, replied, *'We're in Big trouble this time. God is missing and they think we did it!'*

Don't Mess With Mom!

My son came home from school one day, with a smirk upon his face.
He decided he was smart enough, to put me in my place.
'Guess what I learned in Civics Two, that's taught by Mr. Wright?
It's all about the laws today, 'The Children's Bill of Rights.'
It says I need not clean my room, don't have to cut my hair.
No one can tell me what to think or speak or what to wear.
I have freedom from religion and regardless what you say,
I don't have to bow my head and I sure don't have to pray.
I can wear earrings if I want and pierce my tongue & nose.
I can read & watch just what I like and get tattoos from head to toes.
And if you ever spank me, I'll charge you with a crime.
I'll back up all my charges, with the marks on my behind.

Don't you ever touch me, my body's only for my use,
not for your hugs and kisses, that's just more child abuse.
Don't preach about your morals, like your Mother did to you.
That's nothing more than mind control and it's illegal too!
Mum, I have these children's rights, so you can't influence me,
or I'll call Children's Services Division, better known as C.S.D.
Of course my first instinct was, to toss him out the door.
But the chance to teach him a lesson made me think a little more.
I mulled it over carefully, I couldn't let this go.
A smile crept upon my face. He's messing with a pro.
The next day I took him shopping at the local Goodwill Store.
I told him, *'Pick out all you want, there's shirts & pants galore.*
I've called and checked with C.S.D. who said they didn't care
If I bought you K-Mart shoes instead of those Nike Airs.
And I've cancelled that appointment to take your driver's test.
The C.S.D. is unconcerned so I'll decide what's best.'
I said *'No time to stop and eat or pick up stuff to munch.*
And tomorrow you can start to learn to make your own sack lunch.
Just save the raging appetite and wait till dinnertime.
We're having liver and onions, a favourite dish of mine.'
He asked *'Can I please rent a movie, to watch on my VCR?'*
'Sorry, but I sold your TV, for new tires on my car.
I also rented out your room. You'll take the couch instead.
All the C.S.D. requires is a roof for over your head.
Your clothing won't be trendy now and I'll choose what we eat.
That allowance that you used to get, will buy me something neat.
I'm selling off your jet ski, dirt-bike and roller blades.
Check out the 'Parents Bill of Rights.' It's in effect today!'
Hey hot shot, are you crying and why are you on your knees?
Are you asking God to help you out, instead of C.S.D?'

Art Work

A Kindergarten teacher was observing her classroom of children while they were drawing. She would occasionally walk around to see each child's work. As she got to one little girl who was working diligently, she asked what the drawing was.

The girl replied, *'I'm drawing God.'*

The teacher paused and said, *'But no one knows what God looks like.'*

Without missing a beat or looking up from her drawing, the girl replied, *'They will in a minute.'*

Great truths that little children have learned

1.   No matter how hard you try, you can't baptize cats.

2. When your Mum is mad at your Dad, don't let her brush your hair.
3. If your sister hits you, don't hit her back. They always catch the second person.
4. Never ask your 3-year old brother to hold a tomato.
5. You can't trust dogs to watch your food.
6. Don't sneeze when someone is cutting your hair.
7. Never hold a Dust-Buster and a cat at the same time.
8. You can't hide a piece of broccoli in a glass of milk.
9. Don't wear polka-dot underwear under white shorts.
10. The best place to be when you're sad is Grandpa's lap.

Biology

A teacher was giving a lesson on the circulation of the blood. Trying to make the matter clearer, she said, *'Now, class, if I stood on my head, the blood, as you know, would run into it and I would turn red in the face.'*

'Yes,' the class said.

'Then why is it that while I am standing upright in the ordinary position, the blood doesn't run into my feet?'

A little fellow shouted, *'Cause your feet ain't empty.'*

Ten Commandments

A Sunday school teacher was discussing the Ten Commandments with her five and six year olds. After explaining the commandment to 'honour' thy Father and thy Mother, she asked, *'Is there a commandment that teaches us how to treat our brothers and sisters?'*

Without missing a beat one little boy (the oldest of a family) answered, *'Thou shall not kill.'*

Photographs

The children had all been photographed and the teacher was trying to persuade them each to buy a copy of the group picture. *'Just think how nice it will be to look at it when you are all grown up and say, 'There's Jennifer, she's a lawyer,' or 'That's Michael, he's a doctor.''*

A small voice at the back of the room rang out, *'And there's the teacher, she's dead.'*

The Apples

The children were lined up in the cafeteria of a Catholic elementary school for lunch. At the head of the table was a large pile of apples. The nun made a note and posted on the apple tray:

'Take only ONE. God is watching.'

Moving further along the lunch line, at the other end of the table was a large pile of chocolate chip cookies.

A child had written a note, *'Take all you want. God is watching the apples.*

Why God made Moms

Brilliant answers given by second-grade school children to the following questions!!

Why did God make Moms?
1. She's the only one who knows where the scotch tape is.
2. Mostly to clean the house.
3. To help us out of there when we were getting born.

How did God make mothers?
1. He used dirt, just like for the rest of us.
2. Magic plus super powers and a lot of stirring.
3. God made my Mom just the same like He made me. He just used bigger parts.

What ingredients are mothers made of?
1. God makes mothers out of clouds and angel hair and everything nice in the world one dab of mean.
2. They had to get their start from men's bones. Then they mostly use string, I think.

Why did God give you your mother and not some other mom?
1. We're related
2. God knew she likes me a lot more than other people's moms like me.

What did mom need to know about dad before she married him?
1. His last name.
2. She had to know his background. Like is he a crook? Does he get drunk on beer?
3. Does he make at least $800 a year? Did he say NO to drugs and YES to chores?

Why did your mom marry your dad?
1. My dad makes the best spaghetti in the world. And my Mom eats a lot.
2. She got too old to do anything else with him.
3. My grandma says that Mom didn't have her thinking cap on.

What kind of little girl was your mom?
1. My mom has always been my mom and none of that other stuff.
2. I don't know because I wasn't here, but my guess would be pretty bossy.

3. They say she used to be nice.

Who's the boss at your house?
1. Mom doesn't want to be boss, but she has to because dad's such a goof ball.
2. Mom. You can tell by room inspection. She sees the stuff under the bed.
3. I guess Mom is, but only because she has a lot more to do than dad.

What's the difference between moms and dads?
1. Moms work at work and work at home and dads just go to work at work.
2. Moms know how to talk to teachers without scaring them.
3. Dads are taller & stronger, but moms have all the real power 'cause that's who you got to ask if you want to sleep over at your friend's.
4. Moms have magic. They make you feel better without medicine.

What does your mom do in her spare time?
1. Mothers don't do spare time.
2. To hear her tell it, she pays bills all day long.

What would it take to make your mom perfect?
1. On the inside she's already perfect. Outside, I think some kind f plastic surgery.
2. Diet. You know; her hair. I'd diet, maybe blue.

If you could change one thing about your Mom, what would it be?
1. She has this weird thing about me keeping my room clean. I'd get rid of that.
2. I'd make my Mom smarter. Then she would know it was my sister who did it and not me.
3. I would like for her to get rid of those invisible eyes on the back of her head.

Kids Are Quick

Teacher: *'Maria, go to the map and find North America?'*
Maria: *'Here it is.'*
Teacher: *'Correct. Now class. Who discovered America?'*
Class: *'Maria.'*
Teacher: *'John, why are you doing your math multiplication on the floor?'*
John: *'You told me to do it without using tables.'*
Teacher: *'Glenn, how do you spell 'crocodile?'*
Glenn: *'K-r-o-k-o-d-i-a-l.'*
Teacher: *'No, that's wrong.'*

Glenn: *'Maybe it is wrong, but you asked me how I spell it.'*
Teacher: *'Donald, what is the chemical formula for water?'*
Donald: *'H i j k l m n o.'*
Teacher: *'What are you talking about?'*
Donald: *Yesterday you said it's h to o.'*
Teacher: *'Winnie, name one important thing we have today that we didn't have ten years ago.'*
Winnie: *'Me!'* (Priceless)
Teacher: *'Glen, why do you always get so dirty?'*
Glen: *'Well, I'm a lot closer to the ground than you are.'*
Teacher: *'George Washington not only chopped down his father's cherry tree, but also admitted it. Now, Louie, do you know why his father didn't punish him?'*
Louis: *'Because George still had the axe in his hand.'*
Teacher: *'Now, Simon, tell me frankly, do you say prayers before eating?'*
Simon: *'No sir, I don't have to. My mom is a good cook.'*
Teacher: *'Clyde, your composition on 'my dog' is exactly the same as your brother's. did you copy his?'*
Clyde: *'No, sir. It's the same dog.'*
Teacher: *'Harold, what do you call a person who keeps on talking when people are no longer interested?'*
Harold: *'A teacher.'*

Daddy's Day at School

Her hair was up in a ponytail, her favourite dress tied in a bow.
Today was Daddy's Day at school and she couldn't wait to go.
But her Mommy tried to tell her, that she probably should stay at home.
Why the kids might not understand, if she went to school alone.
But she was not afraid; she knew just what to say.
What to tell her classmates of why he wasn't there today.
But still her mother worried, for her to face this day alone.
And that was why once again, she tried to keep her daughter home.
But the little girl went to school, eager to tell them all,
About a Dad she never sees. A Dad who never calls.
There are daddies along the wall in back, for everyone to meet.
Children squirming impatiently, anxious in their seats.
One by one the teacher called a student from the class.
To introduce their Daddy, as seconds slowly passed.
At last the teacher called her name, every child turned to stare.
Each of them was searching for the man who wasn't there.
'Where's her Daddy at?' She heard a boy call out.
'She probably doesn't have one,' another student dared to shout.

And from somewhere near the back, she heard a Daddy say,
'Looks like another deadbeat Dad. Too busy to waste his day.'
The words did not offend her, as she smiled up at her Mom.
And looked back at her teacher, who told her to go on.
And with hands behind her back, slowly she began to speak.
And out from the mouth of a child, came words incredibly unique.
'My Daddy couldn't be here, because he is so far away.
But I know he wishes he could be, since this is such a special day.
And though you cannot meet him, I want you to know.
All about my Daddy and how much he loves me so.
He loves to tell me stories, he taught me to ride my bike.
He surprised me with pink roses and taught me to fly a kite.
We share fudge sundaes and ice cream in a cone.
And though you cannot see him, I'm not standing here alone.
Cause my Daddy's always with me, even though we are apart,
I know because he told me, he'll forever be in my heart.'
With that, her little hand reached up and lay across her chest.
Feeling her own heartbeat, beneath her favourite dress.
And from somewhere in the crowd of Dads, her mother stood in tears.
Proudly watching her daughter, who was wise beyond her years.
For she stood up for the love, of a man not in her life.
Doing what was best for her, doing what was right.
And when she dropped her hand back down, stared straight into the crowd.
She finished with a voice so soft, but its message clear and loud.
'I love my Daddy very much, he's my shining star.
And if he could, he'd be here, but Iraq is just too far.'

There wasn't a dry eye in the auditorium full of students and their parents. They clapped and clapped while the little girl basked in the reflected glory of her father who was protecting them all from terrorism.

CHAPTER 10 - SENIORS

The first time

Maude and Claude, both 91, lived in a retirement community. They met in the social centre and discovered over time that they enjoyed each other's company. After several weeks of meeting for coffee, Claude asked Maude out for diner and much to his delight, she accepted.

They had a lovely evening. They dined at the most romantic restaurant in town. Despite his age, Claude was still a charmer. Afterward, Claude asked Maude to loin him at his place for an after-dinner drink. Things continued along a natural course and, age being no inhibitor, Maude soon joined Claude for a most enjoyable roll in the hay. As they were basking in the glow of the magic moments they'd shared, each was lost for a time in their own thoughts.

Claude was thinking, *'If I'd known she was a virgin, I'd have been gentler.'*

Maude was thinking, *'If I'd known he could still do it, I'd have taken off my pantyhose.'*

Disbelievers

No one believes seniors. Everyone thinks they are senile.

An elderly couple were celebrating their sixtieth anniversary. The couple had married as childhood sweethearts and had moved back to their old neighbourhood after they retired.

Holding hands, they walked back to their old school. It was not locked, so they entered and found the old desk they'd shared where Andy had carved *'I love you Sally.'*

On their way back home, a bag of money fell out of an armoured car, practically landing at their feet. Sally quickly picked it up, but not sure what to do with it, they took it home. There, she counted the money - fifty thousand dollars! Andy said, *'We've got to give it back.'*

Sally said, *'Finders keepers'* and she put the money back in the bag and hid it in their attic.

The next day two FBI men were canvassing the neighbourhood looking for the money and knocked on the door. *'Pardon me, but did either of you find a bag that fell out of an armoured car yesterday?'*

Sally said *'No.'*

Andy said, *'She's lying. She hid it up in the attic.'*

Sally said, *'Don't believe him, he's getting senile.'*

The agents turn to Andy and began to question him. One said, *'Tell us the story from the beginning.'*

Andy said, *'Well, when Sally and I were walking home from school yesterday ...'*

The first FBI guy turns to his partner and says, *'We're outta here.'*

The Old Couple

A very elderly couple is having an elegant dinner to celebrate their 75th wedding anniversary. The old man leans forward and says softly to his wife, *'Dear, there is something that I must ask you. It has always bothered me that our tenth child never quite looked like the rest of our children. Now I want to assure you that these 75 years have been the most wonderful experience I could have ever hoped for and your answer cannot take that all that away. But, I must know, did he have a different father?'*

The wife drops her head, unable to look her husband in the eye. She paused for a moment and then confessed. *'Yes. Yes he did.'*
The old man is very shaken. The reality of what his wife was admitting hit him harder than he had expected. With a tear in his eye he asks *'Who? Who was he? Who was the father?'*

Again the old woman drops her head, saying nothing at first as she tried to muster the courage to tell the truth to her husband. Then, finally, she says, *'You.'*

Viagra

Grandma and Grandpa were visiting their kids overnight. When Grandpa found a bottle of Viagra in his son's medicine cabinet, he asked about using one of the pills. The son said, *'I don't think you should take one Dad, they're very strong and expensive.'*

'How much?' asked Grandpa.

'$10.00 a pill,' answered the son.

'I don't care,' said Grandpa, *'I'd still like to try one and before we leave in the morning I'll put the money under the pillow.'*

The next morning the son found $110.00 under the pillow. He called Grandpa and said, *'I told you each pill was $10.00, not $110.00.'*

'I know,' said Grandpa, *'The hundred is from Grandma!'*

Getting Older

Have you ever been guilty of looking at others your own age and thinking, *'Surely I can't look that old?'* well ... You'll love this one!
I was sitting in the waiting room for my first appointment with a new dentist. I noticed his DDs diploma, which bore his full name.

Suddenly, I remembered a tall, handsome, dark-haired boy with the same name had been in my high school class some 40-odd years ago. Could he be the same guy that I had a secret crush on, way back then??

Upon seeing him, however, I quickly discarded any such thought. This balding, gray-haired man with the deeply lined face was way too old to have been my classmate. Hmm or could he???

After he examined my teeth, I asked him if he had attended Morgan Park High School. *'Yes. Yes, I did. I'm a Mustang,'* he gleamed with pride.

'When did you graduate?' I asked.

He answered, *'In 1965. Why do you ask?'*

'You were in my class!' I exclaimed.

He looked at me closely. Then, that ugly, old, wrinkled, bald, fat, gray, decrepit son-of-a-bitch asked, *'What did you teach?'*

Julie Andrews Turns 69

To commemorate her 69th birthday on October 1st, 2006, actress/vocalist Julie Andrews made a special appearance at Manhattan's Radio City Music Hall for the benefit of the AARP. One of the musical numbers she performed was *'My Favourite Things'* from the legendary movie *'Sound of Music.'* Here are the lyrics she used for her own version of the song:

> Maalox and nose drops and needles for knitting,
> Walkers and handrails and new dental fittings,
> Bundles of magazines tied up in string,
> These are a few of my favourite things.
> Cadillacs and cataracts and hearing aids and glasses,
> Polident and Fixodent and false teeth in glasses,
> Pacemakers, golf carts and porches with swings,
> These are a few of my favourite things.
> When the pipes leak,
> When the bones creak,
> When the knees go bad,
> I simply remember my favourite things,
> And I don't feel so bad.
> Hot tea and crumpets and corn pads for bunions,
> No spicy hot food or food cooked with onions,
> Bathrobes and heating pads and hot meals they bring,
> These are a few of my favourite things.
> Back pains, confused brains and fear of sinnin',
> Thin bones and fractures and hair that is thinnin',
> And we won't mention our short shrunken frames,

> When we remember our favourite things.
> When the joints ache,
> When the hips break,
> When our eyes grow dim,
> Then I remember the great life I've had,
> And then I don't feel so bad.

Ms Andrews received a standing ovation from the crowd that lasted over four minutes and repeated encores.

Seniors at Trailer Estates

A little old lady was sitting on a park bench in Trailer Estates, a Florida mobile home park. A man walked over and sat down on the other end of the bench. After a few moments, the woman asks, *'Are you a stranger here?'*

He replies, *'I lived here years ago.'*
'So, where were you all these years?'
'In prison,' he says.
'Why did they put you in prison?'
He looked at her and very quietly said, *'I killed my wife.'*
'Oh!' said the woman. *'So you're single ...?'*

Another two elderly people living in Trailer Estates, he a widower and she a widow, had known each other for a number of years.

One evening there was a community supper in the big activity centre. The two were at the same table, across from one another. As the meal went on, he took a few admiring glances at her and finally gathered the courage to ask her, *'Will you marry me?'*

After about six seconds of careful consideration, she answered, *'Yes. Yes, I will.'*

The meal ended and, with a few more pleasant exchanges, they went to their respective places.

Next morning, he was troubled. *'Did she say 'yes' or did she say 'no'?'* He couldn't remember. Try as he might, he just could not recall. Not even a faint memory.

With trepidation, he went to the telephone and called her. First, he explained that he didn't remember as well as he used to. Then he reviewed the lovely evening past. As he gained a little more courage, he inquired. *'When I asked if you would marry me, did you say 'Yes' or did you say 'No'?'*

He was delighted to hear her say, *'Why, I said, 'Yes, yes I will' and I meant it with all my heart.'*

Then she continued, *'I am so glad that you called, because I couldn't remember who had asked me.'*

A man was telling his neighbour in Trailer Estates, *'I just bought a new hearing aid. It cost me four thousand dollars, but it's state of the art. It's perfect.'*

'Really,' answered the neighbour. *'What kind is it?'*

'Twelve thirty.'

Morris, an 82 year-old man, went to the doctor at The Trailer Estates Medical Clinic to get a physical. A few days later the doctor saw Morris walking down the street with a gorgeous young woman on his arm.

A couple of days later the doctor spoke to Morris and said, *'You're really doing great, aren't you?'*

'Just doing what you said, Doc: 'Get a hot mamma and be cheerful,'" Morris replied.

To which, the doctor said, *'I didn't say that, Morris. I said, 'You've got a heart murmur. Be careful!'"*

Millie and Myrtle were lamenting over the fact that there were so many women and so few men their age to choose from.

'I used to look for retired professional men so that we could at least have good conversation even though we might not have sex.' Millie admitted.

Myrtle added, *'I've changed my mind too. I'm now going for the tradesmen – at least they will be able to fix things up around the house. Professional men usually are useless at that. And besides Tradies are usually more physically fit and many are still able to have sex. Yes, we do have to be careful in choosing a fellow don't we?'*

Ice Cream Parlour

A little old man shuffled slowly into the 'Orange Dipper,' an ice cream parlour in Trailer Estates and pulled himself slowly, painfully, up onto a stool. After catching his breath he ordered a banana split.

The waitress asked kindly, *'Crushed nuts?'*

'No,' he replied, *'arthritis!'*

Coloured panties

Three old black ladies were preparing for their first plane flight. The first lady said, *'I don't know bout y'all, but I'm gonna wear me some hot pink panties on dis flight.'*

'Why you gonna wear dat?' the other two asked.

The first replied, *'Cause, if dat plane goes down and I'm out dere laying butt-up in a corn field, dey gonna find me first.'*

The second lady says, *'Well, I'm gonna wear me some fluorescent orange panties.'*

'Why you gonna wear dem?' the others asked.

The second lady answered: *'Cause if dat plane goes down and I'm floating butt-up in the ocean, dey can see me first.'*

The third old lady says, *'Well, I'm not going to wear any panties at all.'*

'What, no panties?' the others said in disbelief.

'Dat's right,' says the third lady. *'I'm not wearing any panties, cause if dat plane goes down, the first thing they always looks for is da black box.'*

The Fence

The husband leans over and asks his wife, *'Do you remember the first time we had sex together over fifty years ago? We went behind this very tavern where you leaned against the back fence and I made love to you.'*

'Yes,' she says, *'I remember it well.'*

'Okay,' he says, *'How about taking a stroll around there again and we can do it for old time's sake?'*

'Oh Charlie, you old devil, that sounds like a crazy, but good idea!'

There's a police officer sitting in the next booth listening to all this and having a chuckle to himself. He thinks, *'I've got to see these two old-timers having sex against a fence. I'll just keep an eye on them so there's no trouble.'* So he follows them.

They walk haltingly along, leaning on each other for support aided by walking sticks. Finally they get to the back of the tavern and make their way to the fence. The old lady lifts her skirt and the old man drops his trousers.

As she leans against the fence, the old man moves in. Suddenly they erupt into the most furious sex that the watching policeman has ever seen. This goes on for about ten minutes. Both are making loud noises and moaning and screaming. Finally, they both collapse, panting on the ground.

The policeman is amazed. He thinks he has learned something about life and old age that he didn't know. After about half an hour of lying on the ground recovering, the old couple struggle to their feet and put their clothes back on.

The Policeman still watching thinks, this was truly amazing. He thinks, *'I've got to ask them what their secret is.'* As the couple passes, he says to them, *'Excuse me, but that was something else. You must've had a fantastic sex life together. Is there some sort of secret to this?'*

The old man says, *'Fifty years ago that wasn't an electric fence!'*

Wisdom from Grandpa....

- Whether a man winds up with a nest egg or a goose egg, depends a lot on the kind of chick he marries.
- Trouble in marriage often starts when a man gets so busy earnin' his salt that he forgets his sugar.
- Too many couples marry for better or for worse, but not for good.
- When a man marries a woman, they become one; but the trouble starts when they try to decide which one.
- If a man has enough horse sense to treat his wife like a thoroughbred, she will never turn into an old nag.
- On anniversaries, the wise husband always forgets the past - but never the present.
- The bonds of matrimony are a good investment only when the interest is kept up.
- Many girls like to marry a military man - he can cook, sew and make beds and is in good health and he's already used to taking orders.
- Eventually you will reach a point when you stop lying about your age and start bragging about it.
- The older we get, the fewer things seem worth waiting in line for.
- Some people try to turn back their odometers. Not me, I want people to know 'why' I look this way.
- I've travelled a long way and some of the roads weren't paved.
- How old would you be if you didn't know how old you are?
- I don't know how I got over the hill without getting to the top.
- One of the many things no one tells you about aging is that it is such a nice change from being young.
- Ah, being young is beautiful, but being old is comfortable.
- Old age is when former classmates are so gray and wrinkled and bald, they don't recognise you.
- If you don't learn to laugh at trouble, you won't have anything to laugh at when you are old.
- You know you're getting old, when everything either dries up or leaks.
- A foolish husband says to his wife, *'Honey, you stick to the washin, ironin, cookin and scrubbing. No wife of mine is gonna work!'*

Signs of Menopause

1. You sell your home heating system at a yard sale.
2. You have to write post-it notes with your kids' names on them.
3. You change your underwear after a sneeze.

Feeling Old

Just in case you weren't feeling too old today, this will certainly change things. The people who were born in 1989:

1. Are too young to remember the space shuttle blowing up.
2. Their lifetime has always included Aids.
3. The CD was introduced just before they were born.
4. They have always had an answering machine.
5. They have always had cable.
6. Jay Leno has always been on the Tonight Show.
7. Popcorn has always been cooked in the microwave.
8. They never took a swim without thinking about Jaws!
9. They don't know who Mork was or where he was from.
10. McDonald's still came in Styrofoam containers.
11. They never heard: 'We're happy little Vegemites' or 'I like Aeroplane Jelly.'
12. They don't have a clue how to use a typewriter – electronic or manual!

The Amazing Italian

A salesman drove into a small town where a circus was playing. A sign read: 'Don't Miss The Amazing Italian.'

The salesman bought a ticket and sat down. There, under the Big Top, in the centre ring, was a table with three walnuts on it. Standing next to it was an old Italian. Suddenly, the old man dropped his pants, whipped out his huge male member and smashed all the walnuts with three mighty swings! The crowd erupted in applause and the elderly Italian was carried off on their shoulders.

Fifteen years later the salesman visited the same little town, found the same circus and saw the same faded sign that read, 'Don't Miss The Amazing Italian'. He couldn't believe the old guy was still alive much less still doing his act!

He bought a ticket. Again, the centre ring was illuminated. This time, however, instead of walnuts, three coconuts were placed on the table. The Italian stood before them, then suddenly dropped his pants and smashed the coconuts with three swings of his amazing member. The crowd went wild!

Flabbergasted, the salesman requested a meeting with him after the show. *'You're incredible!'* he told the Italian, *'But I have to know* something. I saw your act 15 years ago and you were using walnuts. Why the switch from walnuts to coconuts?'

'Well,' said the Italian, 'My eyes aren't what they used to be.'

Private part

An old man, Mr. Goldstein, was living the last of his life in a nursing home. One day he appeared to be very sad and depressed. Nurse Tracy asked if there was anything wrong.

'Yes, Nurse Tracy,' said Mr. Goldstein, 'My Private Part died today and I'm very sad.'

Knowing her patients were forgetful and sometimes had a little dementia, she replied, 'Oh, I'm so sorry, Mr. Goldstein, please accept my condolences.'

The following day, Mr. Goldstein was walking down the hall with his Private Part hanging out his pajamas. When he met Nurse Tracy she said, 'Mr. Goldstein, you shouldn't be walking down the hall like that. Please put your Private Part back inside your pajamas.'

'But, Nurse Tracy,' replied Mr. Goldstein, 'I told you yesterday that my Private Part died.'

'Yes, you did tell me that, but why is it hanging out of your pajamas?'

(You gotta love this!!!!!!!!!!!)

'Well,' he replied, 'Today's the viewing.'

When I'm an old lady

When I'm an old lady, I'll live with each kid,
And bring so much happiness ... just as they did.
I want to pay back all the joy they've provided,
Returning each deed. Oh, they'll be so excited!
(When I'm an old lady and live with my kids).
I'll write on the wall with reds, whites and blues,
And bounce on the furniture wearing my shoes.
I'll drink from the carton and then leave it out.
I'll stuff all the toilets and oh, how they'll shout!
(When I'm an old lady and live with my kids),
When they're on the phone and just out of reach,
I'll get into things like sugar and bleach,
Oh, they'll snap their fingers and then shake their head,
And when that is done I'll hide under the bed!
(When I'm an old lady and live with my kids).
When they cook dinner and call me to eat,
I'll not eat my green beans or salad or meat.
I'll gag on my okra, spill milk on the table,

And when they get angry I'll run ... if I'm able!
(When I'm an old lady and live with my kids).
I'll sit close to the TV, through the channels I'll click,
I'll cross both my eyes just to see if they stick.
I'll take off my socks and throw one away,
And play in the mud 'til the end of the day!
(When I'm an old lady and live with my kids).
And later in bed, I'll lay back and sigh,
I'll thank God in prayer and then close my eyes.
My kids will look down with a smile slowly creeping,
And say with a groan. *'She's so sweet, when she's sleeping!'*
(When I'm an old lady and live with my kids).

Libido

An Irish woman of advanced age visited her physician to ask for his help in reviving her husband's libido.

'What about trying Viagra?' asks the doctor. *'It really works.'*

'Not a chance,' says she. *'He won't even take an aspirin.'*

'No problem,' replied the doctor. *'Give him an 'Irish Viagra.'* It's when you drop the Viagra tablet into his coffee. He won't even taste it. Give it a try and call me in a week to let me know how things went.'

It wasn't a week later that she called the doctor, who directly inquired as to progress. The poor dear exclaimed, *'Oh, faith, t'was horrid! Just terrible, doctor!'*

'Really? What happened?' he asked.

'Well, I did as you advised and slipped it in his coffee and the affect was almost immediate! He jumped straight up, with a twinkle in his eye and with his pants a-bulging fiercely! With one swoop of his arm, he sent the cups and tablecloth flying, ripped me clothes to tatters and took me then and there, making wild, mad, passionate love to me on the tabletop! It was a nightmare, I tell you, an absolute nightmare!'

'I don't understand,' said the doctor. *'Do you mean the sex your husband provided wasn't good'?*

'Oh, no, no, no, doctor! The sex was fine indeed! 'Twas the best sex I've had in 25 years! But sure as I'm sittin' here, I'll never be able to show me face in Starbucks again!'

Life Perspectives

A very self-important college freshman was attending a recent football game. He took it upon himself to explain to a senior citizen sitting next to him why it was impossible for the older generation to understand his generation.

'You grew up in a different world, actually an almost primitive one,' the student said, loud enough for many of those nearby to hear. *'The young people of today grew up with television, jet planes, space travel, man walking on the moon, our spaceships have visited Mars. We have nuclear energy, electric and hydrogen cars, computers with light-speed processing and ...'* pausing to take another drink of beer.

The senior took advantage of the break in the student's litany and said, *'You're right, son. We didn't have those things when we were young ... so we invented them. Now, you arrogant little shithead, what are you doing for the next generation?'*
The applause was deafening.

Five New Boyfriends!

I'm seeing five gentlemen every day. As soon as I wake up, Will Power helps me get out of bed. Then I go to see John. Then Charlie Horse comes along and when he's here he takes a lot of my time and attention. When he leaves, Art Ritis shows up and stays the rest of the day. He doesn't like to stay in one place very long, so he takes me from joint to joint. After such a busy day, I'm really tired and glad to go to bed with Ben Gay. What a life!
Oh yes, I'm also flirting with Al Zymer.

Memories of a Senior Citizen

'Hey Grandad,' one of my grandkids asked the other day, *'What was your favourite fast food when you were growing up?*

'We didn't have fast food when I was growing up,' I informed him. *'All food was slow.'*

'C'mon, seriously. Where did you eat?'

'It was a place called 'at home.'' I explained. *'My mom cooked every day and when my dad got home from work, we sat down together at the dining room table and if I didn't like what she put on my plate, I was made to sit there until I did like it.'*

By this time, the kid was laughing so hard I was afraid he was going to suffer serious internal damage, so I didn't tell him the part about how I had to have permission to leave the table. But here are some of the other things I would have told him about my childhood if I figured his system could have handled it:

Some parents NEVER owned their own house, wore jeans, set foot on a golf course, travelled out of the country or had a credit card. In their later years they had something called a revolving charge card. The card was good only at department stores.

My parents never drove me to rugby practice. I had a bicycle that weighed probably 50 pounds and only had one speed (slow). We didn't have a television in our house until I was eleven. It was, of course, black and white. Later, they bought a piece of coloured plastic to cover the screen. The top third was blue, like the sky and the bottom third was green, like grass. The middle third was red. It was perfect for programs that had scenes of fire trucks riding across someone's lawn on a sunny day. Some people had a lens taped to the front of the TV to make the picture look larger.

I was 21 before I tasted my first pizza. It was called 'pizza pie.' When I bit into it, I burned the roof of my mouth and the cheese slid off, swung down, plastered itself against my chin and burned that too. It's still the best pizza I ever ate.

Pizzas were not delivered to our home, but milk was.

We didn't have a car until I was twelve. My father called it a 'machine.' It was a special treat to be driven to school instead of walking or riding my bike.

I never had a telephone in my room. The only phone in the house was in the hallway and we were on a waiting list for six years. Before you could dial, you had to listen and make sure some people you didn't know weren't already using the line. Toll calls were booked weeks in advance to England and it was a pound a minute.

All newspapers were delivered by boys and all boys delivered newspapers. I delivered a newspaper six days a week and had to get up at 4 am every morning. It cost 7 cents a paper, of which I got to keep 2 cents. Saturday, I had to collect the weekly accounts of my customers. My favourite customers were the ones who gave me 50 cents and told me to keep the change. My least favourite customers were the ones who never seemed to be home on collection day.

Movie stars kissed with their mouths shut. At least, they did in the movies. Touching someone else's tongue with yours was called French kissing and they didn't do that in movies. I don't know what they did in French movies. French movies were dirty and we weren't allowed to see them. By the way, movies cost 3d for kids and 1/6d for adults (before 6 o'clock it was 2d afterwards).

My Dad was cleaning out my grandmother's house (she died) and he brought me an old Royal Crown Cola bottle. In the bottle top was a stopper with a bunch of holes in it. I knew immediately what it was, but my daughter had no idea. She thought they tried to make it a salt shaker or something. I new it as the bottle that sat on the end of the ironing board to 'sprinkle' clothes with because we didn't have steam irons. Man, I am old!

If you grew up in a generation before there was fast food, you may want to share some of these memories with your children or grandchildren. Just don't blame me if they bust a gut laughing.

Growing up isn't what it used to be – is it?

You're old if you remember the following:
- Headlight dimmer switches on the floor.
- Ignition switches on the dashboard.
- Heaters mounted on the inside of the firewall.
- Real ice boxes.
- Pant leg clips for bicycles without chain guards.
- Soldering irons you heat on a gas burner.
- Using hand signals for cars without turn signals.
- No air conditioning in a home.
- Spearmint chewing gum.
- Wax Coke-shaped bottles with coloured sugar water.
- Blue rinse bombs for washing (also used for bee stings)
- Candy cigarettes.
- First coffee shops.
- Home milk delivery in glass bottles with cardboard stopper.
- Soda pop machines that dispensed glass bottles.
- Party lines.
- Newsreels at the movies.
- Drive-in movies.
- Telephone numbers with only three or four digits.
- Peashooters.
- Home made Ginger Beer.
- 45 RPM records.
- Gramophones.
- Hi-fi's.
- Howdy Doody.
- Blue flashbulbs.
- Coffee shops or diners with tableside juke boxes.
- Metal ice trays with lever.
- Street photographers.
- Model A's.
- Roller skate keys.
- Cork popguns.
- Matinees at 2 pm with serialised westerns, Spiderman and superman.
- Coppers (washtubs – not policemen!)
- Washing machines with wringers.

Prenuptials

An elderly couple in their 70's were about to get married.

She said: *'I want to keep my house.'*
He said: *'That's fine with me.'*
She said: *'And I want to keep my Cadillac.'*
He said: *'That's fine with me.'*
She said: *'And I want to have sex 6 times a week.'*
He said: *'That's fine with me ... put me down for Fridays'*

Test for Dementia

Below are four (4) questions and a bonus question. You have to answer them instantly. You can't take your time. Answer all of them immediately. Okay? Let's find out just how clever you really are ... Ready? GO!!!

First Question:
You are participating in a race. You overtake the second person. What position are you in?
Answer: If you answered that you are first; then you are absolutely wrong! If you overtake the second person and you take his place, you are second! Try not to screw up next time. Now answer the second question, but don't take as much time as you took for the first question, okay?

Second Question:
If you overtake the last person, then you are ...?'
Answer: If you answered that you are second to last; then you are wrong again. Tell me, how can you overtake the LAST person?
You're not very good at this, are you?

Third Question:
Very tricky arithmetic! Note: This must be done in your head only Do NOT use paper and pencil or a calculator. Try it.
    Take 1000 and add 40 to it. Now add another 1000. Now add 30. Add another 1000. Now add 20. Now add another 1000. Now add 10. What is the total?
Answer: Did you get 5000? The correct answer is actually 4100.
If you don't believe it, check it with a calculator! Today is definitely not your day, is it? Maybe you'll get the last question right ... Maybe.

Fourth Question:
Mary's father has five daughters: 1. Nana 2. Nene 3. Nini 4. Nono. What is the name of the fifth daughter?
Answer: Did you Answer Nunu? NO! Of course it isn't. Her name is Mary. Read the question again!

Okay, now the **bonus round:**
A mute person goes into a shop and wants to buy a toothbrush. By imitating the action of brushing his teeth he successfully expresses himself to the shopkeeper and the purchase is done.

Next, a blind man comes into the shop who wants to buy a pair of sunglasses. How does HE indicate what he wants?

Answer: He just has to open his mouth and asks ... It's really very simple.

Perks of being 50 and over

1. Kidnappers are not very interested in you unless you're rich.
2. In a hostage situation you are likely to be released first.
3. No one expects you to run - anywhere.
4. People no longer view you as a hypochondriac.
5. There is nothing left to learn the hard way.
6. Things you buy now won't wear out.
7. You can eat dinner at 4 pm.
8. You can live without sex but not your glasses.
9. You get into heated arguments about pension plans.
10. You no longer think of speed limits as a challenge.
11. You quit trying to hold your stomach in no matter who walks into the room.
12. You sing along with elevator music.
13. Your eyes won't get much worse.
14. Your investment in health insurance is finally beginning to pay off.
15. Your joints are more accurate meteorologists than the national Weather service.
16. Your secrets are safe with your friends because they can't remember them either.
17. Your supply of brain cells is finally down to manageable size.
18. You can't remember who sent you this list.
19. And you notice these are all in Big Print for your convenience.

The Mean Cop

Working people frequently ask retired people what they do to make their days interesting.

Well, for example, the other day my wife and I went shopping. We were only in there for about 5 minutes. When we came out, there was a cop writing out a parking ticket. We went up to him and said, *'Come on man, how about giving a senior citizen a break?'*

He ignored us and continued writing the ticket. I called him a Nazi turd. He glared at me and started writing another ticket for having worn tyres. So my wife called him a sh*thead. He finished the second ticket and put it on the windshield with the first. Then he started writing a third ticket. This went on for about 20 minutes. The more we abused him, the more tickets he wrote.

Personally, we didn't care. We came into town by bus. We try to have a little fun each day now that we're retired. It's important at our age.

Ain't it Hell getting old?!

Four old mischievous Grandmas were sitting at a table in a nursing home. About then an old Grandpa walked in. One of the old Grandmas yelled out saying, *'We bet we can tell exactly how old you are.'*

The old man said, *'There's no way you can guess it, you old fools.'*

One of the old Grandmas said, *'Sure we can! Just drop your pants and under shorts and we can tell your exact age.'*

Embarrassed just a little, but anxious to prove they couldn't do it, he dropped his drawers. The Grandmas asked him to first turn around a couple of times and to jump up and down several times. Then they all piped up and said, *'You're 87 years old!'*

Standing with his pants down around his ankles, the old gent asked, *'How in the world did you guess?'*

Slapping their knees and grinning from ear to ear, all four old ladies happily yelled in unison – *'We were at your birthday party yesterday'*

Bullshit and brilliance

An old lady decides to go on a photo safari in Africa, taking her faithful aged poodle named Cuddles along for company. One day the poodle starts chasing butterflies and before long, Cuddles discovers that he's lost. Wandering about, he notices a leopard heading rapidly in his direction with the intention of having lunch.

The old poodle thinks, *'Oh, oh! I'm in deep doo-doo now!'* Noticing some bones on the ground close by, he immediately settles down to chew on the bones with his back to the approaching cat. Just as the leopard is about to leap, the old poodle exclaims loudly, *'Boy, that was one delicious leopard! I wonder if there are any more around here?'*

Hearing this, the young leopard halts his attack in mid-strike, a look of terror comes over him and he slinks away into the trees. *'Whew!'* says the leopard, *'That was close! That old poodle nearly had me!'*

Meanwhile, a monkey who had been watching the whole scene from a nearby tree, figures he can put this knowledge to good use and trade it for protection from the leopard. So off he goes, but the old poodle sees him heading after the leopard with great speed and figures that something must be up. The monkey soon catches up with the leopard, spills the beans and strikes a deal for himself with the leopard.

The young leopard is furious at being made a fool of and says, *'Here, monkey, hop on my back and see what's going to happen to that conniving canine!'*

Now, the old poodle sees the leopard coming with the monkey on his back and thinks, *'What am I going to do now?'* but instead of running, the dog sits down with his back to his attackers, pretending he hasn't seen them yet and just when they get close enough to hear, the old poodle says, *'Where's that damn monkey? I sent him off an hour ago to bring me another leopard!'*

Moral of this story: Don't mess with old farts - age and treachery will always overcome youth and skill! Bullshit and brilliance only come with age and experience.

The Medical Exam

An elderly married couple scheduled their annual medical examination the same day so they could travel together. After the examination, the doctor then said to the elderly man, *'You appear to be in good health. Do you have any medical concerns you would like to ask me?'*

'In fact I do,' said the elderly man. *'After I have sex with my wife the first time, I am usually hot and sweaty and then, after I have sex with her the second time, I am usually cold and chilly.'*

The doctor said he would make a note of that and see what some lab tests revealed. After examining the elderly lady, the doctor said, *'Everything appears to be fine. Do you have any medical concerns that you would like to discuss with me?'*

The lady replied that she had no questions or concerns.

The doctor then asked, *'Your husband had an unusual concern. He claims that he is usually hot and sweaty after having sex the first time with you and then cold and chilly after the second time. Do you know why that could be?'*

'Oh that crazy old fart!' she replied. *'That is because the first time is usually around July and the second time is usually in December!'*

The Pond

The old farmer decided to go down to his pond. He grabbed a five gallon bucket to bring back some fruit. As he neared the pond, he heard voices shouting and laughing with glee. As he came closer he saw it was a bunch of young women skinny-dipping in his pond.

He made the woman aware of his presence and they all went to the deep end. One of the women shouted to him, *'We're not coming out until you leave!'*

The old man frowned, *'I didn't come down here to watch you ladies swim naked. Or make you get out of the pond naked.'*

Holding the bucket up he said, *'I'm here to feed the alligator.'*

Moral: Some old men can still think fast ...

Like Old Times

A couple had been married for 50 years. They were sitting at the breakfast table one morning when the wife says, *'Just think, fifty years ago we were sitting here at this breakfast table together.'*

'I know,' the old man said. *'We were probably sitting here naked as a jay-bird fifty years ago.'*

'Well,' Granny snickered. *'Let's relive some old times.'*

Where upon, the two stripped to the buff and sat down at the table.

'You know, honey,' the little old lady breathlessly replied, *'My nipples are as hot for you today as they were fifty years ago.'*

'I wouldn't be surprised,' replied Gramps. *'One's in your coffee and the other is in your oatmeal.'*

Harold & Mildred

Harold is 92 and lives in a senior citizens' home. Every night after dinner, Harold goes to a secluded garden behind the Centre to sit, smoke a cigar, listen to music, ponder his accomplishments and reflect on his long life.

One evening, Mildred, aged 86 wandered into the garden. They began to chat and before they knew it several hours had passed. After a short lull in their conversation, Harold turned to Mildred and asked, *'Do you know what I miss most of all?'*

She asked, *'What?'*

'Sex' he replied.

Mildred exclaimed, *'Why you old fart, you couldn't get it up if I held a gun to your head!'*

'I know,' Harold said, *'but it would be nice if a woman could just hold it for a while.'*

'Well, I can oblige,' said Mildred as she unzipped his trousers, removes his manhood and proceeded to hold it.

Afterward, they agreed to meet secretly each night in the garden where they would sit and talk and Mildred would hold Harold's manhood. One night, Harold didn't show up at their usual meeting place. Alarmed, Mildred decided to find him and make sure he was okay. She walked around the centre and found him sitting by the pool with another female resident. It was Ethel and she was holding Harold's manhood!

Furious, Mildred yelled. *'You two-timing creep! What does Ethel have that I don't have?'*

Old Harold smiled happily and replied, *'Parkinson's.'*

Sex Therapist

A couple, aged 67, went to the doctor's office. The doctor asked, *'What can I do for you?'*

The man replied, *'Will you watch us have sexual intercourse?'*

The doctor looked puzzled but agreed. When they were finished, the doctor said, *'There's nothing wrong with the way you have intercourse.'* And he charged them $10.

This happened several weeks in a row. The couple would make an appointment, have intercourse, pay the doctor and leave. Finally the doctor asked, *'Just exactly what are you trying to find out?'*

The old man replied, *'We're not trying to find out anything. She is married and we can't go to her house. I'm married and we can't go to my house. Holiday Inn charges $22; the Hilton charges $27. We do it here for $10 and I get $8 back from Medicare for a visit to the doctor's office.'*

The loving husband

A man and his wife went on vacation to Jerusalem. While they were there, the wife died. The undertaker said, *'You can have her shipped home for $5,000 or have her buried here in the Holy Land for $150.'*

The man thought about it and told him he would have his wife shipped home.

The undertaker asked, *'Why would you spend $5,000 to ship your wife home. Wouldn't it be wonderful if she was buried here and you would spend only $150?'*

The man replied, *'Long ago a man died here, was buried here and three days later he rose from the dead. I can't take that risk.'*

Senior Sex

This old couple was sitting in their chairs in the back yard when the old lady reached over and knocked the old man out of his chair.

The old man got up, sat back down in his chair and asked, *'What was that for?'*

The old lady replied, *'That was for fifty years of bad sex.'*

A couple of minutes later, the old man reached over and knocked the old lady out of her chair. She got up and asked, *'What was that for?'*

'For knowing the difference!'

An eighty year-old man was having an annual physical. As the doctor was listening to his heart with the stethoscope, he began muttering, *'oh, oh!'*

The man asked the doctor what the problem was.

'Well,' said the doc, *'you have a serious heart murmur. Do you smoke?'*

'No.'

'Do you drink in excess?'

'No.'

'Do you have a sex life?'

'Yes, I do!'

'Well,' said the doc, *'I'm afraid with this heart murmur, you'll have to give up half your sex life.'*

Looking perplexed, the old man said, *'Which half? The looking or the thinking?'*

A 97-year-old man goes into his doctor's office and says, *'Doc, I want my sex drive lowered.'*

'Sir,' replied the doctor, *'you're 97. Don't you think your sex drive is all in your head?'*

'You're damned right it is!' replied the old man. *'That's why I want it lowered!'*

My nookie days are over,
My pilot light is out,
What used to be my sex appeal,
Is now my water spout.
Time was when of its own accord,
From my trousers it would spring,
But now I have a full time job,
Just to find the blasted thing.
It used to be embarrassing,
The way it would behave,
For every single morning,
It would stand and watch me shave.
As old age approaches,
It sure gives me the blues,
To see it hang its withered head
And watch me tie my shoes.

Romantic

An older couple was lying in bed one night ... The husband was falling asleep but the wife felt romantic and wanted to talk. She said, *'You use to hold my hand when we were courting.'*

Wearily he reached across, held her hand for a second and then tried to get back to sleep.

A few moments later she said, *'Then you used to kiss me.'*

Mildly irritated, he reached across, gave her a peck on the cheek and settled down to sleep.

Thirty seconds later she said, *'Then you used to nibble my neck.'*

Angrily, he threw back the bed covers and got out of bed.

'Where are you going?' she asked.

'To get my teeth!'

Special poem for senior citizens!!

A row of bottles on my shelf
Caused me to analyse myself.
One yellow pill I have to pop
Goes to my heart so it won't stop.
A little white one that I take
Goes to my hands so they won't shake.
The blue ones that I use a lot
Tell me I'm happy when I'm not.
The purple pill goes to my brain
And tells me that I have no pain.
The capsules tell me not to wheeze
Or cough or choke or even sneeze.
The red ones, smallest of them all
Go to my blood so I won't fall.
The orange ones, very big and bright
Prevent my leg cramps in the night.
Such an array of brilliant pills
Helping to cure all kinds of ills.
But what I'd really like to know ...
Is what tells each one where to go!
There's always a lot to be thankful for if
you take time to look for it. For example
I am sitting here thinking how nice it is
that wrinkles don't hurt ...

Games for when we are older

1. Sag, you're It.
2. Hide and go pee.
3. 20 questions shouted into your good ear.
4. Kick the bucket.
5. Red Rover, Red Rover, the nurse says Bend Over.
6. Musical recliners.

7. Simon says something incoherent.
8. Pin the Toupee on the bald guy.

At the Bar

An elderly man was sitting next to me at the bar and was getting very drunk. I picked him up off the floor after he fell off the bar stool and offered to take him home. He accepted. On the way to my car, he fell down three more times. When I got him to his house, I helped him out of the car and he fell four more times. I rang the bell and said, *'Ma'am, here's your husband.'*

She replied, *'So, where's his wheelchair?'*

Secret to a long marriage

With a couple celebrating their 50th anniversary at the church's marriage marathon, the minister asked Ralph to take a few minutes and share some insight into how he managed to live with the same woman all these years.

The husband replied to the audience, *'Well, I treated her with respect, spent money on her, but mostly I took her travelling on special occasions.'*

The minister inquired trips to where? *'For our 25th anniversary, I took her to Beijing, China.'*

The minister then said, *'What a terrific example you are to all husbands, Ralph. Please tell the audience what you're going to do for your wife on your 50th anniversary?'*

Brother Ralph: *'I'm going to go get her.'*

How to stay young

- Throw out non-essential numbers. This includes age, weight and height. Let the doctors worry about them. That is why you pay them.
- Keep only cheerful friends. The grouches pull you down. (Keep this in mind if you are one of those grouches!)
- Keep learning: Learn more about the computer, crafts, gardening, whatever. Never let the brain get idle. *'An idle mind is the devil's workshop.'* And the devil's name is Alzheimer's!
- Enjoy the simple things
- Laugh often, long and loud. Laugh until you gasp for breath. And if you have a friend who makes you laugh, spend lots and lots of time with her/him!
- The tears happen: Endure, grieve and move on. The only person, who is with us our entire life, is ourselves. LIVE while you are alive.

- Surround yourself with what you love: Whether it's family, pets, keep-sakes, music, plants, hobbies; whatever. Your home is your refuge.
- Cherish your health: If it is good, preserve it. If it is unstable, improve it. If it is beyond what you can improve, get help.
- Don't take guilt trips. Take a trip to the mall, even to a foreign country, but NOT to where the guilt is.
- Tell the people you love, that you love them - at every opportunity.

Grandpa

A grandson came to visit his grandparents and noticed his grandfather sitting on the porch in the rocker, wearing only a shirt, naked from the waist down.

'Grandpa, whatcha' doing? You're weenie's out in the wind for all to see!' he exclaimed.

Grandpa looked off in the distance, not answering.

'Grandpa, whatcha' doin' sitting out here with nothing on below the waist?' he asked again.

Grandpa looked at him and said, *'Last week I sat here with no shirt on and got a stiff neck. This is grandma's idea ...'*

Old Ladies

The next time you see a little old lady with shaky hands, you'll remember this lady: A little old lady, well into her eighties, slowly enters the front door of a sex shop. Obviously very unstable on her feet, she wobbles the few feet across the store to the counter. Finally arriving at the counter and grabbing it for support, stuttering she asks the sales clerk: *'Dddooo youuuu hhhave dddddiillllldosss?'*

The clerk, politely trying not to burst out laughing, replies: *'Yes we do have dildos. Actually we carry many different models.'*

The old woman then asks: *'Dddddoooo yyyouuuu ccaarrryy aaa pppinkk onnee, tttenn inchessss lllong aaandd aabboutt ttwoo inchesss ththiickk...aaand rrunns by bbaatteries?'*

The clerk responds, *'Yes we do.'*

'Ddddooo yyoooouuuu kknnnooww hhhowww tttooo ttturrrnnn ttthe ssunoooffabbitch offffff?'

Viagra

An elderly gentleman went to the local drug store and asked the pharmacist for Viagra. The pharmacist said, *'That's no problem. How many do you want?'*

'Just a few, maybe 4, but cut each one in 4 pieces.'

'That won't do you any good,' said the pharmacies.

The elderly gentleman said, *'That's all right. I don't need them for sex any more as I'm over 80 years old. I just want it to stick out far enough so I don't pee on my shoes or to roll over and fall out of bed.'*

Gettin' Old

- They keep telling us to get in touch with our bodies. Mine isn't all that communicative, but I heard from it the other day after I said, *'Body, how'd you like to go to the six o'clock class in vigorous toning?'* Clear as a bell my body said, *'Listen fatty ... do it and you die!'*
- Reason to smile: Every seven minutes of every day someone in an aerobics class pulls a hamstring.
- My mind not only wanders, it sometimes leaves completely.
- The nice part about living in a small town: when you don't know what you're doing - someone else always does.
- The best way to forget all your troubles is to wear tight shoes.
- Amazing! You hang something in your closet for a while and it shrinks two sizes!
- Just when I was getting used to yesterday, along came today.
- Sometimes I think I understand everything; then I regain consciousness.
- It is well documented that for every mile that you jog you add one minute to your life. This enables you at 80-years-old to spend an additional 5 months in a nursing home at $5,000 per month.
- My grandmother started walking five miles a day when she was 60. She's now 97 and we don't know where the Hell she is.
- The only reason I would take up jogging is so that I could hear my breathing again,
- I joined a health club last year. I spent $400 and haven't lost a pound. Apparently you have to show up.
- I have to exercise early in the morning before the brain figures what I am doing.
- Actually I don't exercise at all. If God meant us to touch our toes, he would have put them further up in our body.
- I like long walks, especially when they are taken by people who annoy me.
- I have flabby thighs, but fortunately my stomach covers them.
- The advantage of exercising each day is that you die healthier.
- If you are going cross-country skiing - start with a small country.

- I don't jog. It makes the ice jump right out of my gin and tonic.
- Maybe it's true that life begins at fifty, but everything else starts to wear out, fall out or spread out.
- There are three signs of old age. The first is your loss of memory. The other two I've forgotten.
- You're getting old when 'getting lucky' means you find your car in the parking lot.
- You're getting old when you don't care where your spouse goes, just as long as you don't have to go along.
- You're getting old when you wake up with that morning-after feeling and you didn't do anything the night before.
- I'm getting just like my great-grandchildren - wearing diapers and using a walker.
- Going bra-less pulls all the wrinkles out of your face.
- An all-nighter means not getting up to pee!
- The cardiologist's diet: if it tastes good - spit it out.
- It's hard to be nostalgic when you can't remember anything.
- My grandfather is getting forgetful, but he likes to give me advice. One day he took me aside and left me there.
- Middle age is when it takes longer to rest than to get tired.
- By the time a man is wise enough to watch his step, he's too old to go anywhere.
- At my age, 'getting a little action' mans I don't need to take a laxative.
- Don't worry about avoiding temptation. As you grow older, it will avoid you.
- I have everything I had twenty years ago, only it's all a little bit lower.
- Middle age is when you have stoped growing at both ends and have begun to grow in the middle.
- Of course I'm against sin. I'm against anything that I'm too old to enjoy.
- A man has reached middle age when he is cautioned to slow down by his doctor instead of by the police.
- Middle age is having a choice of two temptations and choosing the one that will get you home earlier.
- You know you're into middle age when you realise that caution is the only thing you care to exercise.
- The ageing process could be slowed down if it had to work its way through Congress.
- You can live without sex, but not without your glasses.
- Your back goes out more than you do.

- You quit trying to hold your stomach in, no matter who walks into the room.
- Your best friend is dating someone half his or her age ... and isn't breaking any laws.
- Your arms are too short to read the newspaper.
- You sing along with the elevator music.
- You enjoy hearing about other people's operations.
- You consider coffee one of the most important things in life.
- You no longer think of speed limits as a challenge.
- People call at 9:00 pm and ask, *'Did I wake you?'*
- You wear black socks with sandals.
- Your ears and nose are hairier than your head.
- When you talk about 'good grass' you're referring to someone's lawn.
- You get into a heated argument about pension plans.
- You have a party and the neighbours don't even realise it!

Ain't Love Grand?

An 80 year-old woman was arrested for shoplifting. When she went before the judge he asked her, *'What did you steal?'*

She replied: *'A can of peaches.'*

The judge then asked how many peaches were in the can.

She replied, *'Six.'*

The judge then said, *'I will give you six days in jail.'*

Before the judge could pronounce the punishment, the husband spoke up and said, *'She also stole a can of peas.'*

Sounds of Life

It seems an elderly gentleman had serious hearing problems for a number of years. He went to the doctor and the doctor was able to have him fitted for a set of hearing aids that allowed him to hear perfectly again. He returned to the doctor's office in a month for a final check on the new equipment. After some tests, the doctor proclaimed, *'Your hearing is perfect!'*

'Thank you for helping me,' replied the elderly man.

'You're welcome,' said the doctor. *'Your family must be really pleased that you can hear again.'*

'Oh, I haven't told them yet. I just sit around and listen to the conversations I used to miss,' replied the man.

'Really?' questioned the doctor. *'You must still be marvelling at being able to hear again and just not ready to believe it yourself. That must be why you haven't told them.'*

'Well, no, that's not it exactly, but I have changed my will three times!'

Aged Wisdom

- Inside every older person is a younger person wondering what the hell happened. - Cora Harvey Armstrong.
- Inside me lives a skinny woman crying to get out. But I can usually shut the bitch up with cookies. - unknown
- The hardest years in life are those between ten and seventy. - Helen Hayes (at 73)
- I refuse to think of them as chin hairs. I think of them as stray eyebrows. - Janette Barber.
- My second favourite household chore is ironing. My first one being - hitting my head on the top bunk bed until I faint. - Erma Bombeck.
- Old age ain't no place for sissies. - Bette Davis.
- Thirty-five is when you finally get your head together and your body starts falling apart. - Caryn Leschen.
- If you can't be a good example, then you'll just have to be a horrible warning. Catherine.
- I'm not going to vacuum 'til Sears makes one you can ride on. - Roseanne Barr.
- Behind every successful man is a surprised woman. - Maryon Pearson.
- Nobody can make you feel inferior without your permission. - Eleanor Roosevelt.
- When life hands you lemons, ask for tequila and salt and call me over!! - unknown

Music of the 60's

It was fun being a baby boomer ... until now. Some of the artists of the '60s are revising their hits with new lyrics to accommodate an aging public. They include:

1. Herman's Hermits: *'Mrs. Brown, you've got lovely walker.'*
2. The Bee Gees: *'How can you mend a broken hip.'*
3. Bobby Darin: *'Splish, splash, I was havin' a flash.'*
4. Ringo Starr: *'I get by with a little help from Depends.'*
5. Roberta Flack: *'The first time ever I forgot your face.'*
6. Johnny Nash: *'I can't see clearly now.'*
7. Paul Simon: *'Fifty ways to lose your liver.'*
8. The Commodores: *'Once, twice, three times to the bathroom.'*
9. Marvin Gaye: *'Heard it through the grape nuts.'*

10. Procol Harem: *'A whiter shade of hair.'*
11. Leo Sayer: *'You make me feel like napping.'*
12. The Temptations: *'Papa's got a kidney stone.'*
13. Abba: *'Denture queen.'*
14. Tony Orlando: *'Knock three times on the ceiling if you hear me fall.'*
15. Helen Reddy: *'I am woman, hear me snore.'*
16. Willie Nelson: *'On the commode again.'*
17. Leslie Gore: *'It's my procedure and I'll cry if I want to.'*

New Standard Living Will Form

I, ..., being of sound mind and body, do not wish to be kept alive indefinitely by artificial means. Under no circumstances should my fate be put in the hands of pinhead politicians who couldn't pass ninth-grade biology if their lives depended on it or lawyers/doctors interested in simply running up the bills.

If a reasonable amount of time passes and I fail to ask for at least one of the following:

A Bloody Mary,
A Margarita,
A Scotch and soda,
A Dirty Martini,
A Miller draft,
A steak,
Chicken Fried Steak with mashed potatoes and gravy, lobster or crab legs,
The remote control,
A bowl of French vanilla ice cream,
Chocolate or sex,

It should be presumed that I won't ever get better. When such a determination is reached, I hereby instruct my appointed person and attending physicians to pull the plug, reel in the tubes and call it a day.

Signature: ....
Date: ....

The Joys of growing older

Three men were discussing aging on the steps of the nursing home. *'Sixty is the worst age to be,'* announced the sixty-year-old. *'You always feel like you have to pee. And most of the time, you stand at the toilet and nothing comes out!'*

'Ah, that's nothing,' said the seventy-year-old. *'When you're seventy, you can't take a crap anymore. You take laxatives, eat bran - you sit on the toilet and nothing comes out!'*

'Actually,' said the eighty-year-old, *'Eighty is the worst age of all.'*

'Do you have trouble peeing too?' asked the sixty-year-old.

'No ... not really. I pee every morning at 6 am. I pee like a race horse - no problem at all.'

'Do you have trouble taking a crap?' asked the seventy-year-old.

'No ... not really. I have a great bowel movement every morning at 6:30 am.'

With great exasperation, the sixty-year-old said, *'Let me get this straight. You pee every morning at six o'clock and take a crap every morning at six thirty. What's so tough about being eighty?'*

'I don't wake up till ten!' explained the eighty-year-old.

The Baby

With the help of a fertility specialist, a 65 year-old woman has a baby. All her relatives come to visit and meet the newest member of their family. When they ask to see the baby, the 65 year-old mother says, *'Not yet.'*

A little later they ask to see the baby again. Again the mother says, *'Not yet.'*

Finally they say, *'When can we see the baby?'*

And the mother says, *'When the baby cries.'*

So they ask, *'Why do we have to wait until the baby cries?'*

The new mother says, *'Because I forgot where I put it.'*

Getting Old

Reporters interviewing a 104-year-old woman: *'And what do you think is the best thing about being 104?'* the reporter asked.

She simply replied, *'No peer pressure.'*

Just before the funeral services, the undertaker came up to the very elderly widow and asked, *'How old was your husband?'*

'98,' she replied. *'Two years older than me.'*

'So you're 96,' the undertaker commented.

She responded, *'Hardly worth going home, is it?*

I really know I'm old! I've had two bypass surgeries; a hip replacement, new knees, fought breast cancer and diabetes. I'm half blind, can't hear anything quieter than a jet engine; take 40 different medications that make me dizzy, winded and subject to blackouts.

Have bouts with dementia. Have poor circulation; hardly feel my hands and feet anymore. Can't remember if I'm 85 or 92. Have lost all my friends. But, thank God, I still have my driver's license.

An elderly woman decided to prepare her will and told her preacher she had two final requests. First, she wanted to be cremated and second, she wanted her ashes scattered over Wal-Mart.
   'Wal-Mart?' the preacher exclaimed.
   'Why Wal-Mart?'
   'Then I'll be sure my daughters visit me twice a week.'

Senior Moments:

- It's scary when you start making the same noises as your coffeemaker.
- How do you get four old ladies to swear? Get the fifth old lady to say, *'Bingo.'*
- The nice thing about being senile is you can hide your own Easter eggs.
- The good news is that even as we get older, guys still look at our boobs. The bad news is they have to squat down first.
- These days about half the stuff in my shopping cart says, *'For fast relief.'*
- I've tried to find a suitable exercise video for women my age, but they haven't made one called *'Buns of Putty.'*
- Don't think of it as getting hot flashes. Think of it as your inner child playing with matches.
- Don't let aging get you down. It's too hard to get back up!
- Remember: You don't stop laughing because you grow old; you grow old because you stop laughing.
- Now, I think you're supposed to send this to five or six, maybe ten people. Oh heck, send it to a bunch of your friends if you can remember who they are!

Mid-Life

- I've seen two shows lately that went on and on about how mid-life is a great time for women. Just last week Oprah had a whole show on how great menopause will be. Puhleeeeeeeze! I've had a few thoughts of my own and would like to share them with you. Whether you are pushing 40, 50, 60 (or maybe even just pushing your luck) you'll probably relate.
- Mid-life is when the growth of hair on our legs slows down. This gives us plenty of time to care for our newly acquired moustache.

- In mid-life women no longer have upper arms, we have wing spans. We are no longer women in sleeveless shirts we are flying squirrels in drag.
- Mid-life is when you can stand naked in front of a mirror and you can see your rear without turning around.
- Mid-life is when you go for a mammogram and you realise that this is the only time someone will ask you to appear topless.
- Mid-life is when you want to grab every firm young lovely in a tube top and scream, *'Listen honey, even the Roman Empire fell and those will too.'*
- Mid-life brings wisdom to know that life throws us curves and we're sitting on our biggest ones.
- Mid-life is when you look at your-know-it-all, beeper-wearing teenager and think*: 'For this I have stretch marks?'*
- Mid-life is when you've still got 'it' but nobody wants it.
- Mid-life is when you reach your sexpiration date.
- In Mid-life your memory starts to go. In fact, the only thing we can retain is water.
- Mid-life means that you become more reflective. You start pondering the 'big' questions. *'What is life? Why am I here? How much Healthy choice ice cream can I eat before it's no longer a healthy choice?'*
- But mid-life also brings with it an appreciation for what is important. We realise that breasts sag, hips expand and chins double, but our loved ones make the journey worthwhile. Would any of you trade the knowledge that you have now, for the body you had way back when? Maybe our bodies simply have to expand to hold all the wisdom and love we've acquired. That's my philosophy and I'm sticking to it!

Old Groom

At 85 years of age, Roger married Jenny, a lovely 25 year old. Since her new husband is so old, Jenny decides that after their wedding she and Roger should have separate bedrooms, because she is concerned that her new but aged husband may overexert himself if they spend the entire night together.

After the wedding festivities Jenny prepares herself for bed and the expected knock' on the door. Sure enough the knock comes, the door opens and there is Roger, her 85-year-old groom, ready for action. They unite as one. All goes well, Roger takes leave of his bride and she prepares to go to sleep.

After a few minutes, Jenny hears another knock on her bedroom door and it's Roger. Again he is ready for more 'action.'

Somewhat surprised, Jenny consents for more coupling. When the newly weds are done, Roger kisses his bride, bids her a fond good night and leaves.

She is set to go to sleep again, but, aha you guessed it - Roger is back again, rapping on the door and is as fresh as a 25-year-old, ready for more 'action.' And, once more they enjoy each other.

But as Roger gets set to leave again, his young bride says to him, *'I am thoroughly impressed that at your age you can perform so well and so often. I have been with guys less than a third of your age who were only good once. You are truly a great lover, Roger.'*

Roger, somewhat embarrassed, turns to Jenny and says: *'You mean I was here already?'*

The moral of the story: Don't be afraid of getting old. Alzheimer's has its advantages.

I'm not old ... Just mature!

Today at the drugstore, the clerk took off ten percent. I asked for the cause of the lesser amount and he answered, *'Because of the seniors' Discount.'* I went into McDonald's for a burger and fries; and then once again, got quite a surprise. The waiter poured some coffee, which he handed to me and said, *'For you seniors, the coffee is free.'*

Understand - I'm not old - I'm merely mature; but some things are changing, temporarily, I'm sure. The newspaper print gets smaller each day and people speak softer - can't hear what they say.

My teeth are my own (I have the receipt.) and my glasses identify people I meet. Oh, I've slowed down a bit, not a lot, I'm sure. You see, I'm not old. I'm only mature.

The gold in my hair has been bleached by the sun; you should see all the damage that chlorine has done. Washing my hair has turned it all white, but don't call it grey, saying 'blonde' is just right.

My car is all paid for, not a nickel is owed. Yet a kid yells, *'Old duffer ... get off the road!'*

My friends all get older, much faster than me. They seem much more wrinkled, from what I can see. I've got 'character lines,' not wrinkles for sure, but don't call me old; just call me mature.

The steps in the houses they're building today are so high that they take your breath all away; and the streets are much steeper than ten years ago, that should explain why my walking is slow.

But I'm keeping up on what's hip and what's new and I think I can still dance a mean boogaloo. I'm still in the running; in this I'm secure, I'm not really old. I'm only mature.

This has got to stop!

Have you noticed that stairs are getting steeper; groceries are heavier and everything is farther away? Yesterday I walked to the corner and I was dumbfounded to discover how long our street had become.

And you know – people are less considerate now – especially the young ones. They speak in whispers all the time! If you ask them to speak up, they just keep repeating themselves, endlessly mouthing the same silent message until they're red in the face! What do they think I am - a lip reader?

I also think they are much younger than I was at the same age. On the other hand, people my own age are so much older than I am. I ran into an old friend the other day and she has aged so much that she didn't even recognise me. I got to thinking about the poor dear while I was combing my hair this morning and in doing so, I glanced at my own reflection. Well, really now – even mirrors are not made the way they used to be!

Another thing is that everyone drives so fast these days! You're risking life and limb if you happen to pull onto the freeway in front of them. All I can say is their brakes must wear out awfully fast, the way I see them screech and swerve in my rear view mirror.

Clothing manufacturers are less civilised these days. Why else would they start labelling a size 10 or 12 dress as 18 or 20? Do they think no one notices that these things no longer fit around the waist, hips, thighs and bosom?

The people who make bathroom scales are pulling the same prank, but in reverse. Do they think I actually believe the number I see on the dial? HA! I would never let myself weigh that much! Just who do these people think they're fooling?

I'd like to call up someone in authority to report what's going on – but the telephone company is in on the conspiracy too: they've printed the phone books in such small type that no one could ever find a number in there.

All I can do is pass along this warning: We are under attack! Unless something drastic happens, pretty soon everyone will have to suffer these awful indignities.

The Golden Years

Suppositories set in place,
Spectacles upon my face,
Microphones in both my ears,
and they call these the Golden Years?
Partial dentures, hard to eat,
Circulation bad in both my feet,

Getting fat like all my peers,
Who share with me these Golden Years.
Prostate problems - aching back,
Lots of trouble in the sack,
Many problems - damned few cheers,
Greet me in my Golden years.
I worked and saved and shed some tears,
Preparing for these Golden Years,
These years of Gold seem more like brass,
And you can shove them up your ass!

Grandpa

A man goes to visit his 85-year-old grandpa in hospital.
'How are you grandpa?' he asks.
'Feeling fine,' says the old man.
'What's the food like?'
'Terrific, wonderful menus.'
'And the nursing?'
'Just couldn't be better. These young nurses really take care of you.'
'What about sleeping? Do you sleep okay?'
'No problem at all - nine hours solid every night. At ten o'clock they bring me a cup of hot chocolate and a Viagra tablet ... and that's it. I go out like a light.'

The grandson is puzzled and a little alarmed by this, so he rushes off to question the nurse in charge. *'What are you people doing?'* he exclaims. *'I'm told you're giving an 85-year-old Viagra on a daily basis. Surely that can't be true?'*

'Oh yes,' replies the nurse. *'Every night at ten o'clock we give him a cup of hot chocolate and a Viagra tablet. It works wonderfully well. The chocolate makes him sleep and the Viagra keeps him from rolling out of bed!'*

Remembering

An 80-year-old couple were having problems remembering things, so they decided to go to their doctor to get checked out to make sure nothing was wrong with them. When they arrived at their doctor's, they explained their problem. After checking the couple out, the doctor tells them that they are physically okay, but they might want to start writing things down and make notes to help them remember things.

The couple thank their doctor and leave. Later that night while watching TV, the old man got up from his chair and his wife asks, *'Where are you going?'*

He replies, *'To the kitchen.'*
'Will you get me a bowl of ice cream?'
'Sure,' he replies.

She then asks him, *'Don't you think you should write it down so you can remember it?'*

He replies, *'No I can remember that.'*

She then says, *'Well, I also would like some strawberries on top. You had better write that down cause I know you'll forget that.'*

He says, *'I can remember that, you want a bowl of ice cream with strawberries.'*

'I'd also like some whipped cream on top. I know you will forget that, so you'd better write it down.'

With irritation in his voice, he says, *'I don't need to write that down. I can remember that.'* He fumes into the kitchen.

After about 20 minutes, he returns from the kitchen and hands her a plate of bacon and eggs. She stares at the plate for a moment and says, *'You forgot my toast.'*

The Punker

A young punker got on the cross-town bus. He had spiked, multi-coloured hair that was green, purple and orange. His clothes are a tattered mix of leather and rags. His legs are bare and he's without shoes. His entire face and body are riddled with pierced jewellery and his earrings are big bright feathers. He sits down in the only vacant seat, directly across from an old man who just glares at him for the next ten miles.

Finally, the punker gets self-conscious and barks at the old man, *'What are you looking at you old fart. Didn't you ever do anything wild when you were young?'*

Without missing a beat, the old man replies: *'Yeah, back when I was in the Navy, I got really drunk one night in Singapore and had sex with a parrot. I thought maybe you were my son.'*

Chocolate Chip Cookies

A 98-year-old man lay on his deathbed at home. According to his doctors he would not live to see another sunrise. All of a sudden, he became aware of the ever-increasing scent of freshly baked chocolate chip cookies coming from the kitchen two floors below. He thought, *'Before I leave this world, I must have just one of my wife's wonderful chocolate chip cookies.'* After all, it was such a batch of cookies made by his wife that first won his heart more than 80 years before when they were first dating. What better way to depart this life than with the warm and loving taste of his wife's cookies still lingering on his palate?

The man bravely and arduously rolled himself in his bed till he was finally able to fall off the bed onto the floor. He pulled himself by his elbows out of the room into the hallway. He continued to pull himself to the stairwell where he backed himself down the two flights of stairs, painfully sliding down one step at a time. The man then pulled himself through the parlour, living room, dining room and finally into the kitchen.

Tears swelled in his eyes as he contemplated all of the love that his wife had put into that final batch of cookies. This was a most appropriate final act of love offered to him by the woman who had shared her life with him for more than 80 years.

He pulled himself to the counter top where the cooling batch of cookies lay, sending their aroma deep into his nostrils and announcing to the world that his wife's love for him was most certainly as fresh and warm today as on the day she married him.

He rested his body weight on his left elbow and with shaking determination, ever so slowly raised his right arm to a point that put his fingers so close to the cookies that he could feel the heat rising and caressing his fingertips.

His wife turned her head and noticed her husband in his valiant struggle to reach for the cookies. She grabbed his hand and declared, *'Oh no you don't! Those are for the funeral.'*

Age Activated Attention Deficit Disorder

This is how it manifests: I decide to water my garden. As I turn on the hose in the driveway, I look over at my car and decide my car needs washing.

As I start toward the garage, I notice that there is mail on the porch table that I brought up from the mailbox earlier.

I decide to go through the mail before I wash the car.

I lay my car keys down on the table, put the junk mail in the garbage can under the table and notice that the can is full.

So, I decide to put the bills back on the table and take out the garbage first.

But then I think, since I'm going to be near the mailbox, when I take out the garbage anyway, I may as well pay the bills first.

I take my cheque book off the table and see that there is only 1 check left. My extra checks are in my desk in the study, so I go inside the house to my desk where I find the can of Coke that I had been drinking.

I'm going to look for my checks, but first I need to push the Coke aside so that I don't accidentally knock it over. I see that the Coke is getting warm and I decide I should put it in the refrigerator to keep it cold.

As I head toward the kitchen with the Coke, a vase of flowers on the counter catches my eye - they need to be watered.

I set the Coke down on the counter and I discover my reading glasses that I've been searching for all morning.

I decide I better put them back on my desk, but first I'm going to water the flowers.

I set the glasses back down on the counter, fill a container with water and suddenly I spot the TV remote. Someone left it on the kitchen table.

I realise that tonight when we go to watch TV, I will be looking for the remote, but I won't remember that it's on the kitchen table, so I decide to put it back in the den where it belongs, but first I'll water the flowers.

I pour some water in the flowers, but quite a bit of it spills on the floor.

So, I set the remote back down on the table, get some towels and wipe up the spill.

Then, I head down the hall trying to remember what I was planning to do.

At the end of the day:

The car isn't washed,

The bills aren't paid,

There is a warm can of Coke sitting on the counter,

The flowers don't have enough water,

There is still only 1 cheque in my cheque book,

I can't find the remote,

I can't find my glasses and

I don't remember what I did with the car keys.

Then, when I try to figure out why nothing got done today, I'm really baffled because I know I was busy all day long and I'm really tired. I realise this is a serious problem and I'll try to get some help for it, but first I'll check my e-mail. Do me a favour will you? Forward this message to everyone you know, because I don't re member to whom it has been sent.

Don't laugh - if this isn't you yet, your day is coming!

P.S. I just remembered. I left the water running in the driveway!

Yearly Check-up

I went to the doctor for my yearly physical. The nurse started with the basics. *'How much do you weigh?'* she asks.

'61 kg,' I said. The nurse put me on the scale. Turns out I'm 76 kg.

The nurse asks, *'What's your height?'*

'*5 foot 8,*' I said. The nurse checked and sees that I'm 5' 5'.

She sat me down on the exam table and took my blood pressure and told me it's very high. '*Of course it's high!*' I screamed. '*When I came in here I was tall and thin, now I'm short and fat!*'

Old age, I decided, is a gift

I am now, probably for the first time in my life, the person I have always wanted to be. Oh, not my body! I sometime despair over my body ... the wrinkles, the baggy eyes and the sagging butt. And often I am taken aback by that old person that lives in my mirror, but I don't agonise over those things for long.

I would never trade my amazing friends, my wonderful life, my loving family for less gray hair or a flatter belly. As I've aged, I've become kinder to myself and less critical of myself. I've become my own friend.

I don't chide myself for eating that extra cookie or for not making my bed or for buying that silly cement gecko that I didn't need, but looks so avante garde on my patio.

I am entitled to overeat, to be messy, to be extravagant. I have seen too many dear friends leave this world too soon; before they understood the great freedom that comes with aging.

Whose business is it if I choose to read or play on the computer until 4 am and sleep until noon? I will dance with myself to those wonderful tunes of the 60's and if I, at the same time, wish to weep over a lost love I will.

Sure, over the years my heart has been broken. How can your heart not break when you lose a loved one or when a child suffers or even when a beloved pet gets hit by a car? But broken hearts are what give us strength and understanding and compassion. A heart never broken is pristine and sterile and will never know the joy of being imperfect.

I am so blessed to have lived long enough to have my hair turn gray and to have my youthful laughs be forever etched into deep grooves on my face. So many have never laughed and so many have died before their hair could turn silver.

I can say '*no,*' and mean it. I can say '*yes,*' and mean it.

As you get older, it is easier to be positive. You care less about what other people think. I don't question myself any more. I've even earned the right to be wrong.

I will walk the beach in a swim suit that is stretched over a bulging body and will dive into the waves with abandon if I choose to, despite the pitying glances from the bikini set. They, too, will get old.

I know I am sometimes forgetful. But there again, some of life is just as well forgotten ... and I eventually remember the important things.

So, to answer your question, I like being old. It has set me free. I like the person I have become. I am not going to live forever, but while I am still here, I will not waste time lamenting what could have been or worrying about what will be.

And I shall eat dessert every single day.

Life would be great if it were backwards!

- You'd start out dead and get it out of the way.
- Then, wake up in an old age home feeling better every day.
- You get kicked out for being too healthy; go collect your pension and then when you start work, you get a gold watch on your first day.
- You work 40 years until you're young enough to enjoy your retirement.
- You drink alcohol, you party, you're generally promiscuous and you get ready for High School.
- You go to primary school, you become a kid, you play, you have no responsibilities, you become a baby and then ...
- You spend your last 9 months floating peacefully in luxury, in spa-like conditions; central heating, room service on tap, larger quarters every day,
- And then, you finish off as an orgasm.

I rest my case.

20 Things that it took me 50 years to learn

- Never under any circumstances take a sleeping pill and a laxative on the same night.
- If you had to identify, in one word, the reason why the human race has not achieved and never will achieve its full potential - that word would be 'meetings.'
- There is a very fine line between 'hobby' and 'mental illness.'
- People who want to share their religious views with you almost never want you to share yours with them.
- And when God, who created the entire universe with all of its glories, decides to deliver a message to humanity, he will not use, as His messenger, a person on Cable TV with a bad hairstyle.

- You should not confuse your career with your life. No matter what happens, somebody will find a way to take it too seriously.
- When trouble arises and things look bad, there is always one individual who perceives a solution and is willing to take command. Very often, that individual is crazy.
- Nobody cares if you can't dance well. Just get up and dance.
- Never lick a steak knife.
- Take out the fortune before you eat the cookie.
- The most powerful force in the universe is gossip.
- You should never say anything to a woman that even remotely suggests that you think she's pregnant unless you can see an actual baby emerging from her at that moment.
- There comes a time when you should stop expecting other people to make a big deal about your birthday. That time is aged 11.
- The one thing that unites all human beings, regardless of age, gender, religion, economic status or ethnic background, is that, deep down inside, we all believe that we are above-average drivers.
- The main accomplishment of almost all organised protests is to annoy people who are not in them.
- The person who is nice to you, but rude to the waiter, is not a nice person.
- Your friends love you anyway.

So never be afraid to try something new. Remember that amateurs built the ark. Professionals built the Titanic.

Don't Mess with Grandma

An elderly Florida lady did her shopping and, upon returning to her car, found four males in the act of leaving with her vehicle. She dropped her shopping bags and drew her handgun, proceeding to scream at the top of her voice, *'I have a gun and I know how to use it! Get out of the car!!'*

The four men didn't wait for a second invitation. They got out and ran like mad. The lady, somewhat shaken, then proceeded to load her bags into the back seat of the car and got into the driver's seat. She was so shaken that she couldn't get her key into the ignition. She tried and tried and then it dawned on her why.

A few minutes later, she found her own car parked four or five spaces further down. She loaded her bags into the car and drove to the police station. The sergeant to whom she told the story couldn't stop laughing. He pointed to the other end of the counter, where four pale men were reporting a car jacking by a mad, elderly woman described as white, less than five feet tall, glasses, curly white hair and carrying a large handgun.

Moral of the story: If you're going to have a Senior Moment, make it a memorable one!

The Clothesline

For those who are older, this should bring memories. For those of you who are younger, it gives a glimpse into the past.

1. You had to wash the clothes line before hanging any clothes. Walk the length of each line with a damp cloth around the line.
2. You had to hang the clothes in a certain order and always hang whites with whites and hang them first.
3. You never hung a shirt by the shoulders, always by the tail (easier to iron when dry – yes, ironing also was a chore).

A clothesline was a news forecast to neighbours passing by. There were no secrets you could keep when clothes were hung to dry. It also was a friendly line, for neighbours always knew if company had stopped by to spend a night or two. For then you'd see the fancy sheets and towels upon the line. You'd see the 'guest' tablecloths with intricate design.

The line announced a baby's birth to folks who lived inside, as brand new infant clothes were hung so carefully with pride. The ages of the children could so readily be known, by watching how the sizes changed, you knew how much they'd grown.

It also told when illness struck, as extra sheets were hung. Then nightclothes and a bathrobe too, haphazardly were strung.

It said, *'Gone on vacation now'* when lines hung limp and bare. It told, *'We're back!'* when full lines sagged without an inch to spare.

New folks in town were scorned upon if wash was dingy gray, as neighbours raised their brows and looked disgustedly away.

Most clotheslines are of the past for dryers save time and effort. Now, what goes on inside a home is anybody's guess. I really miss that way of life. It was a friendly sign, when neighbours knew each other best by what hung on the line!

Dreams

The first day of school, our professor introduced himself and challenged us to get to know someone we didn't already know. I stood up to look around when a gentle hand touched my shoulder. I turned around to find a wrinkled, little old lady beaming up at me with a smile that lit up her entire being. She said, *'Hi handsome. My name is Rose. I'm eighty-seven years old. Can I give you a hug?'*

I laughed and enthusiastically responded, *'Of course you may!'* and she gave me a giant squeeze.

'Why are you in college at such a young, innocent age?' I asked.

She jokingly replied, *'I'm here to meet a rich husband, get married, have a couple of children and then retire and travel.'*

'No seriously,' I asked. I was curious what may have motivated her to be taking on this challenge at her age.

'I always dreamed of having a college education and now I'm getting one!' she told me.

After class, we walked to the student union building and shared a chocolate milk shake. We became instant friends. Every day for the next three months we would leave class together and talk non-stop. I was always mesmerised listening to this 'time machine' as she shared her wisdom and experience with me. Over the course of the year, Rose became a campus icon and she easily made friends wherever she went. She loved to dress up and she revelled in the attention bestowed upon her from the other students. She was living it up.

At the end of the semester, we invited Rose to speak at our football banquet. I'll never forget what she taught us. She was introduced and stepped up to the podium. As she began to deliver her prepared speech, she dropped her three by five cards on the floor. Frustrated and a little embarrassed she leaned into the microphone and simply said, *'I'm sorry I'm so jittery. I'll never get my speech back in order, so let me just tell you what I know.'*

As we laughed, she cleared her throat and began. *'We do not stop playing because we are old; we grow old because we stop playing. There are only four secrets to staying young*

1. Be happy;
2. Achieve success;
3. Laugh and find humour every day; and
4. Have a dream.

When you lose your dreams, you die. We have so many people walking around who are dead and don't even know it! There is a huge difference between growing older and growing up. If you are nineteen years old and lie in bed for one full year and don't do one productive thing, you will turn twenty years old. If I am eighty-seven years old and stay in bed for a year and never do anything, I will turn eighty-eight. Anybody can grow older. That doesn't take any talent or ability. The idea is to grow up by always finding the opportunity in change. Have no regrets. The elderly usually don't have regrets for what we did, but rather for the things we did not do. The only people who fear death are those with regrets.'

She concluded her speech by courageously singing *'The Rose.'* She challenged each of us to study the lyrics and live them out in our daily lives. At the years' end, Rose finished the college degree she had begun all those years ago.

One week after graduation, Rose died peacefully in her sleep. Over two thousand college students attended her funeral in tribute to the wonderful woman who taught by example that it's never too late to be all you can possibly be.

- Growing older is mandatory,
- Growing up is optional
- Laughing at yourself is therapeutic!

CHAPTER 11 - BLONDE JOKES

More Blonde Jokes

- Why are all dumb blonde jokes one or two liners? So men can understand and remember them.
- Why do blondes have TGIF on their shoes? Toes go in first.
- Why do blondes have TGIF on their shirts? Tits go in front.
- What do you call a brunette with a blonde on either side? An interpreter.
- What do you call a blonde between two brunettes? A mental block.
- What do you call a smart blonde? A golden retriever.
- How do you change a blonde's mind? Blow in her ear or buy her another beer.
- What do you say to a blonde that won't give in? *'Have another beer.'*
- What do blondes do with their arseholes in the morning? Pack their lunch and send them to work.
- Why do blondes take the pill? So they know what day of the week it is.
- Why did the blonde stop using the pill? Because it kept falling out.
- Why did the blonde have a sore navel? Because her boyfriend was also blonde!
- What happens when a blonde gets Alzheimer's disease? Her IQ goes up.
- What is the difference between a blonde and the Titanic? They know how many men went down on the Titanic.
- What do a blonde and a beer bottle have in common? They're both empty from the neck up.
- What do peroxide blondes and black men have in common? They both have black roots.
- How many blondes does it take to make chocolate-chip cookies? One to mix the dough and nine to peel the smarties.
- What do you get when you offer a blonde a penny for her thoughts? Change.
- What do you see when you look into a blonde's eyes? The back of her head.
- What did the blonde name her pet zebra? Spot.
- How do you make a blonde laugh on Monday mornings? Tell them a joke on Friday night.

- What did the blonde say when she looked into a box of Cheerios? *'Oh look! Donut seeds!'*
- Why does a blonde only change her baby's diapers every month? Because it says right on it 'good for up to twenty pounds.'
- What's the difference between a blonde and a supermarket trolley? The supermarket trolley has a mind of its own.
- How do you get a blonde to marry you? Tell her she's pregnant.
- What do you call a blonde behind a steering wheel? An air bag.
- Did you hear about the blonde couple that were found frozen to death in their car at the drive-in movie theatre? They went to see *'Closed for the winter.'*
- What did they name the offspring of a blonde and a Puerto Rican? Retardo.
- What do you call a blonde in an institution of higher learning? A visitor.
- What about the blonde guy whose wife gave birth to twins? He wanted to know who the other man was.
- How do blondes get pregnant? And I thought blondes were dumb!
- What is the best blonde secretary in the world to have? One that never misses a period.
- What does a blonde think an innuendo is? An Italian suppository.
- What two things in the air can get a blonde pregnant? Her feet!
- Government studies show that blondes do have more fun - they just don't remember who with.
- What do you call a blonde mother-in-law? An air bag.
- Why should you never take a blonde out for coffee? It's too hard to re-train them.
- What's the difference between a pit bull and a blonde with PMS? Lipstick.
- To a blonde, what is long and hard? Grade 4.
- Why do blondes like lightening? They think someone is taking their picture.
- What did the blonde do when she heard that 90% of accidents occur around the home? She moved.
- Did you hear about the blonde who tried to blow up her husband's car? She burned her lips on the tailpipe.
- What does a blonde make best for dinner? Reservations.
- What do you call a blonde lesbian? A waste.

- What are the worst six years in a blonde's life? Grade 3.
- What do you call a blonde wearing a leather jacket on a motorcycle? Rebel without a clue.
- Why did the blonde fail her driver's licence? She wasn't used to the front seat.
- What do you call a blonde with half a brain? Gifted.
- How do blonde brain cells die? Alone.
- What do you call a blonde with two brain cells? Pregnant.
- What do you call it when a blonde dies her hair brunette? Artificial intelligence.
- Why is it good to have a blonde passenger? You can park in the handicapped zone.
- What is the blonde psychic's greatest achievement? An in-body experience.
- How do you make a blonde's eyes light up? Shine a flashlight in her ear.
- How can you tell if a blond has been using the computer? There's whiteout on the screen.
- Why do blondes have more fun? Because they don't know any better.
- How can you tell when a blonde reaches orgasm? She drops her nail file.
- How does a blonde like her eggs? Unfertilised.
- How does a blonde high-5? She smacks herself in the forehead.
- What do you get when you cross a blonde and a lawyer? I don't know. There are some things even a blonde won't do.
- What does a blonde answer to the question, *'Are you sexually active?' 'No, I just lie there.'*
- Why can't blondes make ice cubes? They forget the recipe.
- How many blondes does it take to screw in a light bulb? Blondes screw in back seats, not in light bulbs, silly.
- Did you hear about the blonde who bought an AM radio? It took her two weeks to figure out that she could play it at night.
- Did you hear about the blonde who stood in front of a mirror with her eyes closed? She wanted to see what she looked like asleep.
- Did you hear about the new form of birth control for blondes? They take off their makeup.
- Why did the blonde get fired from the sperm bank? Her employer found out she was embezzling.
- How can you tell when a fax has been sent from a blonde? There's a stamp on it.

- What do you give a blonde that has everything? Penicillin.
- Why did the blonde climb up to the roof of the bar? She heard that the drinks were on the house.
- How can you steal the window seat of a blonde going to London on a plane? Tell her the seats that are going to London are all in the middle.
- How does a spoiled rich blonde girl change a light bulb? She says, *'Daddy, I want a new apartment.'*

Three blondes run across a genie and he said that he would grant them each one wish.

The first blonde wished to be 50% smarter. *poof* she's a brunette.

The second one wished to be 25% smarter. *poof* she's a redhead.

The third one wished to be 50% dumber *poof* she's a blonde man.

Need Money

A blonde was hard up for money, so she walked around her neighbourhood trying to find a job. She met a nice man who said he would give her work. All she had to do was paint his porch white. He gave her a bucket of paint and left. He walked into his house, laughing. He told his brunette wife what he had done.

'Frank, our porch covers half of the house! You're so mean.' His wife replied.

Three hours later, the blonde went into the house and gave the bucket of white paint back to the man. The astonished man handed her a $100 bill and asked how she had finished it so quickly.

'It took time, but it was easy' was her reply. *'And it's a Ferrari, not a Porsche.'*

Secured Loan

A blonde walked into a bank in New York City and asked for the loan officer. She said she was going to Europe on business for two weeks and needed to borrow $5,000. The bank officer said the bank would need some kind of security for the loan, so the blonde handed over the keys to a new Rolls Royce. The car was parked on the street in front of the bank, she had the title and everything checked out. The bank agreed to accept the car as collateral for the loan.

The bank's president and its officers all enjoy a good laugh at the blonde for using a $250,000 Rolls as collateral against a $5,000 loan. An employee of the bank then proceeds to drive the Rolls into the bank's underground garage and parks it there.

Two weeks later, the blonde returns, repays the $5,000 and the interest, which comes to $15.41. The loan officer says, *'Miss, we are very happy to have had your business and this transaction has worked out very nicely, but we are a little puzzled. While you were away, we checked you out and found that you are a multi-millionaire. What puzzles us is, why would you bother to borrow $5,000?'*

The blonde replies, *'Where else in New York City can I park my car for two weeks for only $15.41 and expect it to be there when I return?'*

Finally, a smart blonde joke.

Stranded

There were three people stranded on an island, a brunette, a redhead and a blonde. The brunette looked over the water to the mainland and estimated about twenty kilometres to shore. So she announced, *'I'm going to try to swim to shore.'* So she swam out ten kilometres and was too tired to go on so she drowned.

The redhead said to herself,' *'I wonder if she made it. I guess it's better to try to get to the mainland than stay here and starve.'* So she attempts to swim. She had a lot more endurance than the brunette, but after fifteen kilometres she was too tired to go on, so she drowned.

So the blonde thought to herself, *'I wonder if they made it! I think I'd better try to make it too.'* So she swam ten, then fifteen and then nineteen kilometres from the island. The shore was just in sight, but she said, *'I'm too tired to go on!'* So she swam back.

Dandruff

A blonde and brunette were talking one day. The brunette said that her boyfriend had a slight dandruff problem but she gave him Head and Shoulders and it cleared up. The blonde asked inquisitively, *'How do you give shoulders?'*

Tracks

Two blondes were walking through the woods when one looked down and said, *'Oh, look at the deer tracks.'* The other blonde looks down and says, *'Those aren't deer tracks - they're wolf tracks!'* They keep arguing and arguing and one half hour later a train killed them both.

Locked out

Two blondes were observed in a parking lot trying to unlock the door of their Mercedes with a coat hanger. Blonde #1 says, *'I can't seem to get this door unlocked!'*

Blonde #2 responds with, *'Well, you'd better hurry up and try harder, it's starting to rain and the top is down!'*

Disneyland

The blonde was driving down the highway to Disneyland when she saw a sign that said, *'Disneyland left.'* After thinking for a minute, she said to herself *'Oh well!'* turned around and drove home.

Broke

A blonde finds herself in dire trouble. Her business has gone bust and she's in serious financial trouble. She's so desperate that she decides to ask God for help. She begins to pray, *'God, please help me. I've lost my business and if I don't get some money, I'm going to lose my house as well. Please let me win the lotto.'*

Lotto night comes and somebody else wins it. She again prays, *'God, please let me win the lotto! I've lost my business, my house and I'm going to lose my car as well.'*

Lotto night comes and she still has no luck. Once again, she prays, *'My God, why have you forsaken me? I've lost my business, my house and my car. My children are starving. I don't often ask you for help and I have always been a good servant to you. Please just let me win the lotto this one time so I can get my life back in order.'*

Suddenly there is a blinding flash of light as the heavens open and she is confronted by the voice of God himself: *'At least meet me half way on this - buy a ticket!'*

Clean Restrooms

A blonde saw a sign that said, 'Clean restrooms eight miles.' By the time she had driven eight miles, she had cleaned forty-three restrooms and was desperate to go.

Snow Plow

A blonde got lost in her car in a snowstorm. She remembered what her Dad had once told her. *'If you ever get stuck in a snow storm, wait for a snow plow and follow it.'*

Pretty soon a snow plow came by and she started to follow it. She followed the plow for about forty-five minutes. Finally the driver of the truck got out and asked her what she was doing. She explained what her Dad had advised her. The driver nodded and said, *'Well, I'm done with the Wal-Mart lot, now you can follow me over to the K-Mart.'*

Wrong Way

A policeman pulls a blonde over after she was driving the wrong way on a one-way street. The cop asked, *'Do you know where you're going?'*

Blonde: *'No, but wherever it is, it must be bad 'cause all the people are leaving.'*

Bad News

A blonde goes into work one morning crying her eyes out. Her boss, concerned about all his employees' well-being, asked sympathetically, *'What's the matter?'* to which the blonde replies, *'Early this morning I got a phone call saying that my mother had passed away.'*

The boss feeling very sorry at this point explains to the young girl, *'Why don't you go home for the day ....we aren't terribly busy. Just take the day off to relax and rest.'*

The blonde very calmly states, *'No, I'd be better off here. I need to keep my mind off it and have the best chance of doing that here.'*

The boss agrees and allows the blonde to work as usual. *'If you need anything, just let me know.'*

Well, a few hours pass and the boss decides to check on the blonde. He looks out over his office and sees the blonde hysterically crying!! He rushes out to her asking, *'What's so bad now ... Are you gonna be okay?'*

'No,' exclaims the blonde. *'I just got a call from my sister. She told me that her mom died too!!'*

Final Exam

The Blonde reported for her university final exam that consists of 'yes/no' type questions. She takes her seat in the examination all, stares at the question paper for five minutes and then in a fit of inspiration takes her purse out, removes a coin and starts tossing the coin and marking the answer sheet - Yes for Heads and No for Tails.

Within half an hour, she is all done whereas the rest of the class is sweating it out. During the last few minutes she is seen desperately throwing the coin, muttering and sweating. The moderator, alarmed, approaches her and asks what is going on. *'I finished the exam in half an hour, but I'm rechecking my answers.'*

Trick Question

The executive was interviewing a young blonde for a position in his company. He wanted to find out something about her personality so he asked, *'If you could have a conversation with someone, living or dead, who would it be?'*

The blonde quickly responded, *'The living one.'*

Space Travel

A Russian, an American and a Blonde were talking one day. The Russian said, *'We were the first in space!'*

The American said, *'We were the first on the moon!'*

The Blonde said, *'So what, we're going to be the first on the sun!'*

The Russian and the American looked at each other and shook their heads. *'You can't land on the sun, you idiot! You'll burn up!'* said the Russian to which the Blonde replied, *'We're not stupid you know. We're going at night!'*

Driver's Licence

A police officer stops a Blonde for speeding and asks her very nicely if he could see her license. She replied in a huff, *'I wish you guys would get your act together. Just yesterday, you took away my license and then today you expect me to show it to you!'*

The Vacuum

The Blonde was playing Trivial Pursuit one night. It was her turn. She rolled the dice and landed on 'Science and Nature.' Her question was, *'If you are in a vacuum and someone calls your name, can you hear it?'*

She thought for a time and then asked, *'Is it on or off?'*

The Flight Attendant

An airline captain was breaking in a very pretty new blonde flight attendant. The route they were flying had a stay-over in another city, so upon their arrival, the captain showed the flight attendant the best place for airline personnel to eat, shop and stay overnight. The next morning as the pilot was preparing the crew for the day's route, he noticed the new flight attendant was missing. He knew which room she was in at the hotel and called her up wondering what happened to her. She answered the phone, sobbing and said she couldn't get out of her room.

'You can't get out of your room?' the captain asked, *'Why not?'*

The flight attendant replied, *'There are only three doors in here,'* she cried, *'one is the bathroom, one is the closet and one has a sign on it that says, 'Do Not Disturb!''*

Blonde Cowboy

The Sheriff in a small town walked out in the street and saw a blonde cowboy coming down the walk with nothing on but his cowboy hat, gun and his boots, so he arrested him for indecent exposure.

As he was locking him up, he asked, *'Why in the world are you dressed like this?'*

The Cowboy answered, *'Well it's like this Sheriff. I was in the bar down the road and this pretty little red head asks me to go out to her motor home with her. So I did. We go inside and she pulled off her top and asks me to pull off my shirt ... So I did.*

Then she pulled off her skirt and asked me to pull off my pants ... So I did. Then she pulled off her panties and asked me to pull off my shorts ... So I did. Then she got on the bed and looked at me kind of sexy and said, 'Now go to town cowboy ...' And here I am.'

Son of a Gun, Blonde Men do exist.

Alligator shoes

A young blonde was on vacation in the depths of Louisiana. She wanted a pair of genuine Alligator shoes in the worst way, but was reluctant to pay the high prices the local vendors were asking. After becoming very frustrated with the 'no haggle' attitude of one of the shopkeepers, the blonde shouted, *'Maybe, I'll just go out and catch my own alligator so I can get a pair of shoes at a reasonable price!'*
The shopkeeper laughingly snorted, *'By all means; be my guest. Maybe you'll luck out and catch yourself a big one!'*

Determined, the blonde headed for the swamps, set on catching herself an alligator.

Later in the day, the shopkeeper was driving home, when he spotted the young woman standing waist deep in the water, shotgun in hand. Just then, he saw a huge nine-foot alligator swimming quickly towards her. She took aim and shot, killing the alligator and with a great deal of effort hauls it onto the swamp bank. Lying nearby were several more of the dead creatures. The shopkeeper watched in amazement.

Just then the blonde flipped the alligator on its back and frustrated, shouted out, *'Damn it, this one isn't wearing any shoes either!!'*

The Indian

A cute blonde was driving through the West when her car ran out of gas. An Indian came along on a horse and gave her a ride to a gas station.

Every few minutes he let out a wild whoop that would curdle milk. Finally, he dropped her off with a final, *'Yiiiee-yiiieee-yiiieee!'*

'My God!' said the gas station attendant. *'What were you doing to that Indian to make him holler like that?'*

'Why, nothing.' Said the girl, *'I just sat behind him with my arms around him, holding onto his saddle horn.'*

'Lady ...' says the attendant, *'Indians don't use saddles.'*

The Year in Review ... for a Blonde

January - Took new scarf back to store because it was too tight.
February - Fired from pharmacy job for failing to print labels. Bottles won't fit into typewriter!!!

March - Got excited. Finished jigsaw puzzle in 6 months. Box said 2 - 4 years!

April - Trapped on escalator for hours. Power went out!!!

May - Tried to make Kool Aid - 8 cups of water won't fit into those little packets!!

June - Tried to go water skiing. Couldn't find a lake with a slope.

July - Lost breast stroke swimming competition. Learned later that other swimmers cheated – they used their arms!!

August - Got locked out of car in rainstorm. Car swamped, because top was down.

September - Lost on a TV quiz show. I was asked to list the fifty states. I told them, *'T-bone, sirloin, chops ...'*

October - Hate M & M's. They are so hard to peel.

November - Couldn't call 911 because there's no eleven button on the phone.

December - Baked Christmas turkey for 4 days. Instructions said one hour per pound and I weigh 108 pounds.

The rabbit

A man is driving along a highway and sees a rabbit jump out across the middle of the road. He swerves to avoid hitting it, but unfortunately the rabbit jumps right in front of the car. The driver, a sensitive man as well as an animal lover, pulls over and gets out to see what has become of the rabbit. Much to his dismay, the rabbit is dead. The driver feels so awful that he begins to cry.

A beautiful blonde woman driving down the highway sees a man crying on the side of the road and pulls over. She steps out of the car and asks the man what's wrong.

'I feel terrible!' he explains, *'I accidentally hit this rabbit and killed it.'*

The blonde says, *'Don't worry.'* She runs to her car and pulls out a spray can. She walks over to the limp, dead rabbit, bends down and sprays the contents onto the rabbit. The rabbit jumps up, waves its paw at the two of them and hops off down the road.

Ten feet away the rabbit stops, turns around and waves again, he hops down the road another 10 feet, turns and waves, hops another ten feet, turns and waves and repeats this again and again and again, until he hops out of sight.

The man is astonished. He runs over to the woman and demands, *'What is in that can? What did you spray on that rabbit?'*

The woman turns the can around so that the man can read the label. It says ...

(Are you ready for this?)

It says, 'Hair spray - restores life to dead hair and adds permanent wave.'

Best Blonde joke ever!

A blonde calls her boyfriend and says, *'Please come over here and help me. I have a killer jigsaw puzzle and I can't figure out how to get started.'*

Her boyfriend asks, *'What is it supposed to be when it's finished?'*

The blonde says, *'According to the picture on the box, it's a rooster.'*

Her boyfriend decides to go over and help with the puzzle.

She lets him in and shows him where she has the puzzle spread all over the table. He studies the pieces for a moment, then looks at the box, then turns to her and says, *'First of all, no matter what we do, we're not going to be able to assemble these pieces into anything resembling a rooster.'*

He takes her hand and says, *'Second, I want you to relax. Let's have a nice cup of tea and then,'* he said with a deep sigh *'Let's put all the Corn Flakes back in the box.'*

Blonde Fishermen

Two blonde guys go on a fishing trip. They rent all the equipment: the reels, the rods, the wading suits, the rowboat, the car and even a cabin in the woods. They spent a fortune.

The first day they go fishing, but didn't catch anything. The same thing happened on the second day and the third. It goes like this until finally, on the last day of their vacation, one of the men manages to catch a fish.

As they're driving home they're really depressed. One guy turns to the other and says, *'Do you realise that this one lousy fish we caught cost us fifteen hundred dollars?'*

The other blonde guy says, *'Wow! It's a good thing we didn't catch any more!'*

Road Rage

A blonde had just bought a new sports car and was out for a drive when she cut off a truck driver. He motioned for her to pull over. When she did, he got out of his truck and pulled a piece of chalk from his pocket. He drew a circle on the road and told the blonde, *'Stand in the circle and don't move!'*

He then went to her car and cut up her leather seats. When he turned around, she had a slight grin on her face, so he said, *'Oh you think that's funny. Watch this.'*

He got himself a golf club out of his truck and broke every window in her car. When he turned and looked at her, she had a smile on her face. He was getting really mad. He got his knife back out and sliced all her tires. Now she was laughing.

The truck driver was really starting to lose it. He went back to his truck and got a can of gas, poured it on her car and set it on fire. He turned around and she was laughing so hard, she was about to fall down.

'What's so funny?' the truck driver asked the blonde.

She replied, *'When you weren't looking, I stepped outside the circle four times.'*

Contractor

A woman calls a contractor to her house to give her a bid on painting the exterior of her home. She takes him into the first room and tells him that she wants it painted pale green. The contractor writes something on his notepad, goes over to the window and yells, *'Green side up.'*

The homeowner takes him into the next room and tells him that she would like to have it painted rose. The contractor again notes it on his note pad, goes over to the window and opens it. He then yells, *'Green side up.'*

The woman was curious but continued to show him the rest of the house. In each room the contractor notes her colour choice on his notepad and yells out the window, *'Green side up.'*

When the homeowner had completed the tour, she asked the contractor why he always yelled, *'Green side up'* when she told him her colour choice, when the colours were all different. He laughed and replied, *'I have a crew of blondes across the street laying sod.'*

First Class

On a plane bound for New York, the flight attendant approached a blonde sitting in the first class section and requested that she move to coach since she did not have a first class ticket. The blonde replied, *'I'm going to New York and I'm not moving.'*

Not wanting to argue with a customer, the flight attendant asked the co-pilot to speak with her. He went to talk with the woman, asking her to please move out of the first class section. Again the blonde replied, *'I'm going to New York and I'm not moving.'*

The co-pilot returned to the cockpit and asked the captain what he should do. The captain said, *'I'm married to a blonde and I know how to handle this.'*

He went to the first class section and whispered in the blonde's ear. She immediately jumped up and ran to the coach mumbling to herself, *'Why didn't someone just say so?'*

Surprised, the flight attendant and the co-pilot asked what he had said to her that finally convinced her to move from her seat. He said, *'I told her the first class section was not going to New York.'*

Payment time

Walking up to a department store's fabric counter, a pretty girl asked, *'I want to buy this material for a new dress. How much does it cost?'*

'Only a kiss a metre,' replied the smirking male clerk.

'That's fine,' replied the girl. *'I'll take ten metres.'*

With expectation and anticipation written all over his face, the clerk hurriedly measured out and wrapped the cloth, then held it out teasingly. The girl snapped up the package and pointed to a little old man standing beside her, *'Grandpa will pay the bill,'* she said as she walked away with the parcel.

The Date

The young blonde secretary was describing her evening's exploits to a friend. *'After dinner,'* she said, *'he wanted to come back to my* apartment, but I refused. I told him my mother would worry if I did anything like that.'

'That was smart,' her friend said, approvingly. 'Then what happened?'

'He kept insisting and I kept refusing,' the secretary said.

'You didn't weaken your resolve did you?' asked the friend.

'Not one bit. In the end, we went to his apartment. I figured, let his mother worry.'

Getting a man

Sally was seen going into the woods with a small package and a large birdcage. She was gone several days, but finally returned. Her friend Liz had never seen Sally look so sad. Liz said, 'I heard you went off in the woods for a couple of days. Glad you got back okay, but you look so sad. Why?'

Sally replied, 'Because I just can't get a man.'

'Well, you sure won't find one in the middle of the woods.'

'Don't be so silly,' Sally said, 'I know that. I went in the woods because I needed something there that would get me a man. But I couldn't find it.'

Liz said, 'I don't understand what you're talking about.'

Sally replied, 'Well, I went there to catch a couple of owls. I took some dead mice and a bird cage.'

'So, how's that gonna help you get a man?' asked Liz.

Sally said, 'Well, I heard the best way to get a man is to have a good pair of hooters.'

Boating problem

A blonde (of course) new to boating was having a problem. No matter how hard she tried, she just couldn't get her brand new twenty-two foot motor boat to perform. It wouldn't get on a plane at all and it was very sluggish in almost every manoeuvre, no matter how much power she applied. After about an hour of trying to make it go, she putted over to a nearby marina. Maybe they could tell her what was wrong. A thorough topside check revealed everything was in perfect working order.

The engine ran fine, the out drive went up and down; the prop was the correct size and pitch. So one of the marina guys jumped into the water to check underneath the boat. He came up choking on water he was laughing so hard.

Remember - this is true ...

Under the boat, still strapped securely in place, was the trailer.

Letter Box

A man was in his front yard mowing grass when his attractive blonde female neighbour came out of her house and went straight to her letterbox. She opened it, then slammed it shut and stormed back into the house. A little later, she came out of her house and again went to the letterbox, opened it and slammed it shut again. Angrily, back into the house she went.

As the man was getting ready to edge the lawn, she came out again, marched to the mailbox, opened it and then slammed it closed harder than ever. Puzzled by her actions, the man asked her, *'Is something wrong?'*

To which she replied, *'There certainly is!'* (Are you ready?) *'My stupid computer keeps saying 'You've got mail.''*

Smart Blonde

An attractive blonde from Dublin arrived and bet twenty-thousand dollars ($20,000) in a single roll of the dice. She said, *'I hope you don't mind, but I feel much luckier when I'm completely nude.'*

With that, she stripped from the neck down, rolled the dice and yelled, *'Come on, baby, Mama needs new clothes!'*

As the dice came to a stop, she jumped up and down and squealed... *'YES! YES! I WON, I WON!'*

She hugged each of the dealers and then picked up her winnings and her clothes and quickly departed. The dealers stared at each other dumbfounded. Finally, one of them asked, *'What did she roll?'*

The other answered, *'I don't know - I thought you were watching.'*

Moral of the story? – Not all Irish are stupid and not all blondes are dumb, but all men are men.

Six degrees of blonde

First Degree
A married couple were asleep when the phone rang at 2 in the morning. The wife (undoubtedly blonde) picked up the phone, listened a moment and said *'How should I know, that's 200 miles from here!'* and hung up.

The husband said, *'Who was that?'*

The wife said, *'I don't know, some woman wanting to know if the coast is clear.'*

Second Degree
Two blondes are walking down the street. One notices a compact on the sidewalk and leans down to pick it up. She opens it, looks in the mirror and says, *'Hmm, this person looks familiar.'*

The second blonde says, *'Here, let me see!'*

So the first blonde hands her the compact. The second one looks in the mirror and says, *'You dummy, it's me!'*

Third Degree
A blonde suspects her boyfriend of cheating on her, so she goes out and buys a gun. She goes to his apartment unexpectedly and when she opens the door she finds him in the arms of a redhead. Well, the blonde is really angry. She opens her purse to take out the gun and as she does so, she is overcome with grief. She takes the gun and puts it to her head.

The boyfriend yells, *'No, honey, don't do it!!!'*

The blonde replies, *'Shut up, you're next!'*

Fourth Degree
A blonde was bragging about her knowledge of state capitals. She proudly says, *'Go ahead; ask me, I know all of them.'*

A friend says, *'Okay, what's the capital of Wisconsin?'*

The blonde replies, *'Oh, that's easy: W.'*

Fifth Degree
What did the blonde ask her doctor when he told her she was pregnant? *'Is it mine?'*

Sixth Degree
Returning home from work, a blonde was shocked to find her house ransacked and burglarised. She telephoned the police at once and reported the crime. The police dispatcher broadcast the call on the radio and a K-9 unit, patrolling nearby was the first to respond.

As the K-9 officer approached the house with his dog on a leash, the blonde ran out on the porch, shuddered at the sight of the cop and his dog, then sat down on the steps. Putting her face in her hands, she moaned, *'I came home to find all my possessions stolen. I call the police for help and what do they do? They send me a BLIND policeman.'*

CONCLUSION

I hope you have enjoyed these jokes enough to obtain Volumes 2, 3 and 4 that cover humour in different areas, so there's no repetition.

Laughter is an essential ingredient to everyday living. If you haven't had a laugh today - you're depriving yourself of enjoyment in life. Bring the jokes out when you're having a bad day - that's what I do. You'll find that things just get better.

If you wish to read books on more serious topics, please see the following information about how to order my other books and e-Books.

www.dealingwithdifficultpeople.info

www.ingramcontent.com/pod-product-compliance
Lightning Source LLC
LaVergne TN
LVHW051545070426
835507LV00021B/2423